Legal Stagings

Legal Stagings

The Visualization, Medialization and Ritualization of Law in Language, Literature, Media, Art and Architecture

Edited by Kjell Å Modéer
and Martin Sunnqvist

Museum Tusculanum Press
University of Copenhagen
2012

Kjell Å Modéer and Martin Sunnqvist (eds.). Legal Stagings:
The Visualization, Medialization and Ritualization of Law
in Language, Literature, Media, Art and Architecture

Cover design: Erling Lynder
Set and printed in Denmark by Narayana Press
ISBN 978 87 635 3161 0

Cover illustration: Engraving by Giacomo Franco showing
a court scene in Doge's Palace in Venice (1610).

This book is published with financial support from
NOS-HS (Nordisk samarbejdsnævn for humanistisk
og samfundsvidenskabelig forskning)

Museum Tusculanum Press
Njalsgade 126
DK-2300 Copenhagen S
Denmark
www.mtp.dk

Contents

Preface

In tandem with contemporary modern society becoming increasingly dependent upon visuality, new trends have emerged in cultural studies discussing how visual representations influence our perception of society and its institutions. This is an important observation concerning central elements of law and legal thinking, which to a large extent have been shaped and informed by a text-based tradition: legislation, preparatory materials, court decisions, and commentaries almost without exception manifest themselves in the form of texts. Most of the papers in this volume, written by lawyers and scholars working in various fields, address variegated forms of legal staging and visual representation across a range of different disciplines and genres, including architecture, theatre, courtroom art and portraiture, cinema, literature, journalism.

Benefiting from contextual and legal cultural comparative methods, the contributions combine theoretical approaches to the visuality of law with practical experiences, demonstrating how law is so much more than law in action and law in books; law is also part of a visual culture: it contributes to that culture and is, in turn, analyzed, maintained and criticized by that culture. While the majority of the papers explore these ramifications in the new legal landscape developing in the late modern Nordic countries, the volume also broadens its perspective in order to probe legal contexts in other countries where new trajectories, and possibilities, impinge on how cultural manifestations of law change the way we understand law and, thus, changes law itself.

This volume has its roots in the project 'Nordic Legal Maps in Transition', which started in 2005 and was concluded in 2009. Within the project, three symposia were arranged:

- *'1968' – and after. The Importance of Critical Legal Theories for Nordic Legal Science. A Nordic Oral-History Symposium. Lund 2005.*
- *Legal Staging: Visualisation – Medialisation – Ritualisation. Nordic Legal Communication through Language, Literature, Media, Art and Architecture.* Copenhagen 2006.
- *Beyond Nordic Legal Modernity. In Search for New Coordinates. Nordic Jurisprudence Revisited.* Reykjavík 2008.

The steering committee for the project consisted of: Kjell Å Modéer (executive), Lund University, LL.D., h.c.mult., professor emeritus. Håkan Gustafsson, University of Gothenburg, LL.D., docent, associate professor. Henning Koch, University of Copenhagen, LL.D., professor. Toomas Kotkas, University of Helsinki, LL.D., research fellow. Mats Kumlien, Uppsala University, LL.D., professor. Pia Letto-Vanamo, University of Helsinki, LL.D., docent, director. Sigurður Líndal, University of Iceland, professor emeritus. Dag Michalsen, University of Oslo, LL.D., professor. Per Nilsén, Lund University, LL.D., docent, associate professor. Hanne Petersen, University of Copenhagen, LL.D., professor. Inger Johanne Sand, University of Oslo, LL.D., professor. Björg Thorarensen, University of Iceland, professor. Martin Sunnqvist (coordinator), Lund University, LL.Lic., doctoral candidate.

Kjell Å Modéer and Martin Sunnqvist
Lund, August 2011

I.
INTRODUCTION

1

Visualization of a Nordic Legal Modernity

From August Strindberg to Lars von Trier

Kjell Å Modéer

A visual metaphor: Nordic legal mapping

One effect of the dramatic geo-political changes in Europe after the collapse of the Berlin Wall in 1989 has been a visualization of the clash between progressive neo-liberal and traditional welfare-state ideologies. Money laundering and trafficking demonstrate the decline and fall of the dominating empire of modernity of the twentieth century. Scandinavian movies like *Lilja 4-ever* (2002) by Lukas Moodysson and *Dogville* (2003) by Lars von Trier have visualized not only the brutal social reality but also a new morality, urging for law reform and justice. Also the new attitude to visibility of religious symbols has, as an effect of a boundless cultural interaction in the time of multiculturalism and globalization, provoked the enlightened view of a secularized public square in the traditional nation-state. In the western hemisphere there is a discourse on the development of a new *Kulturkampf* in the early twenty-first century.[1]

The legal maps in the northern part of Europe are in transition. Boaventura de Sousa Santos's metaphor of *legal mapping* provides an instrument to construct the contemporary legal culture as a landscape with the legal networks interactively combined as roads and paths in the landscape.[2] The legal map of the Nordic countries can be described as a constructed synthesis within the multicultural and multi-religious societies in the Nordic countries. The enduring thesis in this Hegelian construct is the *pre-modernity* at the end of the nineteenth century with its historically rooted institutions, ideologies and artefacts. It was succeeded by an impressive anti-thesis, in this venture represented by the *modernity* which throughout the twentieth century represented the dominating cognitive structure of legal knowledge. The legal maps of the Nordic countries have been edited in several versions from the early 1910s up to the 1990s. One of the aims of this volume, within the framework of the Nordic research project on 'Nordic Legal Maps in Transition', is to relate the current *late modern* legal map to that of legal modernity, and to try to construct a new edition of the maps of the Nordic legal cultures and traditions.

The legal map of the Nordic countries is one part of the big European map. To be able to construct such a Nordic map we have to relate it to at least the European one. The current construct, however, even goes beyond the European map, with the Nordic legal map of today also fitting in as a part of the global one.

Within comparative law of the post-war modernity, the Nordic legal family was regarded as a special one, neither a distinct civil law nor a common law culture. The Nordic legal family has traditionally been regarded as exceptional – and *in between*. The construct of the current late modern legal map of the Nordic countries contains considerably more differences, singularities and divergences than the corresponding one which was used 25–30 years ago.[3]

Visualization of the law in literature

When the peak of legal modernity of the Nordic countries occurred in the 1970s, the legal maps had another construction than today. In the early 1970s there was still a vision of an ongoing, continuous and evolutionary legal harmonization between the Nordic countries. It was valid for the Nordic legislation as well as for the traditional inter-Nordic comparative network within the legal professions. This form of harmonization was a part of the traditions emanating from the generation of progressive liberals of the 1840s. Two of the most famous Scandinavian authors of the romantic era and the Danish 'golden age' were Carl Jonas Love Almquist (1793–1866), who was also an active Scandinavianist, and the Danish author Hans Egede Schack (1820–1859), his friend and colleague. Almquist wrote legal novels like *Amalia Hillner* (1840), set in a Swedish court of appeal,[4] and in Schack's novel *The Enthusiasts* (*Phantasterne*, 1857) two of the main actors are jurists.[5] It was the generation of Hans Egede Schack which in the 1840s matured the Scandinavian project to harmonize the legislation as well as to increase the cooperation between Scandinavian jurists.

And also in Finland, since 1809 a grand duchy of Russia, was the cultural Swedish heritage taken care of, for instance by an author like Johan Ludvig Runeberg (1804–1877). His national epic *The Legends of Ensign Ståhl* (*Fänrik Ståhls sägner*, 1848–60) became instrumental for a National revivalist movement. The poem 'The County Governor' ('Landshövdingen') told the story of the county governor Olof Wibelius who in the war between Sweden-Finland and Russia in 1808 had to surrender, but never accepted surrendering the national code and its symbols. The illustrations of this poem became icons for generations of Swedish as well as Finnish lawyers of the twentieth century. Interestingly enough, this poem by Runeberg was read at the solemn court session by one of the members of the Norwegian Supreme Court when the members of the court decided to leave their offices due to the Nazi occupation of Norway in 1940. These short examples demonstrate how Nordic jurists were visible in the romantic, liberal and national era even before the dominating age of modernity and how this cultural iconization of the idealistic lawyers endured into modernity.

From pre-modernity to modernity of the law

Modernity had its period of dawn. This period of pre-modernity between 1870 and 1914 is crucial for the whole theme of visualization of late modern law. Legal pre-modernity is related to important keywords like 'the democratic breakthrough,' including the emancipation of women – and especially within family law of the wife, 'the parliamentarian idea', and the 'secularization of the society'.

Germany emerged as victors of the Franco-German War and became for decades an attractive archetype for the nation-state, not least for the jurists. In 1871 the German Second Empire was inaugurated. It started the great legislation projects on the federal level, initially in legal procedure and penal law (1877) and later in commercial and private law (1898). When the Nordic convention of jurists (Nordiska Juristmötet) convened for its first session in Copenhagen in 1872, it was inspired by its German equivalent (Deutsche Juristentag) which was inaugurated in 1865. It initiated an important networking between Nordic jurists, and connected the networks of professional jurists, theorists as well as practitioners, the representatives of the judiciaries and the private bars as well as the law professors.[6]

The concept used to describe the context for the jurists of the late nineteenth century was 'culture'.[7] For Friedrich Carl von Savigny the law professors were proclaimed as private protectors of the legal culture. Rudolph von Jhering turned it into the concept of competing interests – a concept which became increasingly important in the times to come. His pamphlet *Der Kampf ums Recht* (The Struggle for Law, 1872) was mostly read among the idealistic jurists in the Scandinavian countries and who upheld the historical-cultural approach to the concept of law.[8]

The German *Kulturkampf* in the late 1870s was another very important event within the secularization discourses of importance not only in Germany but also in the Nordic countries. The blasphemy in 'Dygdens lön' (Virtue's Reward) – the first story in August Strindberg's collection of short stories, *Giftas* (Get Married), from 1884 – was brought to publicity in a high-profile jury trial. Strindberg had to show up in a Stockholm courtroom, and even though he was acquitted in his trial by the jury, the blasphemy cases continued and became landmark cases. During the period of pre-modernity the blasphemy cases increased and peaked during the first two decades of the twentieth century.[9]

In Max Weber's famous study *The Protestant Ethic and the Spirit of Capitalism* (1907) he tried to explain how the success of modern Western capitalism was to be found in the roots of protestant ethics. Max Weber's theories on the disenchantment of the world, '*die Entzauberung der Welt*', and his fascination with the symbols, artefacts and rituals within the legal cultures were in a way contradictory to the ongoing secularization and discourses on anti-metaphysical views of the law. Weber and Durkheim in their analyses of civilizations and cultures focused on the distinct place of the law, and on the interpretation of its symbols and rituals. The interpretations made by Weber and Durkheim during pre-modernity are very important also for our late-modern constructs.

An extremely important part of the legal context of the early twentieth century was modernism in fields such as art, literature, music and architecture. It has been noted that even if modernism as such is not a Nordic invention it was extremely important for the image of legal modernization. Modernism was a European movement in which representatives from many countries were involved. All the prominent artists and authors of this period were on one hand a part of a European modernist movement, but at the same time they articulated their exceptionalism in a local (national) environment. To that extent modernism in pre-modernity had interesting similarities to the current experiences in Nordic late-modern society.

A couple of examples of Paris-trained Nordic modernists within art can demonstrate this paradigm shift of art into modernity. The Danish painter Jais Nielsen's (1885–1961) painting *Afgang* (Departure) from 1918 depicts the modern hub, the railway station, and modern human beings, man and woman as equals, who with quick steps are on the move into the future. The clocks are showing the new modern time, it's time for departure into the future. The modern steam train is blowing, preparing to leave for the future. Also the contemporary Swedish expressionist artist Gösta Adrian-Nilsson ('GAN', 1884–1965) expressed the complex modernity in his paintings, as a brutal alternative to the impressionists of the late nineteenth century.

Visualization with help of comparison

One of the keywords within pre-modernity one hundred years ago was *comparability*. Events like world exhibitions demonstrated and compared industrial and commercial artefacts from all over the world. At the world exhibition in Paris in 1900, the first organized congress of comparative law, Congrès international de droit comparé, was inaugurated and at the same place in the same year a similar important congress of the scholars of comparative literature was founded.[10] In the concept of the nation-state the national identities and communalities were compared.

Within this intellectual concept, in which the discourses were dominated by a well-educated bourgeoisie, we have to identify the visualization of law in the Nordic countries a hundred years ago. Also at that time the geo-political situation had changed with the break-up of the union between Norway and Sweden in 1905.

Modern criminal procedure visualized the conflicts of society.[11] In 1906, the Swedish legislator introduced the public defence counsel. It was a reform initiated by liberal lawyers in parliament. It was, however, a very controversial reform among the lawyers. The members of the Swedish Bar Association were split between those who were prepared to defend the rights of the accused in the courtroom and those who were afraid that this official task should be noted as a defence of the criminal deed.[12] In Scandinavia the criminal defence lawyer is a part of legal modernity. From a European perspective, Honoré Daumier's *Les gens de justice* (1845) gave an ironical and satirical picture of the Parisian lawyers and their counterparts in the courtrooms of *les palais de justice*. Also the Danish cartoonist Robert Storm Pedersen frequently noted the sarcastic and humorous points of the rituals of the legal procedure.[13]

The visualization of the European legal modernity was to a great extent related to the modernization of the legal procedure in the European countries.[14] The modern European legal procedure was codified firstly in France during the first decade of the nineteenth century and secondly in Germany in the late 1870s. Even if there were ongoing discourses on commensurable procedural reforms in the Nordic countries, the legal reforms occurred later in those countries and then especially with the German criminal procedure as a model. The modern criminal procedure was introduced first in Norway with legislation (*Juryloven*) adopted in 1887 and implemented in 1890. It was followed by a similar reform in Denmark (*Retsplejeloven*) in 1916. Even if, as mentioned, the public defence counsel was introduced in 1906, the great Swedish procedural reform was not realized until the implementation of the new Procedural code (*Rättegångsbalken*) in 1948. In Finland this reform was only introduced in the 1990s. We can observe this time lag in legal reforms in the relation between the positions of legal professions in the Nordic countries as well as in the artefacts which visualize this legal culture.

Swedish legal profession on one hand increasingly adjusted to modern society. During pre-modernity idealistic virtues still dominated the discourses – even if they were increasingly criticized. The virtues of the private, modern bar associations competed with those of the traditional public judiciary. As women were not eligible for public positions they got an arena as lawyers in the private sector. The professional members of the modern bar associations increasingly went public and were visible in different new roles, as law reformers as well as public defenders of the accused in criminal cases. The balance between the legal actors in the courtroom increasingly changed. The abolishment of the inquisitorial procedure and the introduction of the adversarial procedure changed the focus from the judge to the interplay between the professional prosecutor and the lawyer on the public court stage. It also resulted in a Europeanization of the courtrooms in the Nordic countries.[15]

August Strindberg (1849–1912) brought his own legal conflicts to the courtrooms and changed his legal representatives frequently. He did not have trust in either his lawyers nor in the judiciary. Public criticism against the legal actors was commonplace in the public discourses of the late nineteenth century. In 1892 Strindberg published a play about his divorce from his first wife, Siri von Essen. She belonged to the nobility, he to a low bourgeoisie family. In the play *Bandet* (The [Marriage] Bond) the parties have reversed social status. Now it is the husband who belongs to the nobility, and the wife has a lower social position. The setting of the play is a courtroom. The judge is only 27 years old and totally inexperienced, the lawyer is a villain and the parties are totally absorbed by a corrupt legal system and its representatives. *The Bond* is a good example of the visualization of a legal-political claim for reforms. Even if Strindberg's description of the imperfect Swedish legal system in *The Bond* is filled with blunders and inadvertences, it demonstrates how he is using the public arena of the theatre stage to demonstrate his own experiences of law's lack and failures.[16]

Staging the law: Legal problems on the stage

During modernity the visualization of law increasingly was to be identified in public national institutions. The national theatres in the Nordic capitals became instrumental for the creation of national identities. In Copenhagen the Royal Theatre (Det kongelige Teater) upheld the national traditions of Ludvig Holberg – whose comedies to a great extent were about legal problems and legal actors.[17] Nationalteatret in Oslo (The National Theatre) staged the plays of Björnstjerne Björnsson and Henrik Ibsen, again with social realities and modern legal problems.[18] In Sweden August Strindberg dominated the scene, not only at the Dramatiska teatern (National Dramatic Theatre) but also at his own Intima teatern (Chamber Theatre). Several of his plays from the first decade of the twentieth century were produced for this theatre. Several of the plays by Björnsson, Ibsen and Strindberg have been iconic for legal modernity. In Henrik Ibsen's 'social dramas' he 'unmercifully swings the lash over the world's widespread sins, hypocrisy, sophistry, immorality, indifference to women's rights [and] worship of the right of the majority'.[19] Ibsen's play *A Doll's House* (*Et dukkehjem*) has become an international icon for the emancipation of the married woman in the sphere of family relations. Nora leaves the family as a modern emancipated woman. August Strindberg complicated the drama in *Miss Julie* (*Fröken Julie*) when he created an impossible relationship between the aristocratic lady and her servant Jean. Jean belongs to his fiancée Kristina, a devoted Christian believer and upholder of traditional Christian values. *Miss Julie* not only demonstrates the modern class conflict but also the conflict between secular and Christian values.

Christian grace and mercy also plays an important role in August Strindberg's passion play from 1900, *Easter* (*Påsk*). It tells the story of the Heyst family, where the father is sentenced to prison due to having falsified bonds. Strindberg wrote the play during his stay in Lund and the dialogue has several references to a small, academic diocese city. The main part is played by the usurer Lindquist, who has the falsified bonds in his possession, and who holds the destiny of the family in his hands. He offers grace and mercy but the son, Elis Heyst, is not prepared to accept this offer from the usurer.[20]

Usury is a legal concept which was totally modernized during the period of pre-modernity. Bismarck's concept of usury in the German reform legislation in the 1880s focused on the weaker part in the contract situation. If somebody used the weakness or the weaker capacities of one party in the contract for his own benefits he should be punished and the contract annulled. Sweden introduced a similar code of usury in 1901.[21] Usury is also in focus in one of the most played national comedies, *Swedenhielms* by Hjalmar Bergman (1883–1931). It was published in 1925 and belongs to the Swedish modern literary heritage. *Swedenhielms* is about a bourgeoisie family in Stockholm. The father becomes a Nobel laureate in chemistry – the most prestigious and honoured academic prize – but the plot takes a dramatic turn when his sons, to acquire money in order to live a more luxurious life, falsify their father's signature. The usurer again plays the role of visualizer of the eroded morality of the bourgeoisie.

There is a common thread of social consciousness throughout the period of pre-modernism and pre-modernity from August Strindberg to Hjalmar Bergman. The creation of the modern nation-state and its legal problems are continuously visualized on the stage, both nationally and internationally.

Legal palaces and theatres: Courthouses and courtrooms

In the later part of the nineteenth century national public institutions like parliaments and courts were constructed with help of the first generations of modern professional architects. The Assemblée Nationale in Paris and the Reichstag building in Berlin demonstrated the sovereignty of the people principle and parliamentary power. They got their analogue constructs in the Nordic countries like the Folketing at

Christiansborg in Copenhagen, the Storting in Christiania/Oslo and the Riksdag in Stockholm.

The courthouses were parallel artefacts to the parliaments. The petrified legal cultures in courthouses represent what Emile Durkheim called '*faits sociaux*'.[22] Courthouses in Paris, Brussels and Leipzig were constructed as national monuments, as 'Temples of Justice'. The architects combined the long traditions going back to Greek antiquity and Roman temples with its impressive pillars and monumental stairs together with functions for modern legal procedural reform. The courtrooms were constructed for modern oral and public hearings. The Nordic analogues to those European courthouses were introduced during pre-modernity. They combined European influences with national, regional and even local historical identities. In Sweden, the town halls in Helsingborg and Östersund, and the local courthouses in Tranås and Jönköping, are good examples in that respect.

Interestingly enough this type of local courthouse combined architectural modernism with legal modernity. The courthouse in Sölvesborg from 1920 drawn by the architect Erik Gunnar Asplund (1885–1940) demonstrates how the architect combines elements belonging to the deep structures of the European legal culture, the front as a temple gable, the impressive stairs and the clock with functional elements. 'In truth, the functionalism's bird of Phoenix has burrowed itself down into the ashes of the antique ruins, before he lifts his wings towards the red light of dawn', a colleague of Asplund described this famous artefact of legal culture.[23]

Modernism in functional architecture dominated after 1930. The yellow brickstone courthouses in Katrineholm (1935) and Sunne (1937) have representative and modern functional facades. The modern principles in the drafts of the new modern procedural code were also reflected in those buildings. On the other hand, as late as in the 1950s the traditional and prestigious location of the courtrooms were still upheld, even if they are moved to the first floor with elegant interior staircases between the floors – as can be seen, for example, in Skellefteå and Falköping.[24]

The new legal procedure reform from 1948 also introduced new courts of appeal in Gothenburg and Sundsvall. Famous Swedish architects drew these buildings during the years of World War II.[25] Both of them were inaugurated in 1948 and represent the judicial culture of its time with a special *Zeitgeist* due to the political circumstances. Both of them are representatives of a distinct national historical identity and traditional monuments in a modern idiom.

The local courthouses were by tradition constructed, maintained and owned by a local community, 'Tingshusbyggnadsskyldige', the members of which were local farmers. The strong Swedish nation-state in 1970, however, decided to take over the responsibility for the maintenance of the courthouses and confiscated them to the state. With this paradigm shift within the legal culture also legal modernity became visible. In the 1970s a more bureaucratic and homogeneous legal culture of modernity was demonstrated and visualized with a dominating pragmatic agency-like architecture. The new courthouses in Halmstad and Sundsvall from the early 1970s can represent this new trend. The visualization of the courthouse as a state authority is well connected to the role of the judiciary and the courts in the new constitution, Regeringsformen, from 1974. This constitution made the sovereignty of the people principle manifest, and it didn't include a chapter related to the courts and the judiciary. Courts and agencies were combined and were regarded as analogue within modern Swedish constitutional culture.[26] The presence of courthouses in the local communities has been observed in the Nordic countries with recent publications.[27]

Sacral rituals and judicial rites

The visualization of the public legal modernity also takes place in the courtrooms, with the legal procedure a part of traditional rituals and rites. The legal procedure as a whole is filled with ritual elements, iterated in case after case, day after day. There are parallels between the liturgy in the mass in the churches and that of procedural norms and forms in cases in the courtrooms.[28]

Also the judicial robes of the judiciaries which are used in all Nordic countries but Sweden are a part of a European tradition. In the Finnish courts there was a discussion on the topic in the early 1950s when the Court of Appeal in Helsinki was inaugurated, but the judicial robes were introduced.[29] The high courts in Europe as well as the Supreme Court in the US are upholding procedural rituals and a judicial culture with sacral elements.[30] The taking of the oaths[31] and the lawyers' pleadings are examples of medieval procedural traditions still visualizing legal authority and social dramatic conflicts in the courtroom.

Law and mass-media

In this volume different aspects of legal visualization will be demonstrated and discussed. In November 2006 – at the time of the symposium from which the chapters in this volume emerged – the participants could follow the criminal case against Saddam Hussein on TV. At the same time, the participants could follow another historical trial on DVD, the Nuremburg trials from the autumn of 1946. These trials were documented with film cameras and shown to the public. It was, however, first in 2006, sixty years after the court sessions, that the films from these historical court sessions were made available on DVD, which were offered as a complimentary gift to readers who purchased a copy of the German weekly *Der Spiegel*. The old documentary not only made the court sessions public to a new generation of German citizens, it also upheld the discourse on elaborating the national history, '*Bewältigung der Vergangenheit*'.

It was in the criminal case against the American football player O. J. Simpson in 1995 that court cases came into the living rooms of the American citizens. The trial was continuously televised over national American networks and introduced the late-modern way of showing the public the real courtroom case. As during pre-modernity, it demonstrated in a clear way the fight in the courtroom between the strong and the weak party.

In the contemporary Nordic legal culture the national constitutions have been revised. In Nordic countries parliamentary committees are creating discourses on the position of the constitution for a national identity. It is today more visible than in earlier versions of the constitutions. The Swedish constitution of 1974 is, as mentioned, to a great extent devoted to the sovereignty of the people principle. Even if there are claims today for giving visibility to Montesquieu and his separation-of-power principle (like the Norwegian constitution since 1814) there has in Sweden been a great reluctance to give more power back to the judges and the courts. A dissertation at Uppsala Law Faculty recently showed that the Swedish judiciary and its professional judicial culture is slowly adjusting to a European standard.[32]

The dilemma within Swedish judicial culture can be shown by this concluding example from a calendar produced by the National Court Administration (Domstolsverket) and which hung over almost every desk of the employees in the Swedish courts. The picture shows the (former) Minister of Justice Thomas Bodström – the highest representative of the law in the executive branch – mingling at an inauguration of a Swedish courthouse in 2004.[33] In this volume on the visualization of the law one main question is what message this picture is sending to its addressee about judicial independence, the need for an autonomous judiciary and judicial confidence. One relevant comment could be that pictures, metaphors, symbols and icons are still playing an important role in giving identity to the legal cultures – in Sweden as well as in other Nordic countries – and I'm convinced that this volume will richly contribute to this statement. Today we are not only identifying the Nordic legal cultures – we are also trying to identify the living ruins of the past.[34] The living ruins, in the sense of Caspar David Friedrich, belong to the deep – and transnational – structures of the Nordic legal histories.

Notes

1 Stefan Ruppert, *Kirchenrecht und Kulturkampf: Historische Legitimation, politische Mitwirkung und wissenschaftliche Begleitung durch die Schule Emil Ludwig Richters* (Tübingen: Mohr & Siebeck, 2002).

2 Boaventura de Sousa Santos, 'Law. A Map of Misreading: Toward a Post-modern Conception of Law', *Journal of Law and Society* 14, no. 3 (1987), pp. 3 ff.

3 Kjell Å Modéer, 'Östersjöområdets rättsliga kartor – rättskulturella konstruktioner i förändring', in Jukka Kekkonen et al. (eds.), *Norden, rätten, historia: Festskrift till Lars Björne* (Helsinki: Suomen lakimiesyhdistys, 2004), pp. 193 ff.

4 Kjell Å Modéer, 'Carl Jonas Love Almqvist och juridiken. Ett law & literature-perspektiv', in *Festskrift till Johan Hirschfeldt* (Uppsala: Iustus Förlag Uppsala, 2008), pp. 277 ff.

5 Aage Jørgensen, 'Hans Egede Schack's Phantasterne', *Forum for Modern Language Studies 1970* VI(2), pp. 173 ff.; Jørgen Mathiassen, *Hans Egede Schack som jurist og politiker. Dokumentation og dokumenter* (Gad: Copenhagen, 1978).

6 Henrik Tamm, *De nordiske juristmøder 1872–1972: Nordisk retssamvirke gennem 100 år* (Copenhagen: Nyt Nordisk Forlag, 1972).

7 Joseph Kohler, *Das Recht als Kulturerscheinung. Einleitung in die vergleichende Rechtswissenschaft* (Würzburg, 1885).

8 Kjell Å Modéer, 'Jherings Rechtsdenken als Herausforderung für die skandinavische Jurisprudenz', in Okko Behrends (ed.), *Jhering's Rechtsdenken: Theorie und Pragmatik im Dienste evolutionärer Rechtsethik* (Göttingen: Vandenhoeck & Ruprecht, 1996).

9 Kjell Å Modéer, *Strindberg och advokaterna* (Stockholm: Norstedts Förlag, 1987), pp. 41 ff.

10 Carl Fehrman, *Litteraturhistorien i Europaperspektiv: Från komparatism till kanon* (Lund, 1999).

11 Katherine Fischer Taylor, *In the Theater of Criminal Justice: The Palais de Justice in Second Empire Paris* (Princeton: Princeton University Press, 1993).

12 Kjell Å Modéer, 'Den offentlige försvararen: Rättshistoriska studier rörande frågan om rättegångsbiträde åt häktad', in *Rättshistoriska studier tillägnade Gösta Hasselberg, Rättshistoriska studier 5* (Lund, 1977), pp. 252 ff.

13 Peter Borberg, '– Har De været straffet før? Nej, hr. dommer – altid bagefter…' *Advokaten* 3 (2007).

14 Jean-Louis Halpèrin, *La visualisation des differentes procedures en Europe, XVIIIe – XXe siècle*, Sociétés & Représentations, no. 18 (2004), p. 63.

15 Kjell Å Modéer, *Det heliga rummet. Domstolsbyggnadernas roll i det civila samhället* (Helsinki: Lakimies, 2000), pp. 1060 ff.

16 Kjell Å Modéer, *Strindberg och advokaterna*, pp. 94 ff.

17 Klaus Neiiendam and Ditlev Tamm, *Holberg og juristerne: en antologi med indledninger* (Copenhagen: Jurist- og Økonomforbundets Forlag, 1984); Hanne Petersen, 'Ludvig Holberg og europæisk retskultur', in Henning Koch and Anne Lise Kjær (eds.), *Europæisk retskultur – på dansk* (Copenhagen: Thomson/GadJura, 2004).

18 Toril Moi, *Henrik Ibsen and the Birth of Modernism: Art, Theater, Philosophy* (Oxford: Oxford University Press, 2006).

19 Kristofer Janson, *The Religious Views of Björnson and Ibsen*, Reprinted from the Report of the Fifth Universal Congress for Free Christianity and Religious Freedom (Berlin-Schöneberg: Protestantischer Schriftenvertrieb, 1910), p. 9.

20 Anders Jarlert, 'Rätt och nåd i Strindbergs "Påsk" – Rättsteologiska perspektiv', in Bernhard Diestelkamp et al. (eds.), *Liber Amicorum Kjell Å Modéer* (Lund: Juristförlaget i Lund, 2007), pp. 271 ff.

21 Kjell Å Modéer, '"God affär" eller "brottslig gärning": Om tillkomsten av 1901 års lag om ocker', in Per-Edwin Wallén et al. (eds.), *Festskrift till Hans Thornstedt* (Stockholm: Norstedts, 1983), pp. 519 ff.

22 Emile Durkheim, *Critical Assessments*, ed. Peter Hamilton (London: Routledge, 1990), pp. 118 ff.

23 Hakon Ahlberg, *Tidsbilder III. Sölvesborg under 1900-talets första halvsekel* (1993), p. 135.

24 Kjell Å Modéer, 'From Idealistic to Realistic Surroundings for Swedish Legal Actors: Iconography and Architecture in Swedish Courthouses 1900–1970', in *Från Schlyters lustgård: rättshistoriska uppsatser 3* (Lund, 2004), pp. 61 ff.

25 The building for the Court of Appeal in Gothenburg is drawn by the architect Hakon Ahlberg and the Court of Appeal in Sundsvall by the architects Backström & Reinius in Stockholm.

26 Kjell Å Modéer, 'Den svenska och nordiska samhällsreligionen', in Anders Mellbourn (ed.), *Författningskulturer: Konstitutioner och politiska system i Europa, Asien och Asien* (Lund: Sekel Bokförlag, 2009), pp. 175 ff.

27 Eva Löfgren, *Rümmet och rätten. Tingshus som föreställning, byggnad och rum i användning 1734–1970*, Institutet för rättshistorisk forskning, diss. (Gothenburg, University of Gothenburg, Stockholm, 2011). Peter Garde (ed.), *Danmarks tinghuse* (Copenhagen: Jurist- og Økonomforbundets Forlag, 2006); Pia Letto-Vanamo and Timo Honkanen, *Moments of Finnish*

Justice in the 1970's (Helsinki: Edita, 2005); cf. Pia Letto-Vanamo's contribution in this volume.

28 Kjell Å Modéer, 'Religionens plats i det offentliga rummet: Rättshistoriska och rättskulturella perspektiv', *Svensk teologisk kvartalsskrift* 81 (2005), pp. 1 ff.

29 Virpi Harju Toimittaja (ed.), *Oikeuden kuva, Bilden av rätten och rättvisan* (Helsinki: Riksdagsbiblioteket, 2000), pp. 275 f.

30 John E. Semonche, *Keeping the Faith: A Cultural History of the U.S. Supreme Court* (Lanham: Rowman & Littlefield Publ., 1998).

31 Martin Sunnqvist, 'Domareden och dess religiösa inslag', in Kjell Å Modéer (ed.), *Rätt, religion och politik. Ett rättshistoriskt seminarium tillägnat Magnus Sjöberg*, Rättshistoriska skrifter, vol. 9 (Stockholm, 2008), pp. 85 ff.

32 Olof Ställvik, *Domarrollen: Rättsregler, yrkeskultur och ideal* (Stockholm: Jure Förlag, 2009).

33 *Almanacka 2005* (Domstolsverket: Jönköping, 2005).

34 Kjell Å Modéer, 'Living Ruins of the Law: On Legal Change and Legal History in the Late Modernity', *Scandinavian Studies in Law* 53 (2008), pp. 219 ff., Kjell Å Modéer, 'Det historiska argumentet i senmodern rättslig diskurs', in *Svensk Juristtidning* 3 (2009), pp. 340 ff.

2

Visualization of the Law

Peter Wahlgren

This chapter is divided into five sections. The discussion starts with the basic question as to *why* it is relevant to study means of visualizing the law. The second section provides a brief *inventory* of various ways of understanding the concept of visualization of the law. In relation to this some possible connections between established means of legal knowledge representation and the *concept of visualization* are addressed. The third part presents a number of possible *functions* that can be related to different means of representing the law. The discussion continues with an analysis of the *relationships* between various representation forms, and finally some tentative *conclusions* are presented.

Why study visualization of the law?

If one compares law and jurisprudence to other sciences and to the development of knowledge in general several things come to mind. First and foremost it is apparent that law to a large extent is a text-based phenomenon. Legislation, preparatory materials, court decisions, and commentaries almost without exception manifest themselves in the form of texts, and in many situations the law is so intimately correlated to its textual form that it is even difficult to envision any alternatives.

In a broader perspective, however, it appears beyond doubt that well-formed and customised-representation languages can be of great importance for the development of scientific knowledge. Mathematics, chemistry and physics are candid examples where domain-related notations have been important tools during long periods of time, and eventually have become standardized. The digital revolution is another illustration of how means of representation can affect our understanding of various subject matters in the most fundamental way. In all these cases the establishing of non-textual forms of representation has had effects that are difficult to overestimate. It is also noticeable that visual representations, as for example the periodical system and the graphical representations of elements, often function as catalysts when it comes to the accumulation of knowledge. As the tools for representations improve, more details, additional levels, and further aspects can be described and communicated, which in turn leads to an aggregation of knowledge, and in many domains this is an iterative process.

Consequently, it is well-motivated and interesting to investigate whether and to what extent our understanding and use of the law can improve with access to additional tools of representation, or, to use a slightly different terminology, if the law can be visualized.

What are visualizations of the law?

In contrast to pure mental representations of the law there exists a large variety of manifestations that are observable and possible to elaborate. Firstly it must nevertheless be mentioned that also *text* is a form of visualization. It should likewise be underlined that text is, and for the foreseeable future will remain, the most important tool in this respect.

It is furthermore evident that text in the form of phrases and words can be a core element in other types of formalisms. Well-known and already in use in the legal sector are for example semi-formal ways to describe relations between different aspects by means of using *matrices* and *tables*. Text elements are also in various ways more or less crucial components in other forms of visualizations. To study visualizations of the law is therefore not primarily an activity contrasted to traditional jurisprudential studies; rather it should be looked upon as an explorative activity in which established methods also are included.

Looking beyond representations utilizing text elements, and approaching what more easily can be understood as visualizations, it is indisputable that pictures, films, animations, symbols, and icons can be employed in order to depict different aspects of the law. All these types of visualizations exist in large numbers and in practice some of them are used as primary tools. Examples are road traffic signs (symbols) and clickable 'accept icons' on computer screens. In this context it is also reasonable to mention graphical representations. These in turn can take the form of fault trees, flow charts, semantic nets, hierarchical illustrations, and various kinds of so-called mind maps.

In addition to graphical representations there exists a long tradition in the field known as *legal logic*, where numerous notations are utilized in order to describe legal phenomena. Some logical languages have been developed in other fields of science while other forms have been developed with the specific purpose of supporting the legal domain. The latter is for instance the case with deontic logic.

In its broadest sense one can argue that *law in action*, as for example the way it is observable in *court processes*, is a form of visualization, where at least some attributes are elaborated with the intent to communicate legal aspects such as power, legitimacy, etc. Following this line of thought also more *tangible things*, for instance law books, law libraries and court buildings, can be looked upon as visualizations.

The enumeration need not be extended. As this brief overview illustrates, it is possible to understand the concept of visualization in several ways. It is likewise clear that both established means of representation and more unorthodox approaches can be included. An important distinction is also that several tools for representation have been developed in a conscious way, while other kinds of visualization are generated spontaneously and as side effects (e.g. law libraries). It is furthermore noticeable that formal means of representation as well as other visualizations can appear in various combinations.

What are the functions of various visualizations/representations?

Contemplating the existence of various manifestations of the law, it soon becomes quite obvious that most of them primarily fulfil different functions. Equally apparent is that this often is an overlooked fact and sometimes a point of departure for criticism; representations of formal logic are for instance often discarded as being too abstract and difficult to understand, while texts are criticized as being voluminous and thus too time consuming to read and complicated to grasp, etc.

Statements of the latter kind can, however, be confronted rather easily. If one articulates the fact that logic first and foremost is a *tool for analysis*, and not a practicable mean for the communication of comprehensive materials, much of the criticism loses its edge. Similarly, if it is stressed that text primarily is an efficient *vehicle for communication of large quantities of data*, and not the best way of providing quick summaries of a holistic nature, the disapproving attitude may be challenged.

Reflecting further over this state of the matter it becomes clear that various means of representation have different strengths and weaknesses. As mentioned, formal logic is an analytical tool which can be highly efficient for the skilled analyst who wants to deepen his or her knowledge concerning a specific issue. At the same time it is evident that it is a rather useless approach to depend on formal logic if one wants to communicate large volumes of information to broad groups in society.

Symbols, as for example road traffic signs, on the other hand, are doubtlessly efficient means of communication, but as contrasted to logic quite mediocre as tools for analysis. The exemplification can easily be extended: graphical representations and diagrams are primarily ways of summarizing complex matters, matrices are ways of illustrating how different aspects of various components can be related to each other in a more comprehensive way than what can be accomplished with linear text, mind maps can be highly efficient when a field of knowledge first is explored and when various components are to be identified, and so forth.

The functions and the relations between various representations

From the existence of various strengths and weaknesses of various forms of representation follows that it would be possible to elaborate the knowledge concerning the ultimate function of different visualizations, as related to patent requirements in the legal sector. At least two dimensions of requirements seem reasonable to start out from. It may be suggested that

a) There is a need to represent details as well as a need to represent holistic matters and all things in between, i.e. there is a need to manage various levels of description efficiently.
b) There is a need to analyze as well as a need to communicate, i.e. there is a need to manage various forms of transformation of data efficiently.

It can furthermore be suggested that both a) and b) can be looked upon as spectrums in the sense that there exists a continuum from details to holistic matters, as well as a continuum from forms of representation primarily supporting analysis to forms of representation primarily supporting communication. The functions and relations between various forms of representations in law can thus be visualized in the diagram below.

Conclusions

It is quite obvious that various forms of representation have different pros and cons. Equally apparent is that a better understanding of when and why various forms should be utilized, and, most importantly, how they can be combined, in many ways can improve legal knowledge and facilitate legal knowledge management.

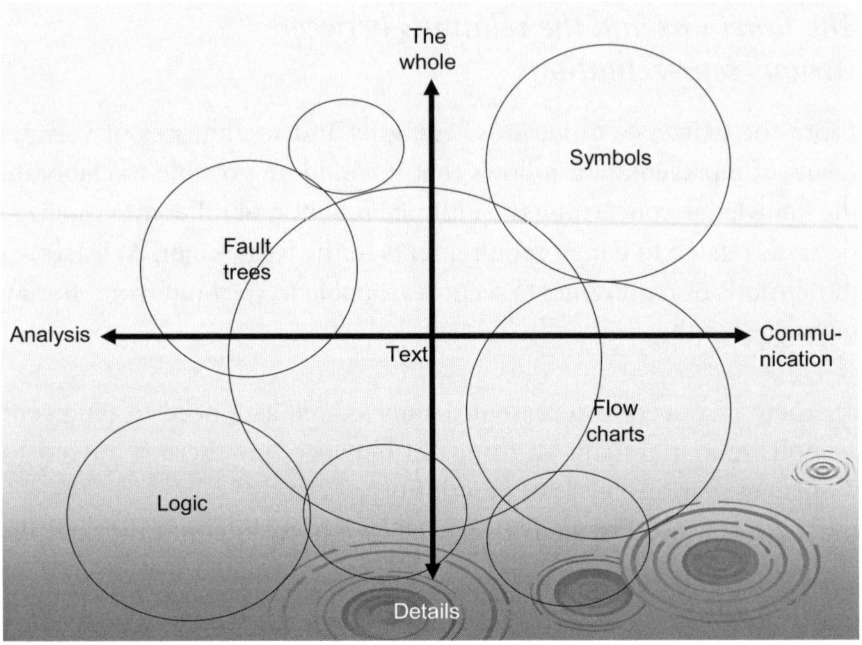

Another conclusion from this brief discussion on visualizations of the law is that the topic should be approached in the broadest possible way. The focal points of research should not only be means of representation. In order to understand what kind of representations are interesting to develop, various kinds of requirements of the law should also be investigated.

Note

An earlier version of this paper appeared in Erich Schweighofer, Anton Geist, Gisela Heindl and Christian Szücs (eds.), *Komplexitätsgrenzen der Rechtsinformatik* (Stuttgart: Boorberg, 2008).

3

On-stage and Off-stage European and Global Legal Scenes

Hanne Petersen

Historical stages and European-inspired repertoire

About three hundred years ago – in 1716 – the Norwegian-Danish academic and writer Ludwig Holberg (1684–1756) published a very influential book on natural law in Danish. The book was an introduction to natural law and international law largely copying Hugo Grotius, Samuel Pufendorf (who had been a professor of international law at the University of Lund) and Thomasius – who was a pupil of Pufendorf. This book was to be re-edited and republished six times in the period from 1728 to 1763, and was translated into German in 1748 and into Swedish in 1789.

During the two decades from 1704 to 1726 Holberg went on a long series of trips to European centres of learning and intellectual life. He was born in the important harbour and commercial city of Bergen, went to Copenhagen, later Amsterdam and stayed at Oxford University for almost two years from 1706 to 1708. He went on trips to Dresden, Leipzig and Halle, and from 1714 to 1716 he travelled without passport and to a large degree on foot from The Netherlands to Paris on to Rome via Marseille and Genoa because he had little money. He returned to Copenhagen via Paris, but never returned to Bergen.[1]

During the twentieth century natural law fell into disrespect among especially Scandinavian legal philosophers, and Holberg's work as a natural lawyer was forgotten and repressed. But Holberg as such was not forgotten. In the nine years from 1718 to 1727 he had written a large number of satirical and critical pieces of literature, and during the last five years of this period he wrote twenty-five comedies which have been played and replayed in Danish and Nordic theatres for countless school classes and adult audiences. They were written during absolutism (which in Denmark lasted from 1660 to 1849), where neither freedom of religion nor freedom of speech was guaranteed, but they were also written during the Enlightenment, and by a writer strongly inspired by this movement.

Holberg continued to be interested in issues concerning politics and political freedom. In 1748 he translated elements from Montesquieu's *L'Esprit de Lois*, protesting against the burning of heretics by the Catholic Inquisition. He was strongly inspired and influenced by Molière (1622–1673), another satirical, critical, and most important moral and normative European writer – who had also studied law. Both of them dealt with issues concerning religious freedom and issues concerning the freedom of women to marry without intervention from fathers and family. Holberg's view on marriage became gradually more liberal through his period of comedy writing, and this was reflected in the revised versions of his natural law treatise. His legal philosophical ideas – presented on the stage – pointed towards the ideas of equality of the French Revolution which would take place some sixty years later. Molière and Holberg can perhaps be seen as forerunners of emerging European legal culture.

It can perhaps be claimed that at least in Denmark and probably also in Norway, liberal human rights-oriented thinking – especially thinking about the close relation between law and justice – has been preserved during a period of legal positivism through the performance of Holberg's comedies, which relied so strongly on a European heritage.[2] This is demonstrated amongst others in Holberg's discussions about women's roles in his *Jean de France*, a comedy that focuses on the arranged marriage between the ridiculous Hans Frandsen, who has renamed himself after having studied in France, and Elsebet, to whom he is engaged because of parental and patriarchal interests. Elsebet is in love with Antonius and has her smart female servant, Marthe, involved in securing her love marriage.[3] In the summer of 2007 both the Norwegian national theatre and the Danish open air theatre, Grønnegårdsteatret, staged *Erasmus Montanus*, Holberg's play about the pompous scholar who learns Latin and logic, and ridicules his family and local fellows from the countryside. The description of the power of knowledge and the word – but also of common sense and pragmatism – is the focus of this piece, still of common Nordic relevance.

Peripheral scenes and European legal repertoire

The Nordic legal – and literary – scenes have for centuries been strongly inspired and influenced by the European legal and cultural repertoire. During absolutism, monarchs were important directors and influencers of the local legal and literary scenes. When the international repertoire changed, they also changed the local repertoire. After the French Revolution Sweden got a democratized constitution in 1809, and the same year Finland was occupied from Sweden by Russia. Norway was transferred from Denmark to Sweden in 1814 after the Napoleonic wars – but tried to establish its own scene with the Eidsvoll Constitution from 17 May 1814. After the European revolutions of 1848 the Danish monarch in 1849 gave the bourgeoisie a constitution and thus transformed absolutism into constitutional monarchy. The Nordic legal scenes gradually shifted to coming increasingly under the control of the parliaments. From 1901 the Danish scene became dominated by the lower chamber – the Folketing – increasingly under control of the social democratic mass party and the agrarian party. The year of the aborted Russian revolution in 1905 was also the year when the Personal union between Norway and Sweden was dissolved, and Norway established its own local national scene. During WWI, in 1915, women and non-landowning men entered the scene in Denmark as voters, but only much later did women become MPs in significant numbers. The Grand Duchy of Finland, which had enjoyed relative autonomy within the Russian empire, provided general voting rights for men and women already in 1906, before it was established as an independent state in 1917.

The Nordic countries were some of the first to allow female actors to enter the legal scene, and that has no doubt also influenced the repertoire of the lawmaker, not least through the rapid introduction of welfare systems. Democratic rule seems to have produced varying, but more local legal scenes with different actors. The Nordic legal scenes do not belong to the central European scenes, but they have struggled to keep up to date, and they have offered some inspiration especially in the twentieth century for the relation between welfare-state and citizen, as well as for gender relations.[4] They have also contributed with authors, actors and some players in the debates on post- or late-modern law and perhaps especially practice. Copenhagen, Oslo, Stockholm, and Helsinki have belonged to the off-stage legal scenery in European history, with its legal repertoire of the local legal scenes having been inspired both by the leading scenes and actors, by the classical European – and increasingly Anglo-American – repertoire, and by the repertoire of the close neighbours.

After WWII the legal scenes shifted again, and a European legal scene emerged on the market. The Kingdom of Denmark entered this scene together with the United Kingdom – its great export market for agricultural products – in 1973, with great enthusiasm on behalf of the political actors, and with very mixed feelings on behalf of the audience, who were and still are reluctant in terms of the new rules of the game. According to Hjalte Rasmussen the Danish constitution has now become 'a mere symbol of national unity.'[5] In Norway the audience opted for the local stage during the same year, and Sweden and Finland only became explicit players on the European scene from 1995 after the collapse of communism, and with the role of the former influential Soviet Union being very unclear and insecure.

Because the scenes are local, small and utilize languages which are more or less mutually understandable but inaccessible to most externals, there is some leeway for both a local repertoire, and for local interpretations of foreign plays.[6]

Leading European normative scenes

Scandinavian legal realism of the twentieth century – and especially its Danish representative, Alf Ross – was strongly inspired by the intellectual scene of Europe and particularly Vienna after the collapse of the Austro-Hungarian Empire in 1918. Ross studied with Hans Kelsen in Vienna in the early 1920s. Kelsen personified the indirect Jewish influence on the legal positivist repertoire of modernity in the beginning of the twentieth century. He moved to Cologne to teach and from there on to Geneva – one of the central European and international legal and political scenes – in 1933, when he could no longer stay in Cologne.[7] After WWI Geneva had become the headquarters of the League of Nations, as The Hague became the seat of the Permanent Court of Justice. Geneva is still a global city and a normative scene housing a large number of global organizations. The Hague has since the end of the Cold War become the stage dealing with the crimes that took place during the dissolution of Yugoslavia – the International Criminal Tribunal for the Former Yugoslavia – and with the International Criminal Court.

The Hague scene has only been used rarely and reluctantly by the Nordic actors it seems. Denmark and Norway met in the Permanent Court of Justice in the beginning of the 1930s in a court case over sovereignty over Eastern Greenland – during the period of colonialism, where indigenous people were considered primitive and uncivilized and understood to populate 'no-man's land', *terra nullius.* Greenlanders were not even imagined to become legal actors at this point. The Nordic actors were competing as 'ordinary' imperial actors and at the same time supported the dominant normative view of the times as to who should be allowed to enter the legal scenes and as to the 'backwardness' of 'primitive peoples'.

During the same period, Hitler used modern mass media to influence and manipulate the masses of especially Germany, but generally also all of Europe. Above all film, the most important normative mass media of the twentieth century, served the purpose of securing popular support for the supremacy of German policy. *Triumph of the Will* produced by Leni Riefenstahl was released in 1935 and rapidly became one of the best-known examples of propaganda in film history.[8] The overriding theme of the film is the return of Germany as a great power, with Hitler as a German Messiah who will bring glory to the nation. The title is a reference to Nietzsche's concept of the 'Will to Power'. Riefenstahl won several awards for the film, not only in Germany but also in the United States, France and Sweden.

The legal repertoire of Nazism and Fascism, based on ideas of totalitarianism, nationalism, racism and exclusivism, influenced the global and European legal scenes – lawmakers, judges and the executive – to greater and lesser degrees.[9] The exclusion of Jews from public service, which led Kelsen and many other Jewish intellectuals to flee Cologne, and the ban on marriage with Jews, were not enforced in the Nordic countries, but Jews were not accepted readily as refugees, and eugenics and forced sterilization of the 'mentally deficient' were widely accepted.[10]

After WWII it was not possible to continue this legal repertoire, and some form of distancing, criticism and renewal was required. Shortly after the end of the war 'The Theatre of the Absurd' was developed especially in France, inspired by existentialist writers, but also by the Swedish writer August Strindberg and his 'dream plays'. Realism was challenged. Meaninglessness in the life of modern and restless humans dominated the descriptive dramas. On the international scene the fight for 'human rights' began with the declaration from 1948, and the tribunals in Nuremberg from 1945 to 1949 dealt with characters of the former regime, who were now representing the wicked and evil. On the local scenes some spectacular showdowns took place dealing with the conflict between former collaborators with former powerful actors.

The shift from the legal positivist repertoire was not felt so strongly in the Nordic countries, all of which, apart from neutral Sweden, had been involved in the war as victims. Especially Germans – including German historians – became involved in '*Vergangenheitsbewältigung*' (the attempt to come to terms with the past). One of more recent and influential expressions of this attempt is *Der Vorleser* (The Reader), a novel from 1995 by legal historian Bernhard Schlink on the postwar relationship between a female guard of a concentration camp and a twenty-year-younger boy of 15, who would later become a lawyer. This novel, which was originally published in 1995, has been translated into thirty-nine languages.[11] The novel deals with fear, shame, aggression, illiteracy and responsibility, ambivalence and powerlessness.

These are issues which the modern, realist *legal* repertoire influential in the Nordic countries has rarely dealt with. The role of the victim during WWII has allowed the repertoire of welfare states to focus more upon assumptions about own moral superiority, pride, security, and how to influence the scenes from the periphery and the subordinate parts. Scandinavians have to a large extent considered themselves the *exception* in a European history of atrocities. A novel by Danish author Christian Jungersen, *Undtagelsen* (The Exception) from 2004, about the tense and paranoic relations between four women working at a fictitious Danish Center for Genocide Information, is based on this assumption while at the same time questioning it.[12] Kjell Åke Modéer has discussed Scandinavian exceptionalism in legal cultures on different occasions – describing Scandinavian legal culture as neither civil law nor common law. A period of harmonization of Nordic legislations in several fields in the homogeneous countries of the beginning of the twentieth century was followed by a more 'individualized' state repertoire after the 1970s. Modéer claims that the Scandinavian exceptionalism is eroding from both inside and outside at this moment.[13]

We do not know yet to what extent the communist and socialist normative repertoire of the years from the 1920s to 1989 have influenced European legal culture and the European generations after WWII at large. Without the influence of the socialist agenda and repertoire, it is hard to imagine the development of the 'welfare state scenery' which is so characteristic of the Nordic legal landscapes, but which also generally influenced the Western European legal scene.[14] The demise of this player and its dominant repertoire is bringing new conflicts to the stages. So far the criticism of former left wing welfare law has characterized parts of the so-called 'cultural war' which in Denmark was declared by the incoming neo-liberal government of 2001. The criticism of legal positivism especially in Denmark has grown after 1989, and justice has again become an argument to be taken seriously.[15]

Emerging legal scenes after WWII – the United States, Europe and global scenes

As a reaction to the depraved legal repertoire of Nazism and Fascism – to the moral collapse of great parts of European thinking including legal thinking – a shift of legal stages took place in the United States and Europe after WWII.

Natural law inspired especially Western legal performance, and human rights (re)turned to the stage. The US which had for some time been the land of the American Dream of social mobility and material gain, as well as the symbol of freedom from the class divided societies of the old world – was to set the new normative agenda. Europe still had some important and emerging legal stages, but people began to long for the Promised Land across the great seas. States may be seen as aesthetic and moral theatres claims the Chinese-American cultural geographer Yi-Fu Tuan,[16] and the attraction of the American moral and aesthetic scene has been extraordinarily powerful during the last half century.[17]

Paul Tillich (1886–1965), a German Lutheran theologian and philosopher, described as one of the most influential theologians of the twentieth century, was, like many others, dismissed from his position in Germany in 1933 – where he was a professor in Frankfurt – and immigrated to the US. In a small book from 1954 called *Love, Power and Justice*, he noted that every power group experiences growth and disintegration. It tries to transcend itself and to preserve itself at the same time. Power is never only physical force, but is also the power of symbols and ideas in which the life of a social group expresses itself. For some groups – as for the Americans – this consciousness about symbols and ideas has become a feeling of a special vocation. It is, however, also a consciousness which, as Tillich foresaw less than ten years after the end of World War II, may with time disintegrate:

> America's vocational consciousness has been called 'the American dream', namely to establish the earthly form of the kingdom of God by a new beginning. The old forms of oppressive power were left behind

> and a new start was made. In the Constitution and the living democracy (both are quasi-religious concepts in the United States) the will is embodied to actualize what is felt as the American vocation. This was originally meant for America alone. Now it is meant explicitly for one-half of the world and implicitly for the whole world. The actual power drive working together with this vocational feeling is still rather limited. But the historical situation increases it more and more. And it is already justified to speak of half-conscious American imperialism.
>
> Vocational consciousness expresses itself in laws. In these laws both justice and law are actual. The justice of the empires is not only ideology or rationalization. The empires not only subject, they also unite. And in so far as they are able to do this, they are not without love. Therefore those who are subjected acknowledge silently that they have become participants of a superior power of being and meaning. If this acknowledgement vanishes because the uniting power of the empire, its strength, and its vocational idea vanish, the empire comes to an end. Its power of being disintegrates and external attacks only execute what is already decided.[18]

The United States, its Supreme Court and democratic spirit were to play the lead role – in some competition with the Soviet Union during the era of the Cold War. The Nordic States were situated in between these leading players, but increasingly oriented towards the North Atlantic.

Paris, Rome and Berlin had all lost moral power and legitimacy. Madrid and Lisbon were captured by totalitarian powers for decades to come. London was on the verge of losing its empire, and thus its status and global normative influence, even though it had come out of WWII as a victor and a part of the allied forces. But exactly for that reason it received no economic support for re-establishing society.

The new and upcoming stages were North American and other European political and commercial stages. The new United Nations was now to assemble in New York and no longer in Geneva. The Council of Europe was established in 1949 and located in Strasbourg – the contested French and earlier German Alsatian border city with a painful history dating back to the Prussian-French war of 1871. Ten years later the European Court of Human Rights was established in the same city, and has now become a major player on both the European and global legal scenes. Major issues in its repertoire are cases concerning religion and family matters – themes already treated in Molière's and Holberg's plays.

The Nordic countries have tried to avoid being summoned to Strasbourg, as they have avoided the scene in The Hague. And due to the overlap between the socialist and the Scandinavian realist approach they seem to have succeeded. But with the increased influence of a natural law, individualist and neo-liberal repertoire this is no longer possible. So again the style and performance is changing.

A Swedish example is a case from 2005 where the public prosecutor had accused a Pentecostal pastor, Åke Green, of general discrimination ('hets mot folkgrupp') against homosexuals. In a sermon in 2003 the pastor had described homosexuality as a cancer in the societal body (and also criticized the possibility of registering homosexual relationships). The Swedish Supreme Court acquitted the pastor from charges of discrimination arguing that a judgement following the allegation of the general prosecutor would have violated religious freedom and freedom of expression as protected in the European Convention on human rights and by the precedents of the European Court of Human Rights.[19]

Thus the perhaps more liberal Nordic legal scene limits its interpretation according to the dominant European custom and usage. This case demonstrates that for the public actors and audiences the role of the European Court is the important stage to look for interpretive influence.

Even if Brussels must be described as the main stage for European law-making – closest to old-style legislation – it has a repertoire so expansive that it seems to be quite confusing to the broad European audience. The EU has not really succeeded in becoming a convincing and uniting player. Only major ceremonial plays on currency and constitutional issues seem to catch the interest of the audience at large, and not always positively. Brussels is a central legal stage but mainly for a specialized audience of the European and neighbouring elite. The European Economic Community, which celebrated its 50th anniversary in 2007 – under the German leadership of a GDR-born natural scientist and daughter of a protestant pastor – has never become really popular with large audiences.

While the *law makers* were the modern legal heroes on the national and especially on the Nordic scenes, the *courts* have now become the post-modern legal heroes on the post-national scenes. In Europe the major legal judicial scenes are to be found in Strasbourg, in Luxemburg, and in Karlsruhe in Germany, where the German Constitutional Court was established following the influence of the Allied Forces and especially the American model on the establishment of the German constitution after WWII. None of the Nordic courts have managed to play a role in this league. The networking among constitutional lawyers on a European and global scale has taken place since the beginning of the 1970s. This network does not have coercive power, but only the 'soft power of information'. It works through '*attraction rather than coercion*' and is creating a 'European constitutional culture', Jutta Limbach, former member of the German constitutional court, informed the audience at a plenary panel on 'Globalization and Constitutional Law' in Berlin in July 2007.[20] These scenes are, however, still viewed with some reluctant interest from the North.

The new normative scenes after WWII were set in the New World and New York, the seat of the new United Nations which experienced an ever expanding membership of new states created after post-colonialism and later after the end of the Cold War. The United Nations is, however, still a centre of *traditional* international law and persuasive power. Its strength in the twenty-first century may lie in its appeal to emerging '*global* dreams', and its ability to ally with new and old non-state global normative players. Its big conference events open to very broad audiences during the last part of the twentieth century indicated the potential for a world audience rather than only an inter-state audience. The recent World Trade Organization (WTO) established in 1995 is located in Geneva, but is also on the move, giving performances and organizing events all over the world it seems, and providing 'Third Country Actors' a stage to perform upon.

New and old normative scenes

Geneva has been called the 'Protestant Rome', and besides the national legal scenes with their divided competences, the old religious normative powers are re-entering the global scene after the collapse of communism. The normative role of the Vatican for European and colonial legal history cannot be overlooked, and the present and future role of religious normativity in general and especially in Europe has been growing and surfacing considerably over the last few decades. During the long reign of John Paul II (from 1978 to 2005) the Vatican Church started to use the new media as a means to convince believers and non-believers alike of the importance of the religious – and political – message. The importance and influence of the Vatican on the fall of communism and the dominance of the capitalist repertoire on the local and global legal scenes has not yet been investigated, but there is no doubt that it played a major role. The burial of John Paul II on 8 April 2005 probably became one of the most globally watched media-events ever. The message was one of both the importance of religiosity in a post-modern world of weaker states, and of cooperation between religions, as several religious and national leaders were present. This Catholic orientation perhaps also diminishes the Nordic, Protestant and secularized influence on the global scenes. Nordic actors seem to have difficulties in operating in an environment where religious rhetoric and values are (again) upgraded.

This also shows in relation to Israel and Jerusalem, which have long been stages and centres for religiously influenced and highly conflictual dramas of very broad importance. The roles of Mecca and Medina seem to become increasingly important for global society, but so far they are viewed as the new villains on the scene by Western and Nordic audiences.

The importance of the media for the emergence of new actors and for political and legal role playing has grown everywhere. The elections in Italy in April 2006 led to the fall of the Italian media mogul Silvio Berlusconi, but in 2008 he was again re-elected. Since 1994 he has a number of times combined the status of owner of media stations and football teams with that of prime minister of Italy. His regime has combined politics and media in a 'media-cracy', unparalleled in Europe after WWII. Berlusconi has been called a 'media-dictator' by Umberto Eco, and Berlusconi's reign has been described in satirical films and on Italian traditional stages.[21] His continued re-election demonstrates both the power of the stage and his popularity as a player for the Italian audience.

The media has in general been a very important stage for the preparation and dissemination of normative messages in the global village. During the last twenty-five years global cable television networks have conquered the media scene and changed it. CNN celebrated its 25-year anniversary in 2005.

Al Jazeera was created in 1996, and claims to be the only politically independent television station in the Middle East. It now rivals the BBC in worldwide audiences with an estimated 50 million viewers. The development of network media and satellite TV is changing the conditions for the creation of norms, for evaluations of normativity and probably also for the execution of normative power.

The destabilization of national sovereignty and the growing importance of religion, market and media have led to the emergence of new forms of authority and government or 'non-governmental forms of power', as it has been witnessed earlier in history.[22] Among the recent actors on the global scene, globalized musicians and singers have increasingly become involved in humanitarian work, legitimizing their general 'political roles'. Bob Geldof is probably the most well-known. He was recently involved in arranging the so-called Live 8 concerts in 2005. As his younger fellow countryman Bono, Bob Geldof is an Irish singer, songwriter, actor and political activist. He is quoted to have said that '[t]hese concerts are the start point for The Long Walk To Justice, the one way we can all make our voices heard in unison.'[23]

Running parallel with the UK's 'Make Poverty History' campaign, the Live 8 shows planned to pressure world leaders to drop the debt of the world's poorest nations, increase and improve aid, and negotiate fairer trade rules in the interest of poorer countries. Ten simultaneous concerts were held on 2 July and one on 6 July 2005 prior to the

G8 meeting in Scotland. More than 1,000 musicians performed at the concerts, which were broadcast on 182 television networks and 2,000 radio networks. On 7 July the G8 leaders pledged to double 2004 levels of aid to Africa from US$ 25 to US$ 50 billion by the year 2010.

In 2007 Al Gore 'imitated' the normative legitimacy and power of these public global events in his initiative and involvement in the Live Earth concerts. In Copenhagen politicians looked forward to hosting a big UN conference on climate change in 2009, and never had so many 'great actors' shown up on the stage simultaneously only to demonstrate that this was not a successful way to run a show. The performance demonstrated the competition between the American and the Chinese stars, none of whom were at this moment able to hold or take over the stage. Nobody emerged as a rising global star, but the power of the American repertoire – or 'vocational idea' in Tillich's term – was clearly challenged.

Scenes and screens

In February 2006 Denmark witnessed the changing and expanding scenes of normative competitive performance first hand in a kind of global wake-up call. What has been termed the 'Cartoon War', the 'Cartoon Controversy' or 'Cartoon Crisis' and in Denmark the 'Mohammed Case', teaches amongst other things that fights about normativity are also fights about 'good stories' for hard pressed media, both old style paper media, and new style satellite media. Good normative stories deal with conflicts, sensations, possibilities of identification, issues of competition – and they appeal to emotions. A local normative performance in an old fashioned local print media, *Jyllands-Posten* (The Jutland Daily), used caricature as a means of criticizing Islam and scapegoating Muslim immigrants in a language nobody presumably understood. Due to technological developments and increased communication in a globalizing world this local performance became part of a global normative event, where the local scene came under strong global pressure to adapt its style and interpretation. Issues of freedom of expression and religion were at stake, but also relations between norms and emotions. Perhaps the fight between the peripheral scenes of the Nordic countries and other powerful regional scenes and actors may become symbols and examples of how globalized scenes and screens influence central players in fights about how to combine, or fuse, a legal repertoire, which has for a long period been mainly mono-cultural.

Domestic 'law-making' in transition – or a neo-liberal repertoire for a new opera?

Monumental architecture is frequently a setting for state theatre, writes Yi-Fu Tuan.[24] The global scenes which present legal culture are not only former castles – turned into parliaments – but also other stages which gradually open their doors to broader audiences:

> New York City Opera opened in February, 1944, at the height of the battles of Anzio and Truk. If sceptics thought it frivolous to start an opera company in the middle of a world war, Fiorello LaGuardia straightened them out: the music-loving Mayor believed that opera was essential to city life, and he wanted lower- and middle-class New Yorkers to have it at affordable prices, without pretension. The company was then part of City Center, on West Fifty-fifth Street, which now concentrates on dance and musical theatre. The composer-critic Deems Taylor called the City Center Opera 'democracy in action, a democracy realizing the work of the individual'. Tickets started at eighty-five cents—nine and a half dollars, in today's currency—and topped out at $2.20.[25]

In the late 1990s the social democratic mayor of Copenhagen, originally a school teacher, Jens Kramer Mikkelsen, was frustrated about the lack of life and dynamics in the city. An architectural competition for a new waterfront was announced. The director of the Royal Theatre (a lawyer) had long wanted a new theatre building, but had not succeeded in convincing the politicians. Politicians in Christiansborg, the seat of the parliament, had started negotiations about an agreement on the future of the Royal Theatre – thus practising the 'negotiational democracy' which Hjalte Rasmussen has described as a 'style of governance that can be likened to the particularities of corporate governance – if one does not forget that Denmark is not a private corporation but a sovereign state.'[26]

While the politicians battled, Mærsk Mc-Kinney Møller (born 1913), shipowner and owner of one of the world's biggest companies – dealing, amongst other things, with container shipping and making big business on globalization – prepared a plan behind the scenes. He bought the Dock Island (Dokøen) situated in alignment with Amalienborg, the royal palace, on an axis with one of the biggest churches of Copenhagen, Marmorkirken (The Marble Church). The church, an imitation of St. Peter's in Rome, was finished by another great Danish industrialist and businessman, C. F. Tietgen, in 1894, 145 years after the laying of the foundation by the absolutist King Frederik V in 1749. The king did not manage to finish it, and neither did his successor nor the state, which took over in 1849. The state sold the construction site to Tietgen, who took about twenty years to finish the church.

Around the turn of the twentieth century shipowner Møller, now close to 90, visited the Queen, the Prime Minister and the Minister of Culture. He offered to donate an opera house to the city and to the Danes. It turned out that the costs of the construction would be tax deductible. Under these conditions Møller would pay all costs and take all decisions regarding architecture, adaptation and artistic arrangement and embellishment. Formally the opera house was donated by the A.P. Møller and Chastine Mc-Kinney Møller Foundation in August 2000 (A.P. Møller, the present shipowner's father, was a co-founder of the company now known as Mærsk). The opera was finished within less than five years and officially opened on 15 January 2005 a few months after the 100-year anniversary of the company and surpassing Tietgen's churchbuilding in efficiency with many years.

This was a gift economy in practice, sidelining democratic procedures for decision-making, and demonstrating the fragility and weakness of local democracy as well as the decision-making power of the shipowner, as described in a film on the process around the construction of the opera house called *Den store gave* (The big gift).[27] The process demonstrated the huge importance and influence of the multinational company in Danish politics and legislation, something which is normally not very public.[28]

Similarly Mærsk was given monopoly rights to drill and extract oil from the North Sea in 1962 by the Danish parliament, and the profits from this lucrative business have been taxed very lightly. Other privileges have been granted to the company through the legislation about business foundations, which are not taxed or publicly controlled. Salaries of foreign seamen working for the shipping company are taxed not according to Danish rules, but to rules of their country of origin, which relieves the company of big financial pressure. When President George Bush, Sr. got involved in the first Gulf War in 1991, Mærsk offered free transportation of american weapons to the war zone.[29] And during the second war against Iraq from 2003, which Denmark supported as a member of the coalition of the willing, a subcompany of one of the Mærsk companies established a billion dollar contract with the American minister of defence on the operation of eight supply ships.[30]

The shipowner, who does not have a reputation as a patron of the arts, is both a very national-minded person and a historically interested person, and the foundation has supported a number of construction projects and other projects for the Danish minority in Germany and projects – amongst them churches, schools and a new Danish gymnasium in the city of Schleswig opened in 2008 – in South Jutland, where the family origins lie.[31]

The support for national projects has perhaps been important in terms of political legitimacy during much of the twentieth century, but the Opera House may indicate a need for a more post-national form of legitimacy of governance, which includes European culture and the construction of a post-national identity.

This local Nordic example may demonstrate how (Nordic) citizens of cities and nations in the twenty-first century experience a situation where national sovereignty is destabilized from outside through the EU and globalization processes, but also from within through the influence of multinational capital firms and local 'business heroes'. Important regulations about use of vital resources and decisions about representative and performative monumental constructions are gradually strongly influenced or in practice transferred from public to 'private' actors. Market economy becomes legitimized through gift economy, and private (contract) law and decision-making may be secured through patronship of national and artistic interests. This development can also be understood as a move from a *bourgeois public*, which is a social sphere of discussion, to a *representative public* related to a feudal society. The representative public – and its monumental constructions – become a 'status symbol' for the local society, and one where royalty (and former clergy and new global saints) may meet with the new wealth aristocracy. In the era of the 'representative public' the spheres of public and private were/are not divided.[32] The decision-making processes in relation to the construction of the Opera House in Copenhagen demonstrate this inter-mingling between private and public spheres, forms of representation and decision-making. Perhaps we can see a 'refeudalization' of the legal landscape, where the division of state power is in practice weakened and the lawmaker, the decision-maker and the judge again meet in one person or institution.

Impermanent legal scenes and landscapes?

Opera director Peter Sellars claims that 'opera … lives in your imagination: it's simultaneously very realistic and at the same time utterly metaphysical, utterly taking place in this dream world where things that *could be* suddenly *are*, and things that "are" *could be* transformed.'[33] This idea that things are in flux is shared by Francesca von Habsburg, one of the members of the pre-democratic feudal world's huge dynasties, who is herself an art patron. She writes about her visions of 'lasting impermanence' in relation to the patronage of art. In the summer of 2007 'Your Black Horizon Art Pavilion' commissioned by von Habsburg for the Vienna Biennale 2005, and created by Icelandic-Danish artist Olafur Eliasson and British architect David Adjaye (born to Ghanaian parents in Dar es Salaam, Tanzania), was exhibited on the island of Lopud close to Dubrovnik in the former Yugoslavia, now in Croatia on the Adriatic coast. In the catalogue von Habsburg writes:

> Most importantly this project celebrates impermanence, which is a driving force in my decision-making process. I do not want to allow something that is inherently private and fluid to freeze into a structure that can only be institutionalized and/or nationalized. When this happens to a collection, a certain chill sets in that never existed before and it begins to distance itself from the intimate realm of the private which should remain its essence... Maybe finding new ways of sharing art and providing means to facilitate projects that otherwise would never see the light of day is the task for the private sector to undertake in the art world as it is presently evolving...
>
> The intrinsically private altruistic discourse with art is most compelling, maybe more because of the complexities and risks involved than despite them. Through this approach, we can allow and encourage our own creativity as collectors and philanthropists to evolve. Hopefully, generosity overcomes our egos, creating a comforting and stimulating environment for artists to work and develop their practice, apart from the commercialization of the art world. Achieving this through site-specific projects that benefit local communities on a larger scale is a true challenge... Could it not help open a dialog between the practitioners of sustainable development and those of the contemporary art movement? To me it seems needed just as much as the shift from market-driven to project-driven paradigm in the art world itself.[34]

In a biography on Danish-Swedish industrialist and patron Einar Hansen, from Malmö, Kjell Åke Modéer writes that perhaps what produces sites or meeting places of creativity are capital, heterogeneous culture and idealists.[35] National Nordic legal scenes have during the welfare era relied very much on religious, ethnic and social homogeneity and on bureaucratic and economic equality. This may have led to a certain lack of creative energy and development on the political and legal scenes.

Contemporary global and local audiences are witnessing a change of the Nordic legal scenes and landscapes. There are still national scenes and national landscapes – influenced by both bourgeois and feudal repertoire and heritage and by modern homogeneous positivism. These scenes and landscapes *could be* transformed into local departments of global scenes where new and economically very powerful quasi-absolutist directors will be setting many of the rules and taking many of the decisions – together with the informal networks working to make a European legal culture attractive.

The audiences are also witnessing the actors of a diluted national democracy trying to stick to their influential roles as earlier periods witnessed the absolutist monarchs gradually being swept off the scene through the dilution of absolutist monarchies.[36] With immigration, new and contested actors are appearing. Audiences and actors have to conceive of 'new' forms of power, as they observe 'commerce, family, religion and the arts and sciences'[37] returning to the scenes to ask for their share of authority and law-making often in a market-modified form.

In one of the novels by the contemporary Norwegian author (originally educated in theology) Jan Kjærstad, the protagonist Jonas Wergeland tells that he celebrates the birthday of Grotius every year. Wergeland claims that at some point in the future people will think with disbelief about the historical period where it was possible for countries to own natural resources – such as the oil which has made Norway the richest Nordic country at present and The A.P. Moller-Maersk Group the largest shipping business and container ship and supply vessel operator in the world. The protagonist of the novels about the seducer, the conqueror, and the discoverer, who is himself a media-star, envisions that national ownership of oil will in the future be regarded as slavery is today – as something unacceptable.[38] The onlookers, map-readers and audiences are witnessing transitions, resistances, confusion and insecurity but also senses of new possibilities and new trajectories and routes for new groups. The role of the stage for the creation of 'new' normative repertoires is likely to grow. And the backstage influence as well.

Notes

An earlier version of this text was presented at a seminar in Istanbul on 'Centres and Peripheries in Europe' as part of the Nordic Research Project 'Nordic Legal Maps in Transition' April 2006. Thanks to Lisbet Christoffersen for comments on this version.

1 I have dealt with Holberg's influence on Danish legal culture in an article from 2004, 'Holberg – den store formidler af europæisk rets/kultur', in Henning Koch and Anne Lise Kjær (eds.), *Europæisk retskultur – på dansk* (Copenhagen: Thomson/GadJura, 2004).

2 The Danish Holberg expert Billeskov-Jansen, in *Ludvig Holberg og menneskerettighederne … og andre Holbergstudier* (Copenhagen: C.A. Reitzel, 1999), claims that Holberg's comedies can only be understood on the background of his writings on natural law.

3 See my article 'Holberg – den store formidler af europæisk rets/kultur', pp. 47–52, for a presentation of this example.

4 See for instance Tove Stang Dahl, *Women's Law: An Introduction to Feminist Jurisprudence* (Oslo: Norwegian University Press, 1987); Hanne Petersen and Henrik Zahle (eds.), *Legal Polycentricity. Consequences of Pluralism in Law* (Dartmouth: Dartmouth Publishing Group, 1995); Hanne Petersen, *Home Knitted Law: Norms and Values in Gendered Rule Making* (Dartmouth: Dartmouth Publishing Group, 1996); Hanne Petersen (ed.), *Love and Law in Europe* (Aldershot: Ashgate, 1998); Anne Hellum, *Women's Human Rights and Legal Pluralism in Africa: Mixed Norms and Identities in Zimbabwe* (Oslo and Harare: TANO Aschehoug/Mond Books, 1999); Kevät Nousianinen, Åsa Gunnarsson, Karin Lundström and Johanna Niemi-Kiesilainen (eds.), *Responsible Selves: Women in the Nordic Legal Culture* (Aldershot: Ashgate, 2001); Eva-Maria Svensson, Anu Pylkkänen and Johanna Niemi-Kiesiläinen (eds.), *Nordic Equality at a Crossroads: Feminist Legal Studies Coping with Difference* (Aldershot: Ashgate, 2004); Åsa Gunnarsson, Eva-Maria Svensson and Margaret Davies (eds.), *Exploiting the Limits of Law: Swedish Feminism and the Challenge to Pessimism* (Aldershot: Ashgate, 2007).

5 Hjalte Rasmussen, 'Constitutional Laxity and International High Economic Performance: Is there a Nexus', in John L. Campbell, John A. Hall and Ove

K. Pedersen (eds.), *National Identity and the Varieties of Capitalism: The Danish Experience* (Copenhagen: DJØF Publishing, 2006), p. 242.

6 Ibid., 'It was moreover – and as usual – assumed that the inaccessibility of the Danish language would enhance chances of getting away with the law's irregularities unpunished', Rasmussen writes, commenting on a Danish legislation infringing on EU law.

7 See Håkan Gustafsson, 'Den andre Kelsen', *Retfærd* 71 (1995), pp. 3–18.

8 See Steven Bach, *Leni: The Life and Work of Leni Riefenstahl* (New York: Alfred A. Knopf, 2007), especially Chapter 10 'Triumph'. See also Wikipedia articles on *Leni Riefenstahl* and *The Triumph of the Will.*

9 *Retfærd. Nordisk Juridisk Tidsskrift* 41 (Nationalsocialismen och rätten) (1988).

10 See the books by Lene Koch, *Racehygiejne i Danmark 1920–56* (Copenhagen: Informations Forlag, 1996) and *Tvangssterilisation i Danmark 1929–67* (Copenhagen: Gyldendal, 2000).

11 On German internet sites there are several articles both on the author and on the novel.

12 Christian Jungersen, *Undtagelsen* (The Exception) (Copenhagen: Gyldendal, 2005).

13 Kjell Å Modéer, 'Adjustment or Reluctance? Scandinavian Exceptionalism in Legal Cultures', in Hanne Petersen, Anne Lise Kjær, Helle Krunke and Mikael Rask Madsen (eds.), *Paradoxes of European Legal Integration* (Aldershot: Ashgate, 2008). See also Kjell Å Modéer, 'An American Dilemma and the Scandinavian Dream: The Citizen Meets Modernity and the Strong Nation-State. A Study in Comparative Legal Cultures', in Harry N. Scheiber (ed.), *Earl Warren and the Warren Court: The Legacy in American and Foreign Law* (Lanham: Lexington books, 2007).

14 Peter Sloterdijk, 'The New Grapes of Wrath: Post Communism – Neoliberalism – Islamism', in António Pinto Ribeiro (ed.), *The State of the World* (Manchester: Carcanet Press/Calouste Gulbenkian Foundation, 2006).

15 See for instance Henrik Zahle, *Omsorg for retfærdighed* (Copenhagen: Gyldendal, 2003).

16 There is a section on 'State Theater: Images of Virtue and Splendor' in Epilogue: Shadows and Light' in Yi-Fu Tuan's book *Passing Strange and*

Wonderful: Aesthetics, Nature, and Culture (Washington, D.C.: Island Press/Shearwater Books, 1995), pp. 234–237.

17 In 'Part IV: Synthesis of Space and the State' in *Passing Strange and Wonderful*, Yi-Fu Tuan has a section on 'America the Beautiful and the Moral', pp. 199–209.

18 Paul Tillich, *Love, Power, and Justice: Ontological analyses and ethical applications* (London, Oxford and New York: Oxford University Press, 1960), pp. 103–104.

19 Högsta Domstolens dom 29 November 2005, Riksåklagaren vs. ÅG (General prosecutor vs. ÅG), http://www.domstol.se/Domstolar/hogstadomstolen/Avgoranden/2005/2005-11-29_B_1050-05_dom.pdf, English semi-official translation, see http://www.domstol.se/Domstolar/hogstadomstolen/Avgoranden/2005/Dom_pa_engelska_B_1050-05.pdf (last accessed 5/11/2008): 'Under these circumstances, it is likely that the European Court, in a determination of the restriction of Åke Green's right to preach his Biblically based opinion that a judgment of conviction would constitute, would find that this restriction is not proportionate, and would therefore be a violation of the European Convention on Human Rights' ('Under sådana omständigheter är det sannolikt att Europadomstolen, vid en prövning av den inskränkning i ÅGs rättighet att förkunna sin i bibeln grundade uppfattning som en fällande dom skulle utgöra, skulle finna att inskränkningen inte är proportionerlig och därmed skulle utgöra en kränkning av Europakonventionen').

20 Law and Society Conference on 'Transitions, Resistances and Futures', Berlin 25–28 July 2007, Panel on Globalization and Constitutional Law. Jutta Limbach informed that the first Conference of European Constitutional Courts had been held in Dubrovnik – then in Yugoslavia, now Croatia – in 1972. This informal conference now has thirty-nine members.

21 'I kamp mod mediediktatoren' (Fighting the media-dictator), *Berlingske Magasin*, 31 March 2006.

22 See Erik Bond, *Reading London: Urban Speculation and Imaginative Government in Eighteenth-Century Literature* (Columbus, OH: Ohio State University Press, 2007). http://www.ohiostatepress.org/Books/Book %20PDFs/Bond %20Reading.pdf (last accessed 8/8/2007).

23 http://en.wikipedia.org/wiki/Live_8 (last accessed 9/8/2007).

24 Yi-Fu Tuan, *Passing Strange and Wonderful*, p. 234.

25 Alex Ross, 'Fresh Faces. City Opera's Fall Season', *The New Yorker*, 24 October 2005, http://www.newyorker.com/archive/2005/10/24/051024crmu_music (last accessed 9/8/2007).

26 Rasmussen, 'Constitutional Laxity', p. 204.

27 *Den store gave* (The big gift). Part of a series of twelve films called *Magtens billeder* (Images of power) released by the Danish Film Institute, http://www.dfi.dk/DfiKataloget/Instruktoerer/Filmbeskrivelse.htm?id=15318 (last accessed 9/8/2007). Footage from the film can be viewed at http://www.dr.dk/magtensbilleder/tema.asp?id=temaarkiv/11moller.asp (last accessed 9/8/2007).

28 See also Peter Suppli Benson, Bjørn Lambek and Stig Ørskov, *Mærsk, manden og magten* (Mærsk, the man, the power) (Copenhagen: Politikens Forlag, 2004), which was sold out and republished in 2005 and 2006. The opening chapter of this book is entitled 'A German Opera?', referring to the reservation of Mærsk Mc-Kinney Møller against opening the new Opera House with a Wagner opera as suggested by the minister of culture.

29 Jakob Nerup, 'Mærsk Mc-Kinney Møller. Milliardær på krig og undertrykkelse', in *Socialistisk Arbejderavis,* no. 182 (May 2000), p. 6, http://www.socialister.dk/arkivet/visartikel.asp?arkivnr=18222 (last accessed 9/8/2007).

30 Jakob Nerup, 'imperialisme.dk: Mærsk tjener fedt på krigen', *Socialistisk Arbejderavis*, no. 213 (April 2003), p. 2.

31 See the homepage of the foundation http://www.apmollerfonde.dk/, especially examples of bigger donations.

32 Historian Hilda Rømer Christensen discusses the Habermasian relationship between representative and bourgeois public in her book on the role of the Danish section of YWCA. Her example is the construction of a representative building for the organization in Copenhagen. See *Mellem backfische og pæne piger. Køn og kultur I KFUK 1883–1940* (Copenhagen: Museum Tusculanum Press, 1995), pp. 131–135.

33 Transcript of an interview with Peter Sellars at Glyndebourne on the occasion of the transmission of his television direction and production of *Theodora* on 15 June 1996, http://gfhandel.org/reviews/theodorasellars.htm (last accessed 8/8/2007).

34 *Your Black Horizon Art Pavilion. Olafur Eliasson and David Adjaye. Thyssen-Bornemisza Art Contemporary*. Catalogue edited by Eva Ebersberger and Daniela Zyman (Cologne: Verlag der Buchhandlung Walther König, 2007), pp. 6 and 7.

35 Kjell Å Modéer, *Patriot i gränsland. Einar Hansen – entreprenör och mecenat* (Patriot in border land. Einar Hansen – Entrepreneur and patron of the arts) (Stockholm: Atlantis, 2002).

36 See 'Preface' in Bond, *Reading London*, p. xiii.

37 Ibid.

38 Jan Kjærstad, *Forføreren* (1993). Quoted from memory. The structure of the book is such that it is very difficult to find a quote or thought again. The reader of this article thus has to trust my feeble memory.

II.
LAW AND THE MEDIA

4

Media Industry, Economy and Value in Crisis

The Role of Contemporary Journalism in Relation to the Danish Cartoon Controversy

Khaled D. Ramadan

Value definitions, beliefs and truths, patriotism or professionalism

Credibility is a traditional journalist's most significant asset. For a journalist to be reliable, he or she must be sovereign and critical and transmit events as they are without misleading or antagonizing anyone. In present times, however, most people realize that their access to information is being largely controlled by people they do not know; people who often have predisposed socio-political agendas. More and more often, contemporary journalists and media practitioners can be seen to expand their role from being simply commentators and information providers to becoming the actual conflict generators and event provokers, eager to seek attention.

This effect was made clear to the entire world through the so-called 'Danish Cartoon Crisis' in which the Danish newspaper *Jyllands-Posten* commissioned caricature drawings of the Prophet Muhammad – an act that is considered highly disrespectful by believers of Islam. In this case, the long-established newsmaker could not resist its own temptation to become The News.

While *Jyllands-Posten*'s editorial decision making at one level can be read as a response to local commercial competition and aiming at higher circulation, it is at another level a strong indicator of the growing politicization of the global media industry. The US-labelled 'War on Terror' has alone provided the world with a multitude of examples of strongly patriotic journalism in which the media practitioners are openly biased. Since 9–11, the following sentence has been mentioned repeatedly in various American media: 'Neutrality belongs to a form of classical journalism which is over; in this situation neutrality is not possible'. Or stated differently in the words of political analyst Michael Parenti, 'The corporate news media faithfully reflects the dominant class ideology in their reportage and commentary. At the same time, these media leave the impression that they are free and independent, capable of balanced coverage and objective commentary. How they achieve these seemingly contradictory but legitimating goals is a matter worth a comprehensive study'.

The inconsistency of taboos and counter-taboos

As most people know now, the Danish newspaper *Jyllands-Posten*'s decision to commission and print the drawings of the Islamic prophet ended up as an international crisis. People were killed and great amounts of property destroyed. What fewer people know is that Iran's best-selling newspaper – *Khoramshahi* – decided to give the western paper a dose of it is own challenge in early 2006. Retaliating to the Danish cartoons, the Iranian newspaper presented an international open call inviting cartoonists and caricature artists to submit their works to be put before an international jury.

The topic of the competition was the existence of the Holocaust and the contributors were asked to challenge the western perception of the Holocaust. The result was 400–500 entries from around the world. About sixty of them entered the competition and were put on public display in Teheran. The ten winners selected by the jury were invited to Teheran to collect their cash prices, which ranged from 3,000 to 15,000 US Dollars. The winning works were celebrated across Iran and part of the Islamic world, while it was condemned as an act of violation and violence in countries like Germany, the US, Israel and some other western states, including Denmark.

Most of the selected works can be seen as a visual debate over the Arab–Israeli conflict in cartoon format. The vast majority of the works submitted capitalized on drawing parallels between the widely portrayed and debated Holocaust that took place during the Nazi regime and the unspoken and little criticized activities of the Israeli state in the Middle East. First and foremost, the actions and counter-actions taken by the newspapers *Jyllands-Posten* and *Khoramshahi* read like the story of a media in crisis.

Danish press coverage of the 'cartoon controversy' was predictable

In her book *The Power of Photography: How Photographs Changed Our* Lives (1991), Vicki Goldberg states that when Louis Philippe took the throne in France in 1830, he announced the free press. Only five years later he realized that he had to establish censorship. One kind of visual expression felt the censorship more than others: the caricatures. While pamphlets were considered a 'violation of opinion', caricature was regarded as an 'act of violence'.

Images are a medium of incredible power that can produce even stronger, more persuasive, and more intuitive effects on people than words. Images have a profound impact on every aspect of our lives – they play a major role in our personal lives and in public history as well. The image has also many roles in society, it records public events, performs as a family historian, meditates as a medium of artistic expression, can be used as a tool for influencing public opinion, and so forth. But let us not forget that it can also be misrepresented to change opinion, like the Nazi cartoon of the Jews and the American cartoon of the Japanese.

There are several facts which one cannot ignore in the Danish cartoon affair when addressing the role of the media. Let us first underline again the power of the visual media, and how an image can stop a war. An example of this is the urban execution of a Vietnamese during the Vietnam War – footage captured by war correspondent Peter Arnett. This image or footage was the beginning of the end of the Vietnam War. So if images can stop a war, an image/depiction can very much start a war.

Between our hands we have three specifics about the Danish cartoons. The first is that the cartoons where initiated and published by a newspaper. Secondly, there is the role and reaction of the target masses and their media, which is the Arab media industry. Thirdly, there is the rest of western media, in particular the American media, which chose to ignore the events until the American political establishment addressed the issue.

Both the print and broadcast media in Denmark felt that they needed to support their sister organization in times of crisis. That way it was proved to the critics that whenever and for whatever reason your country is under attack you need to show patriotism, not professionalism. This phenomenon is not restricted to Denmark, it is a global one.

During the cartoon crisis, a controversial documentary about local imams in Denmark, made undercover by Algerian-French Mohamed Sifaoui, managed to infiltrate the Danish TV station TV2. The station's gate keepers themselves acknowledged at a later stage that under normal circumstances such a documentary would never be broadcast on their screen, so it was a desperate act of support and patriotism.

Another observation: when journalist Ulla Terkelsen was at the trial of the British writer David Irving in Austria, who in a book denied the Holocaust, she noticed that an Al-Jazeera film crew was reporting the trial. She decided to interview the film crew about their interest in David Irving's case. The impression Ulla Terkelsen eventually gave the Danish viewers was that Al-Jazeera audiences were Nazi sympathizers. Danish mainstream media proved it is not immune to patriotism during a national crisis and its objectivities and professionalism can be affected.

Pre- and post-cartoon crises

Initially, news accounts of Arab reactions to the Danish cartoons were transferred to back-page reportage. Only when protests turned violent did the story warrant front-page treatment, accompanied by dramatic photos of angry demonstrators and burning embassies. More recently, major papers and press services have attempted backgrounders on the crisis, still limiting themselves to a simple reconstruction of the chronology of events. Without reference to context, or any understanding of deeper realities at work in this confrontation, editorial writers and commentators have played out two contrary but equally shallow themes.

The best of these commentaries cast the problem as simply a clash between loyalty to the absolute principle of 'freedom of the press' and the insult that these harmful cartoons represented to devoted Muslims. The worst saw only the violence and deemed it evidence of the violence inherent in Islam and its message. Missing in all of this has been an effort to understand the deeper forces of history and the fears and insecurities, both bad and good, at work in this story. Ignored by most media, for example, is the fact that the entire controversy began as a deliberate provocation directed not at Arabs and Muslims in general, but particularly at Muslims who live in Europe, according to senior analyst James Zogby.

The Danish newspaper *Jyllands-Posten* has a long history of anti-immigrant attitude in its reporting. By publishing the cartoons, *Jyllands-Posten* wanted both to stick its finger in Muslims' private affairs, especially those living in Denmark, and in doing so make them understand that, in effect, you are our subjects and you will obey our cultural rules and values; we will not accommodate ourselves to yours. In this regard, *Jyllands-Posten* represents a collective European thought shared by some of the continent's – you may call them – liberal elites or nationalist rabble or something else. Unable to resolve the issue of integration of new immigrants into their national self-identity, these Europeans have withdrawn in fear and insecurity in the face of the growing numbers and impatience of their visitors (some of whom are former colonial subjects).

The cartoons were meant to teach a lesson about freedom of the press, but to state, as some have, that such freedom is absolute is of course nonsense since every press and even culture, by definition, has its own taboos. Ignorance about Islam is at the root of much of the coverage of this story.

It would have been important, for example, to note that Muslims were not only insulted by the crude and hostile intent of the cartoons. In a CNN debate the neoconservative political theorist William Bennett called the violent depiction of Muhammad evidenced in the cartoons 'a peek into the soul of that faith'. Ignorance, combined with chauvinism is always a lethal mixture. Given the depth of feelings provoked by the cartoons and the fact that they were intended as a provocation by *Jyllands-Posten*, the reaction should have been understandable.

What was ignored in most press coverage was the degree to which the response was widespread, spontaneous and largely took the form of non-violent action, at least in the start. That is until the world kept witnessing how the Danish Prime Minister showed total defiance when talking to the local Danish media in an attempt to please his voters, ignoring the fact that other media entities were monitoring what he was saying at home.

At later stages he noticed that the problem was getting out of hand and he had to establish a chamber to monitor the Arab media and those who spoke on it, especially Arabs living in Denmark. In the Danish media no one asked why the Prime Minister was talking to his media and people in one language and when appearing on Al-Arabiah TV he was trying to show pragmatism and diplomacy to please the Arabs and Muslims. Yet again even that did not work on the pro-western Al-Arabiah TV station: their final commentary was that he was not sorry, and the protests took an even more dramatic angle with embassy burnings and violence.

In the start of the crisis protests like boycotting Danish goods around the Arab world were used as peaceful tools. The tragedy, of course, is that the acts of violence which occurred at later stages of the crisis were used and misused in the West, and mainly in the Danish media, by the very same entity that published or supported the cartoons in the first place. In this regard, points were raised to confirm that violence is evidence and part of the entire faith, but yet again other remarks were raised by the other side to confirm that the colonial West will always label, twist and manipulate the notion of freedom and democracy as long as it suits its needs.

5

Freedom from Publicity or Right to Information?

Visual Cultures of the Courtroom

Lynda Nead

It has become a truism to say that we live in a society which is dominated by the visual image. If this view carries any remaining insight, then it would appear to be that in the twenty-first century the images with which we are surrounded are electronically generated and digitally mastered. It goes without saying, therefore, that the most important challenge currently facing scholars of the image is how to theorize a regime of visual culture which is composed of pixels and viewed on the monitor. Within the context of this emerging academic and cultural debate, I have found myself drawn to another order of images which appears at first to belong to a different and earlier age. These are images which have their cultural and aesthetic roots in the popular broadsides of the early nineteenth century and whose technical trajectory can be traced to the most revered tradition in Western art, the artist's sketch. This is a pictorial domain in which the photograph is prohibited and digital recomposition unknown, where artifice and artistic agency define the legality of the image. It is also a visual language which mediates between the official rituals and enclosed spaces of the law and the observation of a general public. It makes justice visible to contemporary society and yet it has never been the subject of an extended and serious analysis. For these reasons, I am fascinated by courtroom art; I am curious about its origins and conventions.

Photography and sketching in court and the publication of such photographs or sketches have been prohibited in English law since 1925.[1] Before 1925, photographs of major criminal trials – including pictures of jury members, defendants and witnesses – were commonly reproduced on the main pages of the mass circulation daily and Sunday press. The Criminal Justice Act forbade the making and publishing of such images and since this time the majority of the public attains a visual impression of a trial while it is being heard through the pictorial mnemonics of the courtroom artist. We can all, surely, recall the look of a courtroom sketch; its composition, style and context, for it is one of the most highly conventionalized forms within contemporary visual media. Courtroom art condenses major criminal trials into generic, gently anachronistic images which are then reproduced in newspapers and broadcast on television. The faces of frauds, murderers and hijackers are known to us through the hasty notations of the courtroom artist, made not on the spot but from memory. They are of the trial but they are emphatically not part of it. These are potent, neglected images which raise questions of representation and signification which continue to be central to any study of the history of visual culture. How do images mediate the public world; how are they regulated and for what reasons; how do they perpetuate or transform historical traditions of representation and what is the relationship between actuality and the image?

This essay is necessarily, therefore, a series of reflections on the nature of courtroom art; a sequence of interdisciplinary detours through the history of the press, photography, courtroom reporting and the law in the first decades of the twentieth century. It is both an historical account of the regulation of the visual within the English courts and a conceptual interpretation of the meaning of this imagery.

Rex v. Bywaters and Thompson [1922]

By the first decades of the twentieth century, major criminal trials had become cultural spectacles and a form of popular entertainment.[2] Tickets were issued for seats in the limited public areas of the courtroom, and in especially notorious cases where the demand for places outstripped their supply, admission to the court became part of a nefarious economy with people queuing for tickets in order to sell them on at a substantial profit. But it was only a tiny minority who experienced the live drama of a trial within the court; mass audiences were created by the press, who transformed promising legal cases into sensational news. From the end of the nineteenth century, major trials were reported in detail and often occupied several pages of the daily and Sunday papers during the period of the trial. Newspapers deployed their full battery of journalistic devices – photographic spreads, banner headlines and hectic prose – which had been developed since the 1880s, to draw their readers into compelling narratives of desire, betrayal and violence. Here were all the familiar subjects of Victorian melodrama, with the added frisson of real life. Trials provided the raw materials for character and plot: the villains and the victims, the crimes and the punishments, which the newspapers spun into stories which bound the nation together in the early years of the twentieth century.

The procedure of the trial seemed naturally, fortuitously, to meet the general temporal requirements of the press. Lapses of interest and dramatic lacunae could be excised and the narrative of the case reshaped in order to create a continuous pitch of emotional interest. The progress of the trial could be unfolded day by day, issue by issue, punctuated by strategic highpoints such as the arrival of key witnesses, the testimony of the defendant, and the climax of the verdict and sentence. The dramatic reporting of the criminal trial was, in part, an inevitable and appropriate extension of that supreme form of narrative fiction, the detective story. The trial was the closing postscript to the narrative of detection; it offered the definitive account of the crime, as well as justice and retribution.[3] Shorn of the legal niceties and intervals of the courtroom itself, the trial offered newspaper editors a complete, self-contained narrative module; in other words, a perfect story.

By the 1920s, anyone who was involved in a major trial was considered fair game by the news and picture editors. Witnesses, defendants, members of the jury, counsel, judges, as well as their relatives, might find themselves the target of a press photographer and on the front page of a mass circulation paper the following day. At the most sensational trials, the public itself became an additional element in the story. The queues and crowds outside the court buildings extended the setting of the trial from the space of the law to the space of the street, making public fascination itself part of the drama and conveniently providing far easier locations for the press photographer than the restrictions imposed by the courtroom. Inevitably, murder trials offered the press and the public the most provocative story lines. Defendants in these cases faced the death penalty and, prompted by the papers, verdicts often resulted in public demonstrations and petitions to the Home Secretary.

At all stages of trial reporting, women played a central part in the dramatic potential of the case and its ability to capture the public imagination and win newspaper sales. As victim, women conformed to a familiar enough image of passive object of what was commonly proved to be male violence; but as the accused, they presented a far more fascinating opportunity for a public examination of the nature of modern femininity and the pathology of female violence. The trial in 1922 of Frederick Bywaters and Edith Thompson for the murder of Edith's husband, Percy, had all the elements necessary for the creation of a big newspaper story; there was an adulterous affair, a handsome young lover, an adoring older woman and, most extraordinarily of all, the evidence of a cache of love letters, written by Edith to Frederick, which were shown to the jury, read aloud in the court, reported in the papers, providing the public with a tawdry and explicit true-life tale of crime and passion.[4]

This was a photogenic story; the case hung on the relationship between the two defendants and called out for revealing and lifelike portraits of them. Their appearance before and during the case, as well as their demeanour in the courtroom were reported in detail, in pictures and in words, and scrutinized for signs of innocence or guilt. The newspapers then were obsessed with the case, but it remains a notorious instance of press coverage of criminal trials before the 1925 statutory prohibition of photography and sketching in the courtroom and its precincts.

In October 1922, Percy and Edith Thompson were returning to their home following a theatre visit in London when a man leapt out of the darkness and fatally attacked Percy with a knife.[5] Within days, Edith Thompson and Frederick Bywaters were charged with murder.[6] Bywaters admitted to lying in wait for the Thompsons but claimed that he had never intended to kill Percy. The notoriety of the trial, however, rested largely on the case against Edith Thompson. Although she had been accompanying her husband and was present when he was attacked by Bywaters, she had not actually struck a blow and so the question was whether she was guilty of aiding and abetting the crime by inciting Bywaters to murder. Both were found guilty and sentenced to death. A public petition was presented to the Home Secretary requesting that Edith's sentence be commuted to one of life imprisonment, but no reprieve was given and Thompson was hanged along with Bywaters.

The trial at the Old Bailey in December 1922 aroused unprecedented public interest, reaching a climax in the cross-examination of Edith Thompson, during which lengthy extracts from her letters to Bywaters were read out in the court. The forlorn melodrama of Thompson's life and letters was reconstructed during the trial and then recreated in the newspapers like instalments of a cheap novel. The trial, law itself, was utterly caught up in this tapestry of public drama and popular fantasy. The courtroom could not extract itself from the irresistible production of sensational news reporting, nor could it sustain its image as a discrete and pure space for the exercise of justice, but was drawn into a world of petit bourgeois sexual fantasy and transgression symbolized by Edith Thompson and magnified through the mass readerships of the early twentieth-century popular press.

Through their reporting of trials such as Bywaters and Thompson, the newspapers brought the public into the courtroom; they penetrated its enclosed and rarified space and opened it up to the mass audiences which had been created by the modern press. Each reader had to feel implicated and involved in the progress of the case; they had to feel, through the agency of the paper, part of the live action which was taking place in and around the courtroom.

All the national newspapers carried reports of Bywaters and Thompson and all described at length the crowds who had gathered at the Old Bailey. Although only a tiny number compared to those who were vicariously consuming the case through reading the newspapers, the crowds and queues were photographed and analyzed and became a staple of trial reporting. The crowds were a metonymy for the mass public audience created by the newspapers. Modernity had created new categories of public who now made up the audiences for criminal trials. *The Times* commented on the queue of several hundred unemployed men which had formed the night before the case opened.[7] This was a detached and pragmatic constituency, concerned only with reserving a place so they could sell their tickets to those who had money but were unwilling to face a winter night outside. And there were others – the new consumers of modern romance and film, for whom the trial was simply one other form of drama catering to their indiscriminate taste for 'love, hate, intrigue and passion.'[8] The *Illustrated London News* was one of a number of papers which speculated about the reasons for the growing public interest in murder trials, using a full-page photographic spread to make an explicit visual link between the events of the trial and their recreation in the theatre and the cinema. Three photographs of the crowds outside the court buildings are juxtaposed with stills from a play and a film set during murder trials at the Old Bailey. The paper deploys the pictures from drama and film to take its readers inside the courtroom. Where the press photographer, on this occasion, stopped, the dramatist continued and the director concluded with a close-up of the judge and prosecuting counsel. The seamless transition from fact to fiction on the page of the *Illustrated London News* is symptomatic of what was identified at the time as a more general confusion in the public consumption of the law. In his summing up of Bywaters and Thompson, the judge, Justice Shearman, felt compelled to remind the jury 'that they were in a Court of Justice trying a vulgar and common crime. They were not listening to a play from the stalls of a theatre.'[9]

Of those who made up the modern public for sensational murder trials, one group was of particular interest to the press and was singled out for comment. It was the women, of all ages and different classes, who were defined as the most voracious consumers of murder. Women queued overnight; they scrambled for admission; and packed into the courtroom. Their appetite for murder seemed to call into question the very nature of modern femininity. 'A Woman Reporter' for the *Daily Graphic* observed:

> The scene at the Old Bailey yesterday makes one wonder whether Englishwomen are morbid, cruel or merely sensation-loving. With curious, dispassionate eyes, they sat in their furs and pearl necklaces.
>
> One woman, in a fur coat, never took her lorgnette from her keen, dark eyes. She looked like the kind of person who would bully her maids and nag her husband. Seated behind her was a pretty, fair girl, whom a casual observer would associate more easily with jazz teas than the criminal court.[10]

If Mrs Thompson represented suburban femininity turned bad, then the women in the public areas of the courtroom embodied new types of unprecedented and unpredictable female behaviour. They were well-dressed, fashionable women who worked in and consumed the public spheres of the modern metropolis.[11] Amongst the witnesses were a waitress and the manageress of a teashop, whose photographs shared the front pages with those of the judge, counsel and defendants. The many women caught up in the trial – as defendant, witnesses, onlookers and newspaper readers – seemed indistinguishable. The *Daily Graphic* juxtaposed a photograph of Edith Thompson and two details of women in the crowd, with the caption: 'Among the crowd are to be seen many women in furs and young girls of the age at which the present generation is, as a rule, chiefly interested in the dramas of the film.' Fashion and fiction united these women and, in excess, had brought about Edith Thompson's downfall. These were sensation-loving women, but the questions raised by the trial were: Did these women murder and were they fit to vote and fit to judge innocence and guilt?[12]

Among the many distinctive features of the case was the fact that the jury included one woman. The first female juror was sworn in at an Old Bailey trial in January 1921 and their appearance in court still excited special comment. Photographs of the entire jury in the Bywaters and Thompson case were printed with impunity,[13] but the woman juror was picked out by the press. The *Daily Sketch* showed her on her way into the Old Bailey[14] and the *Illustrated London News* was one of a number of papers to show her returning with the rest of the jury from a Sunday service at St Paul's Cathedral. In her formal attire of furs and black hat, there was little to differentiate the jurist from Edith Thompson or the morbid voyeurs in the public gallery. But these sartorial similarities were precisely the point; the press had turned murder trials into spectacles which compromised respectability and judgement. Modernity had disturbed the certainties of the courtroom.

No one involved in the case was exempt from illustration in the press. For the most part, these photographs seem to have been taken outside the courtroom itself. It is possible, therefore, that in this case Justice Shearman exercised his right to forbid photography during the trial.[15] The *Daily Sketch* scooped the other mass circulation papers with its front page on Friday, 8 December, which included Thompson entering the courtroom and two, poor-quality images of both defendants during the trial, whilst the *News of the World* printed an unusual and evidently touched-up photograph of the prisoners together in the dock. In its retrospective account of the case, the *Illustrated London News* depicted the moment that sentence was pronounced in a full-page artist's sketch. The sketch, however, was not usual in the reporting of this trial.[16] The press needed immediacy and affect and, for these purposes, the photograph was supreme.

In the immediate aftermath of the case, the Corporation of the City of London met to consider the propriety of queuing outside court buildings and of selling places. The Chairman of the Police Committee was reported as saying that 'it would not be in the public interest to prevent the public attending.'[17] To be sure, the public had to be given access to the legal process, but this could be confined to the physical space of the public areas of the courtroom and did not have to extend to the virtual space created on the front pages of the mass circulation papers. Justice had to be seen to be done, but did not have to be made a spectacle of. Bywaters and Thompson showed how far the courtroom had been infiltrated by modern mass culture and the extent to which it was consumed through the narrative structures of theatre, film and photography. By the 1920s, it seemed as though newspaper and photographic technologies had been moving inexorably towards turning the criminal trial into the perfect tabloid story.

Photographs for the papers

Twentieth-century press coverage of major criminal trials had a long and varied tradition of representation on which it could draw. Murders, trials and executions were commonly the subjects of the illustrated broadsides and ballads which were sold on city streets in the eighteenth and nineteenth centuries.[18] These highly formulaic and simple images gave law and order a visual language in this period; they interpreted the major criminal cases of the day for a popular and often illiterate audience. Although the murder sheets referred to specific cases, they drew on stock characters and locations which were repeated and copied from one woodcut to another. These are the true precursors of the news reporting of the 1920s. Their dependency on the current and the newsworthy and their address to popular audiences on the street and in the market place found their modern variant in the front- and centre-page photographic spreads of the early twentieth-century daily and Sunday newspapers. The broadsides and the tabloids shared the transmission of news as gossip and found a common visual expression in the language of sensation. The popular broadsides prioritized dramatic moments and key personalities, which continued to be the goals of the press photographers over a century later.

The imagery of the broadsides was superseded in the nineteenth century by the huge growth of the illustrated press. Illustrations in daily newspapers were still relatively unusual in the first half of the nineteenth century, but it was the appearance from the 1820s of illustrated journals which really changed the look of periodical publishing and the expectations of readers.[19]

Alongside the development of the illustrated press, the establishment of the Sunday papers in the early nineteenth century was also an important antecedent of the twentieth-century mass circulation press.[20] The Sunday papers reworked many of the defining features of the ballads and broadsheets; their focus was on sex scandals and crime, but they included a miscellany of general reports on foreign and home news. By the end of the nineteenth century the conditions were right for the emergence of a mass circulation press. Newspapers looked different and, drawing on the forms of earlier street literature, they were developing a new style for treating the familiar subjects of sex and violence. These new popular styles of journalistic reporting, which Matthew Arnold referred to as the 'new journalism', specialized in sensation, told through personalized stories. They developed a new vivid style of language which was presented in a bold visual form through the use of streamer headlines, captions and varied typefaces.[21]

In terms of the achievement of large-scale readerships at the beginning of the twentieth century, the Sunday papers showed the way, but the mass circulations of the daily newspapers arose chiefly out of the introduction into news reporting of the direct reproduction of photographic images. By the 1890s newspapers were reproducing images printed from half-tone blocks and in 1904 the *Daily Mirror* became the first newspaper in the world to be illustrated exclusively by photographs.[22] Direct reproduction from photographs came into more general use around 1910. The illustrated front page, with its dramatic photographs and bold headlines, became the tabloid papers' chief weapon in the race for mass circulation. And it was effective; in 1911–12 the *Daily Mirror* became the first paper to reach a circulation of one million.

By the second decade of the twentieth century, photography dominated the output of the popular papers and the press photographer had emerged as a new hero of modern life.[23] Of course this supremacy had been achieved on the back of technical advances.[24] Innovations in small hand-held cameras had eliminated the need for cumbersome tripods, and developments in daylight-loading roll film had also vastly improved the responsiveness of the photographer. The introduction in the mid-1920s of lightweight cameras which could also be fitted with a powerful lens revolutionized news photography. Now photography was simple, portable and fast. With the new compact cameras of the late 1920s, press photography became more mobile and more spontaneous.

By 1920, therefore, the news photograph was playing an increasingly important role within newspaper design, and photojournalism had emerged as a new specialization within the industry. Editorial staffs commonly included picture editors, and news agencies were joined by specialist picture agencies. This was the world of the press photographer who, working either freelance or for particular papers, was creating the modern pictorial journalism of the twentieth century. For John Everard, a press photographer and author of *Photographs for the Papers: How to Take and Place Them* (1923), there had never been a better time to take up the camera; demand from the papers was high and there was money to be made. Press photography, Everard claimed, was immediate and reliable and provided the news in a form which suited contemporary lifestyles:

> Nowadays, men and women are too busy to wade through page after page of a bulky newspaper. In the brief intervals of their lives they like to see what is happening around them and in other parts of the world, and the photograph is the only reliable means of imparting that knowledge.[25]

Photography transformed the new journalism; it made sensation topical and created visual information which could be rapidly absorbed. News transmission had become pictorial rather than textual.

The potential of the courtroom as a source of sensational news images was understood from the beginning. There is no reliable documentation of the first appearance of a news camera at a trial, but what is clear is that by the early 1920s still photography of court proceedings was commonplace in the nation's mass circulation papers.[26] Photography in the courtroom was not a straightforward matter, however. If it became intrusive, it could be seen to interfere with the course of justice and to constitute a contempt of court and a judge could choose to prohibit photography throughout a trial. Everard sensed a change in attitude towards press photographers and predicted legal intervention: 'the time may come when photographing without permission where private individuals are concerned will be made an indictable offence.'[27] But in the ambiguous situation of the early 1920s, the cunning veteran press photographer could always find ways of sneaking a camera into the courtroom and taking a photograph which would acquire even greater value because of its clandestine nature.[28] Once taken, the photograph could be published with impunity since before the 1925 Act there was no statutory prohibition of either photography in the courtroom or its publication.

This was the peculiar nature of the relationship between the law and the press in the years immediately leading up to the framing and passing of the Criminal Justice Act. Within a couple of decades of their creation, the popular newspapers had successfully secured mass readerships, and press photography had emerged as the key player in the look and presentation of the modern news. Women and the working classes, the uncritical romance readers and cinema-goers were the new consumers of the law. Melodrama had contaminated justice, and justice had been reduced to little more than a source of popular entertainment. At its most bathetic, trial by jury itself had become nothing more than a trope for an advert for indigestion salts.

Rex v. Mahon [1924]

Patrick Mahon looked like a matinee idol, which made his trial in 1924 for the murder and dismemberment of Emily Kaye especially picturesque. From its beginning photography had played a significant role in the emerging science of forensic investigation and had been quickly absorbed into criminal justice for the purposes of evidence and identification.[29] By the early 1920s, photographic images were a standard feature of many criminal trials and circulated in the court at a number of levels. Photographic likenesses of defendants were used both before arrest and during the trial. Indeed, the capacity of the photograph to draw the past into the present occasionally constituted its inadmissibility as evidence. In 1924 an appeal was made against a conviction for housebreaking and theft on the grounds that during the trial prison photographs of each of the accused were shown to the jury. This was tantamount to informing the court that the accused had previous convictions; the photographs were thus inadmissible and the conviction was quashed.[30] Photography had transformed the detection, punishment and reporting of crime, but it was a complex and apparently still unpredictable medium that might call for rules of use and prohibition.

Police scene of crime photography was central to the case against Patrick Mahon. Mahon, a married man, had met a young woman and arranged to spend some time with her in a bungalow in East Sussex.[31] Mahon's wife had become suspicious and had taken a cloakroom ticket belonging to him for luggage left at Waterloo Station to the police. In the locker a bag was found containing a knife and items of blood-stained clothing. When Mahon was questioned about the contents, he explained to the police that during their stay in the bungalow there had been a quarrel; the woman had become violent and during a struggle she had fallen and hit her head. Realizing that she was dead and fearing the consequences, Mahon had dismembered her body and disposed of the parts by various means. The police went to the bungalow and found a gruesome scene, with body parts and blood stains all over the place. A leading pathologist identified the body as that of Emily Kaye, a London secretary, and Mahon was tried for murder at Lewes Assizes in July 1924. During the trial the jury was shown a series of photographs of the bungalow and of the remains which had been discovered there. As one Sunday paper reported: 'All the terrible scenes which met the detectives' gaze when they entered the bungalow have been pictorially reproduced for the jury.'[32] Readers had to imagine the gore, but they were shown pictures of other evidence, such as a model of the bungalow where the murder took place. Mahon's story of accidental death collapsed; he was found guilty and sentenced to death. After the sentencing, newspapers reported his previous convictions for violent assault on a woman, burglary and forgery, along with his repeated womanizing and adultery. This was the stuff of sensation; a story of evils: 'all housed in one handsome body, all centred in one master brain.'[33] Not surprisingly, large crowds gathered outside the small, hot court at Lewes, reaching their record the day of the verdict. Young and fashionably dressed women were seen to predominate; drawn to the courtroom, the *Daily Sketch* observed: 'as if for the raising of the curtain on an eagerly awaited drama.'[34] The press construction of Mahon's evil good looks was played off against their descriptions of the women in the courtroom; reflecting on the case after sentence had been passed, the *News of the World* sanctimoniously observed: 'the public, especially that portion of the feminine population who found his magnetic eyes an alluring and irresistible attraction, may realise what a black hearted, callous, and cold-blooded criminal he is in reality.'[35] For a moment, every woman following the case is put in the position of Emily Kaye; sharing her fatal pleasure-seeking gullibility and beguiled by Mahon's seductive appearance. Many column inches were devoted to rendering the details of Mahon's clothes and tanned good looks, but reporters assumed an ability to see beneath the surface of his appearance which they were unwilling to attribute to the female observers of the trial. Reporting on the first day of the trial, the *Daily Sketch* described the prisoner: '… looking extraordinarily bronzed and tanned. In his new suit of light cloth, over soft white collar and shirt, he seems rather as though he had just returned from a seaside holiday than as if he were on trial for his life.'[36] And on the second day the reporter for the *Daily Mirror* noticed that '[he] sat down, carefully pulling up his trousers to preserve their crease.'[37] These details and mannerisms were eloquent signs of a dangerous and indifferent informality which was confirmed when a number of reporters perceived that by the final day of the trial Mahon's tan had faded: 'Debonair as ever in his smart grey suit… [But] the tan on his cheeks – tan which he applied artificially, as a sop to his amazing vanity over his appearance – faded…'[38] Mahon was a worthy modern villain. If he did not actually possess all the features and qualities associated with the scoundrels of contemporary melodrama, then the press bestowed them on him. The papers went to town on his testimony, with headlines referring to the 'love experiment' which he and Emily Kaye had planned to carry out in the Sussex bungalow.[39] Illicit sex and extreme violence made the case a perfect true life story in the authentic tradition of the popular broadsides. The press photographers had a field day too and appear to have taken an unprecedented number of pictures inside the courtroom. The entire jury was 'snapped' and their faces printed in the papers; including in one notable case, one figure marked with an 'X', identifying him as the member who fainted twice during the hearing.[40] Mahon was photographed in the dock listening to evidence and in the witness box during his testimony.[41] Most shockingly, the papers got hold of pictures showing him, it was claimed, listening to the judge delivering the death sentence.[42] The images, taken from a limited range of angles, show Mahon in the dock, alone or flanked by police guards. The subject is a horrifying scoop; an austere conclusion to the seedy narrative which had been reported day after day in the papers. In this photograph of the guilty man being sentenced to death, criminal justice is taken back to the streets, to the ballads and rough generic woodcuts of the eighteenth and nineteenth centuries. The question was would modern law continue to tolerate such exposure?

To many members of Parliament and peers it seemed that the press was turning the great legal and moral narratives of the age into a profit-driven circus. After the sentencing, the Sunday paper, *Reynolds's News*, which had only been able to report the Mahon trial in two weekly issues stoked the ongoing popular interest in the case by promising further revelations about Mahon's past over the following weeks.[43] It advised readers to order their copies well in advance in order to avoid disappointment. And immediately after the trial it was reported that the owner of the bungalow in which Emily Kaye had been murdered had opened it as a visitors' attraction, charging one shilling entry: 'In fact, the place has become a fair ground, with its attendant sweet stalls and the like.'[44] Courtroom photography was not an isolated phenomenon, but was part of a sensational, popular discourse surrounding major criminal trials. It was time to separate the conduct of the court from modern mass media; the camera had to be banished from the courtroom and its environs. Against the background of the fragmented politics and rapidly changing governments of Britain in the early 1920s, action was finally taken. In 1923 the Conservative government introduced a Criminal Justice bill; it was unsuccessful, but the following year Ramsay Macdonald's Labour government took over the legislation, adding a clause prohibiting court photography.[45] In 1925, following the sudden collapse of the Labour government, another Conservative government reintroduced the Criminal Justice bill, including the section concerning courtroom photography, and the notoriously puritanical Home Secretary, Sir William Joynson-Hicks, took the issue back to Parliament.[46]

The Criminal Justice Act, 1925

Section 41 of the 1925 Criminal Justice Act states that:

(1) No person shall-

a) take or attempt to take in any court any photograph, or with a view to publication make or attempt to make in any court any portrait or sketch, of any person, being a judge of the court or a juror or a witness in or a party to any proceedings before the court, whether civil or criminal; or
b) publish any photograph, portrait or sketch taken or made in contravention of the foregoing provisions of this section or any reproduction thereof...[47]

The Act thus creates two separate offences: the making of the image and its publication. Furthermore, the prohibition both covers images made in the courtroom itself and those made in the precincts of the building in which the court is held. An offence can thus be committed if a photographer or artist is standing outside and away from the court buildings and makes an image of an individual entering or leaving the court. At the time of writing, Section 41 of the 1925 Criminal Justice Act remains the prevailing law in England and Wales on the matter of photographing and sketching in court.

Section 41 was only one comparatively insignificant clause within a highly complex and controversial piece of legislation.[48] The overall ambition of the bill was to speed up and simplify the administration of justice. The first part of the bill dealt with the probation of offenders and created paid probation officers. The second part concerned jurisdiction and procedure, extending the range of offences made triable at quarter sessions and increasing the power of justices to deal summarily with offences. The third part of the bill dealt with amendments to an assortment of offences – for example, the penalty for drunken driving, and included Section 41. Included in the fourth and final schedule was the abolition of the assumption that if a married woman committed a crime in the presence of her husband she was acting under his coercion. This was significant and symptomatic in that it represented a self-conscious attempt to modernize the criminal law. Commenting on the customary presumption of marital coercion, the *Law Journal* observed: 'This view is not generally shared by persons acquainted with the modern world, and it has not finally prevailed.'[49] Although it asserted that equality between the sexes could have been expanded within this clause, in overall terms it approved of the saving of time and expense embodied in the Act.[50] This was the general view of legal commentaries at the time; the *Justice of the Peace* approved of the various provisions 'aimed at simplifying procedure, saving time and expense in criminal proceedings, and remedying proved defects in the criminal law.'[51]

The point of rehearsing this debate is to contextualize Section 41 within a much broader piece of legislation which was seen at the time to be driven by a modernizing impulse. Can the prohibition on courtroom photography be understood as part of this general framework of simplification and harmonization, or was it simply a retrogressive attempt to resecure the sanctity of the court? For those at the beginning of the twenty-first century who seek to open up the English courts to television and video cameras, the current prohibition is represented as emanating from a conservative and repressive political ideology.[52] But this is not quite the case and is certainly not an accurate picture of the historical moment in which the legislation was created. Can an historical account of that moment complicate, or, at least, helpfully disturb our conventional intellectual assumptions concerning the legal regulation of public access to the courtrooms?

Section 41 was not predictably party political, nor was it necessarily regarded by liberals as an unreasonable or unnecessary restraint. Indeed, across the political spectrum the prohibition was supported as a way of curbing the growing power of commercial popular culture and the ubiquitous tyranny of the press. E. J. Hayward introduced his commentary on the Act with the unambiguous observation: 'By Section 41, judges, jurors, witnesses ... are afforded freedom from the publicity of newspaper photographs etc.', and an article in *Justice of the Peace* confirmed: 'Courts of justice and persons attending them are protected from the press photographer and artist by Section 41.'[53]

The Home Secretary, Joynson-Hicks, took up this language of freedom and protection in his defence of the clause in the House of Commons, describing press photographers around court buildings as 'an intolerable invasion of the liberty of the subject.'[54] The most comprehensive discussion of the issue in the Commons arose on 20 November when a Labour MP, Colonel Wedgwood, moved to leave the clause out of the bill. Wedgwood had been a long-standing member of the Liberal party but had joined the Labour party in 1919. He protested against the gratuitous creation of new offences and argued that the public had a right to know what was going on in the law courts. The clause amounted to censorship of the press and was, moreover, symptomatic of a recent 'habit of grandmotherly legislation in the interests of what is said to be morality.'[55] Wedgwood's amendment was seconded by a Liberal, but vigorously opposed by a coalition of Conservative and Labour MPs. The Conservative member for Cambridge University, who spoke also as the Recorder of Cambridge, defended the clause on the grounds that many people who were involved in legal cases were terrified by the photographers and the thought that their pictures could end up in the papers. He added: 'I do not think it is in keeping with the dignity of the court that it should be used as a studio.'[56] Joynson-Hicks took up the theme of the conduct of the court, confirming that photography and sketching 'did interfere with the administering of justice.' Not only was it contempt in the face of the court, it was also an abuse of press rights; the clause 'was not only in the best interests of the administration of justice but in the interest of the well-being of the people as a whole.'[57]

What is striking about this debate is how swiftly it moved from being a discussion of behaviour in Courts of Law to being a wholesale assault on the popular press. Supporting the removal of the clause, the Liberal MP Captain Wedgwood Benn argued that photography and sketching in court might contravene public taste, but they should not be made a criminal offence. He advised the Home Secretary to turn his attention to the real social problem which was the degrading and demoralizing stories which were published by some newspapers. A number of Labour MPs took their cue from this and launched a passionate attack on the immoral contents of the mass circulation papers and the unregulated profits of their owners. One speaker supported the retention of the clause but felt it did not go far enough to deter the shoddy and shady practices of papers such as the *News of the World*. The Labour MP for Bow and Bromley agreed, suggesting a drastic solution to what he called the 'real evil':

> … namely, the growing manner in which rich men got richer by retailing filth every Sunday. There was a lot of talk about Bolshevism and other 'isms', but they were nothing to the moral degradation caused by these Publications … the pictures and letterpress of these publications Sunday after Sunday were so foul that if he had his way he would take the people who made fortunes by retailing such muck and put them into penal servitude for the rest of their lives.[58]

The move to omit the clause from the bill fell without even going to a vote. The prohibition of photographs and sketches in court had produced an unlikely alliance around the questions of public morality and press freedom. Labour MPs supported a reactionary Conservative Home Secretary and the dignity of the courts was defended alongside a cross-party attack on the modern press.

Section 41 of the 1925 Criminal Justice Act was the product of the historical development of the popular press. Photography had transformed the new journalism and had created the modern tabloid, a compelling combination of nineteenth-century sensation and twentieth-century photographic technologies. In certain respects, government had taken some time to react; photography had, after all, been a staple of the mass circulation press for a number of years. In other ways, however, the politicians had timed it just right. By 1925 criminal trials had become the nub of modern journalism; the narrative of the courtroom possessed all the essential ingredients of the perfect daily or Sunday news story: crime, detection and punishment, scattered liberally with desire, sex and violence. Anyone involved in such a case might find themselves on the front page of a popular, national paper: defendants, jurists, counsel, judges and witnesses. The press had eradicated the distinctions between the administration of justice and mass culture and new kinds of irreverent audiences were now lapping up the intimate details of the great, and ignominious, legal cases of the age. The prohibition was a prescient move. Camera technology was on the brink of further revolutionary change. Within a couple of years they would become smaller, faster and more adaptable; the perfect instrument of the determined and ambitious press photographer. Newsreel cameras would also move further centre stage and access to the courtrooms would be a question not only of the still but also of the moving image. It can come as no surprise, therefore, that this was the moment for the passing of Section 41 and that opposition was not even sufficient to warrant a division.

The art of the courtroom sketch

In his work on the legality of the image, Costas Douzinas has written: 'The law loves and fears images, it both prohibits them and organizes its own operation in a highly spectacular and visual manner.'[59] The courtroom sketch tests this assertion and gives it historical specificity. The sketch is a visual manifestation of law's oscillation between the desire to show and the need to regulate that visual display, of its need to be pictorially represented and the corresponding requirement to police that representation. These are images which are charged with meanings; not simply those which relate to the particular cases concerned, but those which belong to the ongoing relationship between history, law and the image.

We all know what a courtroom sketch looks like; we can visualize its style and picture, its treatment of individuals and settings. The courtroom sketch is highly generic; it obeys rules and conventions which subordinate the particular details of individual cases and identities within general categories of types and location. The *Oxford English Dictionary* defines a sketch as '[a] rough drawing or delineation of something, giving the outlines or prominent features without the detail, especially one intended to serve as the basis of a more finished picture.' The primary characteristics of a sketch, therefore, are a generalized portrayal which ignores detail and which has a preparatory or preliminary status. In this light, the courtroom sketch is unlike other kinds of sketches; it both conforms to and deviates from the general nature of sketches. It is in a state of constant movement between the general and the particular. Its objective is to render an overall impression of the scene, but this has, necessarily, to be scored through with a degree of attention to individual detail. Moreover, the courtroom sketch is the preparation for nothing; it is an end in itself, the final look at a moment of a trial.

There is a universal quality about the courtroom sketch.[60] The viewpoint is everywhere and nowhere: from the dock, the judge's bench, the public gallery. The specificity of the viewpoint ultimately matters less than the general impression of presence within the courtroom. The portraits are a curious synthesis of nobody in particular and potent or notorious individuals. Identities slip in and out of vision; faces resemble people we know, or feel we should know, but features dissolve and are forgotten. The identities of individual artists obey the same cognitive logic and become submerged within a generic category of 'courtroom artist'. The sketch declares its status as 'an artist's impression', but we have no idea who the artist is. We are aware, at some level, that there must be technical differences and individual styles, but they cannot be captured and melt into a homogeneous look and feel. This is a singularly styleless style in which distinctive elements add up to a lack of distinction.

To look at a sketch depicting a dramatic highpoint in the trial narrative – the summing up, the sentencing, etc. – is to feel oneself already familiar with the scene. But what we take to be an understanding of the situation is in fact a grasp of the signs and orthodoxies of the image. Courtroom dramas on film and television provide a lexicon of the legal process which can be mobilized by the viewer of the courtroom sketch. The sketch is a cipher for these other fictional representations. We recognize the conventions of the courtroom sketch and its referents and conflate this recognition with a knowledge of that which is represented. We are present at the trial only by virtue of the courtroom sketch; but the sketch does not have the unmediated presence of the camera. We are aware of its artifice and of the agency of the artist; we are conscious of the act of portrayal. The courtroom sketch acknowledges its own madeness, perhaps, in part, because it appears to show not the scene itself but the impression made on a viewer by the scene: 'This is how I saw it.'

There is a remoteness about the courtroom sketch which is a sign of the gap between the actual trial and its representation. In her outstanding study *Pictures at an Exhibition*, Wendy Lesser argues that the portrayal of murder is always, necessarily, a reflection of the nature of representation itself. She writes:

> To portray murder … is to acknowledge the distance between the act of murder and its rendering. The murder story is always in part about this distance. This is also true of murder trials … the trial is just a rough sketch of what happened, an incomplete and inadequate portrayal, not the thing itself.[61]

I am drawn to Lesser's metaphor of the trial as a sketch of the crime; an evocation of 'the thing itself' which draws us further and further into the world of representations. In these terms, the courtroom sketch is a second-order evocation, a rough sketch of the trial and confirmation of the distance between the actual administration of justice and its representation.

The artist can take written notes during the trial but must leave the courtroom to make the sketch. The image is thus made outside the sitting of the court and is not part of the legal process of the trial. It has a particular temporality. It does not belong to the time of the court; it is not a record or evidence of the trial, but is retrospective and remembered. The courtroom sketch is thus *of* the trial but is not *a part* of the trial; it does not infiltrate the hermetically sealed world of the courtroom as the camera would do, but maintains and strengthens the essential borderline between the inside and the outside of the legal process. The sketch is thus a testimony to the partial and incomplete nature of portrayal and to law's regulation of the visual image. The hasty notations, the sketchy outlines and roughly filled-in blocks of colour, the unfinished edges which dissolve before the frame remind us of what must be imagined and of the gulf between image and event.

The meanings of the courtroom sketch are specific to its medium and making and make it the antithesis of the photographic image. Compared to the sketch, the photograph is seen to be an unmediated representation, both in terms of its means of production and of its consumption. In the process of representation, the photograph is assumed to offer little interference with the truth of its subject. The camera watches and records and offers a first-hand testimony of the trial. It is an automatized image; it seems to eliminate human agency and reflection, thus enabling direct access not simply to an image but to the represented object or event itself. The realistic effect of the photograph creates a direct and affective relationship to the viewer. This assumption has been built into the legal definition and regulation of pornography in which photographs of the body are assumed to be more arousing than comparable images in other, more 'artistic' media.[62] It was the power of the photograph 'to be there', in the court and to motivate its viewers that worried the legislators in 1925. The prohibition of photography effectively removed the mass public from the courtroom and prevented the law being turned into an emotive spectacle.

Courtroom art has been ignored by art history, media studies, sociology and criminology.[63] The academic debate on public access to the courts moved straight to the claims of video and television cameras without ever having considered the history of the visual representation of trials and the circumstances surrounding the prohibition of photography and image-making in the courtroom. An examination of that history can tell us much about the relationship between law, media and the image and about the social and cultural legacy of cameras in the courtroom. Most legal systems have moved much further than the English in allowing the filming of trials. In the United States television coverage and live transmission of trials is routine and in 1991 a case was brought in California to extend the rights of the press to permit television cameras to film an execution.[64] The judge ruled against the case but essentially the terms of the argument were those established at the beginning of the twentieth century. The rights of the press and of the public to see and to know, and the protection of individual privacy and the decorum of the courts continue to structure the debate today. I am shocked now by the photographs from 1924 of Patrick Mahon listening to his death sentence; equally, I am certain that courtroom sketches are anomalous and anachronistic. At the end of 2000, the Labour Government announced that during a second term of office it would introduce legislation to allow television cameras into courtrooms.[65] This must be right; but let us not forget the insights offered by the courtroom sketch. Its foregrounding of artifice and its distance from the moment of the trial, are a constant reminder of the role of representation and ritual at all levels of the legal system. Courtroom art is evidence that our world of electronic imaging is continually compromised by other atavistic forms which bind twenty-first-century pictorial pleasures to older traditions of popular culture and mechanical reproduction.

Notes

This text is a slightly revised version of my 'Visual Cultures of the Courtroom: Reflections on History, Law and the Image', *Visual Culture in Britain* 3, no. 2 (2002), pp. 119–141.

1 Criminal Justice Act, 1925 (15 & 16 Geo. V, c.86), p. 41.

2 On the cultural significance of major trials at the end of the nineteenth century, see Nancy Erber and George Robb, 'Introduction', in George Robb and Nancy Erber (eds.), *Disorder in the Courts: Trials and Sexual Conflict at the Turn of the Century* (London: Macmillan, 1999), pp. 1–11. For a good analysis of one murder trial from this period, see Julie English Early, 'A New Man for a New Century: Dr Crippen and the Principles of Masculinity', in Robb and Erber, *Disorder in the Courts*, pp. 209–230.

3 For an analysis of detective fiction in the context of Walter Sickert's Camden Town Murder series, see Lisa Tickner, *Modern Life and Modern Subjects: British Art in the Early Twentieth Century* (New Haven and London: Yale University Press, 2000), p. 99.

4 The enduring popular interest in this case is suggested by the novels based on it. See Fryniwyd Marsh Tennyson Jesse, *A Pin to See the Peepshow* (London and Toronto: Heinemann, 1934), and Jill Dawson, *Fred and Edie* (London: Sceptre, 2000).

5 Accounts of the case are given in Travers Humphreys, *A Book of Trials* (Melbourne, London, Toronto: William Heinemann Ltd., 1953), pp. 147–155;

Robin Odell, *Landmarks in 20th Century Murder* (London: Headline, 1995), pp. 122–126; Jean Graham Hall and Gordon D. Smith, *R. v. Bywaters and Thompson* (Chichester: Barry Rose Law, 1997).

6 See the *Daily Sketch* (7 October 1922), p. 1; *News of the World* (8 October 1922), p. 5. A transcript of the trial and related papers are kept at the Public Record Office, London. DRIM 1/206/5; HO 144/2685; PCOM 8/22; PCOM 8/436.

7 *The Times* (11 December 1922), p. 12. See also the *News of the World* (10 December 1922), p. 1.

8 *Lloyd's Sunday News* (10 December 1922), p. 1.

9 As cited in the *Illustrated London News* (16 December 1922), p. 986. Shearman's words were quoted in most of the national papers.

10 *Daily Graphic* (7 December 1922), p. 3. See also the *News of the World* (10 December 1922), p. 9, and (17 December 1922), p. 9.

11 On metropolitan working women in the 1920s, see Sally Alexander, *Becoming a Woman and Other Essays in 19th and 20th Century Feminist History* (London: Virago, 1994), pp. 203–224.

12 Women over 31 years of age were first given the vote immediately after World War I, in 1919.

13 See the *Daily Mirror* (9 December 1922), p. 1, and (11 December 1922), p. 1, and the *Daily Graphic* (11 December 1922), p. 1.

14 See also the *Daily Graphic* (9 December 1922), p. 1.

15 There is, however, no reference to such a prohibition in the trial papers at the Public Record Office.

16 Smaller portrait sketches were also used in the *News of the World* (8 October 1922), p. 5; *Daily Sketch* (8 December 1922), p. 2; *Reynolds's Newspaper* (10 December 1922), p. 3. No sketches were printed on front pages.

17 As reported in the *Daily Graphic* (15 December 1922), p. 7.

18 On broadsides and other forms of street literature in this period, see Leslie Shepard, *The History of Street Literature: The Story of Broadside Ballads, Chapbooks, Proclamations, News-Sheets, Election Bills, Tracts, Pamphlets, Cocks, Catchpennies, and Other Ephemera* (Newton Abbott: David and Charles, 1973), and Thomas Gretton, *Murders and Moralities: English Catchpenny Prints 1800–1860* (London: British Museum, 1980).

19 For a helpful account of the illustrated press, see Michael Twyman, *Printing 1770–1970: An Illustrated History of Its Development and Uses in England* (London: Eyre and Spottiswoode, 1970).

20 On the Sunday papers, see Raymond Williams, 'The Growth of the Popular Press', in *The Long Revolution* (Harmondsworth: Penguin, 1965 [1961]), pp. 195–236; Raymond Williams, 'The Press and Popular Culture: An Historical Perspective', in George Boyce, James Curran and Pauline Wingate (eds.), *Newspaper History from the Seventeenth Century to the Present Day* (London: Constable and California: Sage, 1978), pp. 41–50; and Virginia Berridge, 'Popular Sunday Papers and Mid-Victorian Society', in Boyce, Curran and Wingate, *Newspaper History*, pp. 247–264.

21 For a discussion of new journalism in the context of a broader history of the popular press, see Alan J. Lee, *The Origins of the Popular Press in England 1855–1914* (London: Croom Helm, 1976). On the role of the new journalism in the reporting of the trial of Oscar Wilde, see Ed Cohen, *Talk on the Wilde Side: Toward a Genealogy of a Discourse on Male Sexualities* (New York and London: Routledge, 1993).

22 On the early history of news photography, see Ken Baynes (ed.), *Scoop, Scandal and Strife: A Study of Photography in Papers* (London: Lund Humphries, 1971); Ian Jeffrey, *Photograpy: A Concise History* (London: Thames and Hudson, 1981), esp. pp. 242–244; Beaumont Newhall, *The History of Photography from 1839 to the Present* (London: Secker and Warburg, 1982), pp. 251–252; Petr Tausk, *A Short History of Press Photography* (Prague: International Organization of Journalists, 1988).

23 As a contemporary manual put it: 'The press photographer is even more ubiquitous nowadays than the reporter of a few years ago, and few public functions or topical events take place which are not duly recorded by the camera.' F. J. Mortimer, *Photographs for the Press and Photography for Profit* (London: Hazell, Watson and Viney, 1914), p. 7.

24 On technical innovations in photographic equipment, see note 25, also Camfield Wills and Deirdre Wills, *History of Photography: Techniques and Equipment* (London, New York, Sydney, Toronto: Hamlyn, 1980); Alma Davenport, *The History of Photography: An Overview* (Boston and London: Focal Press, 1991), esp. p. 95.

25 John Everard, *Photographs for the Papers: How to Take and Place Them* (London: A. and C. Black Ltd., 1923), p. 9.

26 For an outstanding discussion of the history of courtroom photography in the context of recent debates on televised court proceedings, see Marjorie Cohn and David Dow, *Cameras in the Courtroom: Television and the Pursuit of Justice* (Jefferson, NC and London: McFarland and Co., 1998).

27 Ibid., p. 26. See also '[Photographs taken in court] frequently come very near contempt of court', pp. 42–43.

28 Reminiscing on his career as a press photographer in these years, William R. Turner recalled the tactics used in the courtroom to avoid detection. Experienced photographers would get to know the 'geography' of individual courtrooms and would change their positions throughout the trial to avoid being noticed by officials. He describes other tricks such as resting his small, hand-held camera on the seat beside him and photographing the accused in a murder trial. William R. Turner, *Eyes of the Press* (London: Hutchinson and Co., 1935), p. 208. See also pp. 205 and 217.

29 On the use of photography for forensic investigation, see Wills and Wills, *History of Photography*, pp. 145–149, and Peter Hamilton and Roger Hargreaves, *The Beautiful and the Damned: The Creation of Identity in Nineteenth Century Photography* (Aldershot: Lund Humphries in association with National Portrait Gallery Publications, 2001).

30 Rex *v.* Ferguson and Dwyer, *Law Times*, 132 (28 February 1925), pp. 351–352.

31 For an account of this case, see Odell, *Landmarks*, pp. 128–134. The few remaining documents relating to the trial are in the Public Record Office ASSI/31/55, pp. 386–387.

32 *Reynolds's News* (13 July 1924), p. 11.

33 *Daily Sketch* (21 July 1924), p. 13.

34 *Daily Sketch* (16 July 1924), p.3.

35 *News of the World* (20 July 1924), p. 1.

36 *Daily Sketch* (16 July 1924), p. 3. See also the *Daily Mirror* (16 July 1924), p. 2.

37 *Daily Mirror* (17 July 1924), p. 2.

38 *Daily Mirror* (21 July 1924), p. 2.

39 *Daily Sketch* (18 July 1924), p. 3.

40 *Daily Sketch* (17 July 1924), p. 8.

41 *Daily Sketch* (16 July 1924), p. 1; (18 July 1924), p. 3.

42 See also the *News of the World* (20 July 1924), p. 4; *Reynolds's News* (20 July 1924), p. 11; *Sunday News* (20 July 1924), p. 1; *Daily Sketch* (21 July 1924), pp. 10–11.

43 See *Reynolds's News* (27 July 1924), p. 7; (3 August 1924), p. 7.

44 *Sunday News* (27 July 1924), p. 1.

45 For references to the history of the Criminal Justice bill, see E. J. Hayward, *The Criminal Justice Act, 1925 (Annotated), Together with Rules, Orders and Forms* (London: Butterworth and Co., Shaw and Sons, 1926), p. ix; *Justice of the Peace* LXXXIX (28 February 1925), p. 136; *Manchester Guardian* (21 November 1925), p. 7.

46 See Ronald Blythe, *The Age of Illusion: England in the Twenties and Thirties* (London: Hamish Hamilton, 1963), pp. 15–42.

47 As quoted in Hayward, *Criminal Justice Act*, pp. 129–130. For other commentaries on the Act, see Albert Lieck and A. C. L. Morrison, *The Criminal Justice Act, 1925, with Explanatory Notes* (London: Stevens and Sons, 1926); R. E. Otter and G. B. McClure, *The Criminal Justice Act 1925 with Notes* (London: Solicitors' Law Stationery Society, 1926). For more recent discussion, see Geoffrey Robertson and Andrew G. L. Nicol, *Media Law: The Rights of Journalists, Broadcasters and Publishers* (London: Sage, 1984), pp. 212–213; C. J. Miller, *Contempt of Court*, 2nd edn (Oxford: Clarendon, 1990), pp. 128–132; Nigel Lowe and Brenda Sufrin, *The Law of Contempt*, 3rd edn (London, Dublin and Edinburgh: Butterworths, 1996), pp. 24–27.

48 For analysis of the bill and subsequent Act, see *Law Journal*, vol. 60 (14 March 1925), pp. 252–253; vol. 61 (27 March 1926), pp. 296–297, (3 April 1926), pp. 320–321, (5 June 1926), pp. 484–485; *Justice of the Peace* (28 February 1925), p. 136; F. B. Dingle, *Stones's Justices' Manual*, 58th edn (London: Shaw and Sons Ltd., Butterworth and Co., 1926), pp. 173, 1235.

49 *Law Journal*, vol. 61 (5 June 1926), p. 485.

50 *Law Journal*, vol. 61 (3 April 1926), p. 320.

51 *Justice of the Peace* (28 February 1925), p. 136.

52 See, for example, Robertson and Nicol, *Media Law*, p. 213.

53 Hayward, *Criminal Justice Act*, pp. xii–xiii; *Justice of the Peace*, vol. XC (6 February 1926), p. 86.

54 Reported in *The Times* (24 June 1925), p. 12. The clause changed its number through various amendments to and draftings of the bill. In the following discussion of the bill it will be referred to simply as 'the clause'.

55 *188 H. C. Deb. 5s. (1924–25)* c. 833. A report of the debate is given here (cc. 831–52) and in *The Times* (21 November 1925), p. 6, and the *Manchester Guardian* (21 November 1925), p. 7.

56 *188 H. C. Deb.*, c. 836.

57 *The Times* (21 November 1925), p. 6.

58 Ibid.

59 Costas Douzinas, 'The Legality of the Image', *Modern Law Review*, vol. 63 (November 2000), p. 815.

60 Wendy Lesser uses the term 'Everyman' quality in her description of Howard Brodie's drawings of the execution of Aaron Mitchell in 1967. See *Pictures at an Exhibition* (Cambridge, Mass. and London: Harvard University Press, 1993), p. 166. Lesser's insightful observations on the portrayal of murder in the U.S. offer invaluable ways of understanding courtroom sketches.

61 Lesser, *Pictures at an Exhibition*, pp. 131–132.

62 For a full discussion of the significance of the photographic image and other visual media in relation to pornography, see Lynda Nead, *The Female Nude: Art, Obscenity and Sexuality* (London and New York: Routledge, 1992).

63 See, for example, David Kidd-Hewitt and Richard Osborne, *Crime and the Media: The Post-Modern Spectacle* (London: Pluto, 1995), in which no mention is made of the role of courtroom art in this 'post-modern spectacle'.

64 *KQED v. Vasquez.* This case is the focus of Lesser, *Pictures*. See also the debates surrounding the federal execution of the Oklahoma bomber.

65 As reported in the *Guardian* (27 December 2000), p. 1.

III.
THE VISUALITY OF LAW

6

Law as Visual Communication

Dag Michalsen

Introduction

Contemporary modern society has become increasingly dependent upon visuality. This has led to new trends in cultural studies discussing how visual representations influence our perception of society and its institutions. This is also an important observation concerning central elements of law and legal thinking. But as a research field 'law and visuality' has yet to lead to any distinct research practice founded on a general theoretical basis. To face up to the view of law as something much more than text-based institutions and norms requires another set of theories better suited to the study of the interactions of law and visualization. By and large, legal scientists have not accepted the importance of this connection, presumably because few have seen the relevance of discussing the consequences that visuality might have for the science of law as well as for the understanding of the functioning of law in society. However, during the last two decades some studies on the impact of visual communications on law and justice in modern society have been published internationally. This has especially highlighted the relationship between norm structures in society and filmmaking, both documentary and fictional.

To get an understanding of law suited to a more cultural-oriented research, law might be viewed as a series of communicative processes in society.[1] This perspective might also serve as fruitful access to the interaction between law and visualization. When law is not only understood in the traditional terms of power, institutions and hierarchy, but rather as important means of communicating frameworks for human action in its broadest sense, then the impact of visuality of law gains some relevance. Through the world of visuality, law is being communicated in a number of ways, whether from the point of view of legal institutions, other power groups in society, or from minorities or from alternative political or culture perspectives. Images in the media show this type of visual communication on law all the time.

How are we to interpret this massive visual communication in law and who in particular is suited for such a task? To these questions there are no clear-cut answers, only a number of different ways in which we may reflect upon the issue. In this article I wish to focus on the possible role of legal science as an interpreter of visual communication in law. Usually this has been a task reserved for cultural or media theory or other branches of social and human sciences. But I suggest that legal science is an underrated profession for this type of undertaking.

Legal science/human sciences

Contemporary legal science is so varied that one hesitates to suggest normative approaches to the practices of it. In the last decade, this attitude has come more to the forefront, thus allowing legal scientists greater freedom than before to formulate tasks and perspectives for legal science which go beyond the institutional tasks that the legal order expects from legal science. Therefore, one may ask whether we could make a distinction between the institutional task of legal science and what might be called the cultural-interpretative task. By doing so, legal science also becomes a branch of the human sciences with the specific aim to interpret socio-cultural and aesthetic issues involving law. It goes without saying that this task can only be regarded as a supplement to the dominant institutional function of legal science. Conversely, the cultural-interpretative task of legal science could also be understood as a contribution to the institutional function as knowledge of this kind provides fruitful contexts for legal interpretation and implementation. This has been a common argument for enhancing the mainstream lawyer's interest in law and literature studies.

I would, however, argue that legal science has a competence that makes it suitable to take upon it to become a human science of its own. Based on the traditional arsenal of knowledge and a well-developed methodical vocabulary, legal science is, in my view, able to contribute with specific independent interpretations of socio-cultural and aesthetic issues where law in some way or another is involved. In this role, legal science has a general cultural-interpretative approach allowing it, for example, to show normative structures in aesthetic works, or to interpret texts in a legal-literate way or to contribute with a legal-semiotic perception of a painting or a film.

But why should legal science promote a cultural-interpretative approach to law? The colonization of all parts of society by contemporary law and the fact that legal models have increasingly been influenced by cultural theories have favoured an understanding of law as a system of discourses rather than system of rules. In this manner, the many aspects of law – such as institutional, dogmatic, social and cultural – are seen as interwoven and interconnected, leading legal science to expand its options of legal interpretations.[2] Legal scientists are unable to give an ultimate reading of these complex processes of discourses. What the legal scientist can do, however, is to highlight some of the normative perspectives involved.

W. J. T. Mitchell has called the shift in contemporary culture a pictorial turn compared with the preceding linguistic turn in the mid-twentieth century.[3] This assertion implies not only that the present society is more drained with images than ever before, but it also indicates that the technology of the nineteenth and twentieth centuries has led to new modes of perceptions, also pointing to important historical dimensions in the visual communication of law.[4]

The film media is today the most significant historical contribution to law as visual communication. The visual forms of representation are found in pop culture, in visual aesthetic processes of the views on law within the state or in civil society or in the crime series depicting numerous stories about lawyers, courtrooms and legal and moral destinies of all kinds. Through all these images, society is questioning and thematizing the complex social discourses on law, both as reality and as fictional representations. In these numerous images of representation of law, there is in my view what I would call a *field of law's potentiality* involving a great number of persons elaborating their own views on law compared to what is regarded as the normative structures of society. This wide range of legal visuality seems to be the closest one currently can come to the classical notion of peoples' legal consciousness (or to use a classical German word, *Rechtsbewusstsein*) now having new technological means. This notion seems to have found a new form of reality in the intersection between the universal-virtual space and the private technological room of the individual. Calculating the effect of this new social condition for the formal legal discourse in society is difficult, but these forms of visual communication have become part of what may in the broadest sense be called contemporary law.

In reading these visual legal practices, there may be a differentiation between the two levels of interpretive understanding of film images. The interconnection of image, law and meaning may be investigated with the help of the distinction between the denotation and connotation of the visual communication.[5] The denotation of the image is the immediate reference, what we call the level of information, where one can see the narrative structure unfolding or where the documentary facts are being shown, either as historical reconstructions or as contemporary expressions of law. This type of information is part of the traditional institutional knowledge of legal science.

But the film image also has a *connotative influence,* which opens up for the interpretation of the symbolic universe of the film. Reading the image according to the connotation of the image and as part of the general preconception of legal and social reasoning leads to other forms of reflections than the textual one, reflections that are mediated through the autonomous display of the film images.[6] Consequently, in the difference between denotation and connotation there is a place for cultural-interpretive readings of legal science with regard to legal communication. The level of denotation is only that of referring, and the interpretations of the legal visuality can only be linked to the prevailing hegemonic discourses of law; this is the typical illustrative relationship between law and image in which the image is being structured by a legal textual meaning not the image of law. On the level of connotation, however, there will be another logic than the traditional legal one, as it will further associative reasoning that transcends the legal institution's grip on legal science's legal interpretations.

Gosford Park (2001)

The legal readings of film do not only involve films with the main focus on law, but also those films which have law as a more subordinate theme are interesting for legal cultural interpretations. The visualization processes in society can be just as rewarding also for those films where law is only part of the theme. An interesting film of that kind is Robert Altman's *Gosford Park* from 2001.[7] The film portrays a picture of a weekend party in an upper class house in England in 1932. There are no main characters and there is almost no narrative at all; what we see are subtle images of social structures and social practices. In the centre of the film are the numerous corridors of the house, the many staircases and other physical boundaries that create different social spaces and levels. The film is a visualization of manners in which the normative structures of the collective group of people are being projected by means of Altman's innovative cinematic touches. We are made aware of the neutral functional side of the human actions taking place between people walking in corridors and on staircases and entering and leaving rooms. Despite the fact that many of England's most well-known actors appear in the film, their faces seem unimportant and no one's personality is really being portrayed, only what I would call mechanical social actions are visible. What we see is what Bourdieu called 'embodied social structures'.[8]

Then – not surprisingly – at midnight, the landowner is murdered. When the police appear, when 'Law' is introduced into the narrative, this fact seems quite irrelevant. The reproduction of social structures that is the main theme of the film comes even more into focus as the murder of the proprietor is an integrated part of an upstairs–downstairs conflict. No solution can be ascertained by the ignorant policeman, who cannot see beyond the prevailing social structures. We *see* an aesthetically planned image of law; we *see* a specific interpretation of a plausible historical situation, a fiction, but still very plausible. But these visualizations have in their connotative influence a logic of their own, making it an interesting object of a legal cultural reading and for which legal science seems to be particularly suited.

Altman's *Gosford Park* is, like many important films, part of its own internal film historical universe, particularly referring to Jean Renoir's famous *La Règle du jeu* from 1939 where the plot unfolds at a French château during a weekend. This film's historical reference is an important dimension in *Gosford Park* as it reflects changing forms of discourses concerning law in the twentieth century. The murder in *La Règle du jeu* is visible, an important social event, the climax of the film, executed by human beings. In *Gosford Park*, in 2001, the formal law has become unstable, almost invisible as the social mechanisms lead us to see beyond law. The restless views of the camera visualize a law without a centre, or, rather, a number of possible laws ingrained in social practices are being visualized. Legal science is able to understand this legal visualization by means of cultural readings, thereby demonstrating the film medium's ability to aesthetically conceptualize contemporary law. For legal science, to cultivate a legal semiotics of legal representations seems to me an important task, thus additionally contributing to other branches of the research field.

A long tradition in history of legal science maintains the many identities of the discipline. A legal science will as a matter of fact involve not only a legal and a social theory, but a cultural theory as well. The content of these theories will vary according to the political regime, intellectual hegemonies, social structures and much more. But the capacities of the legal sciences' forms of interpretations ought to be reformulated continually as part of an ongoing legal historical reflection.

Notes

1 Niklas Luhmann, *Recht der Gesellschaft* (Berlin: Suhrkamp, 1995); Mark Van Hoecke, *Law as Communication* (Oxford: Hart Publishing, 2002).
2 Werner Gephart, *Recht als Kultur. Zur kultursoziologischen Analyse des Rechts* (Frankfurt am Main: Vittorio Klostermann, 2006), 289 ff.
3 W. J. T. Mitchell, *Picture Theory: Essays on Verbal and Visual Representation* (Chicago: University of Chicago Press, 1994).
4 Jonathan Crary, *Suspensions of Perception: Attention, Spectacle, and Modern Culture* (Cambridge, MA: The MIT Press, 1999).
5 Roland Barthes, 'Rhetoric of the Image', in *Image, Music, Text*, ed. Stephen Heath (New York: Hill and Wang, 1977), 32 ff. and Atle Kittang, *Sju artikkler om litteraturvitskap* (Oslo: Gyldendal 2001), 97 ff.
6 Gilles Deleuze, *Cinema 2: The Time Image* (London: The Athlone Press, 1989 [1985]), 262 ff.
7 See http://en.wikipedia.org/wiki/Gosford Park (last accessed 09/09/2010).
8 Pierre Bourdieu, *Distinction: A Social Critique of the Judgement of Taste* (London: Routledge and Kegan Paul, 1984 [1979]), 467 ff.

7

The Patron–Client Relation Visualized

Cecilie Schjatvet

What sources may inform us about the professional ethics of the lawyer–client relationship? Existing legal professional codes are unduly limited to a pair of archetypes that are possibly outdated and ideologically charged, the hired gun and the officer of the court, as they hardly manage to look beyond the needs of the profession and to the needs of the client. In everyday practice, the clients pose more varied demands of the lawyer than what the two archetypes may offer. Clients from all walks of life are more empowered than the archetypes inform, and they fail to encompass a social structure that carries a sizeable ambivalence towards lawyers. Social and cultural observations also indicate that all lawyer–client relationships have an element of mutual dependence. Lawyers' ethical codes would therefore achieve greater precision if based on an actual social and cultural context, rather than a professional code with a possible ideological slant. One source that may prove valuable to better understand the lawyer archetypes are the many films that describe the lawyer–client relationship. As a cultural expression, films are particularly relevant as they are usually mass distributed, easily accessible and a dominant cultural expression across social mores. As a source of knowledge about legitimate lawyer archetypes, films may add a needed coloring to the traditional historical approach and a sense of continuity to traditional sociological approaches.

A possible liberal bias in the existing international professional legal ethics

The International Code of Ethics for lawyers[1] is based on a particular *liberal* and *system-oriented* understanding of the patron–client relationship. In part it is shaped by nineteenth-century liberal ideas of individual autonomy,[2] and in part it is based on the much older perception that the protection of lawyer special privileges is key to the rule of law and good governance.[3] Belief in individual autonomy and the rule of law also forms the ideological basis for the two lawyer archetypes that have been developed in US academic writings:[4] *the hired gun* who represents and respects the client's interests and autonomy as a neutral, morally detached partisan,[5] and *the officer of the court* who balances the pure interest of the client with the interest of justice.[6]

The image of the heroic or unscrupulous lawyer who never gives up on the client *is* undoubtedly an influential and viable archetype. The belief that individual effort makes a difference is deeply embedded in public consciousness, and the idea is especially well-represented in US culture.[7] It is also true that the concept of the lawyer as a pillar of society whose allegiance is to the interest of justice is often seen as one prerequisite to a working democratic society, both in science and in popular culture. As to the latter, the Indian director Satyajit Ray's adaptation of Henrik Ibsen's *An Enemy of the People* portrays one famous example of a lawyer who makes sacrifices to uphold the rule of law and security in the local community.[8] Still, as important and central to the lawyer–client relationship as 'the hired gun' and 'the officer of the court' may be, they do not tell the whole story.

First, there is nothing in legal profession's nature or in the science of law that forces lawyers to subscribe only to purely liberal and narrowly set systemic values. The existing international professional legal ethics simply assumes a necessary ideological tie that (no longer) is representative of its members. Jurists are a mixed group of men, women and ethnic minorities, some with lower class background and with varied political attachments. The cases the lawyers defend may also challenge pure liberal ideas and the lawyer may be pushed to find ethical balances that society does not have an impetus to produce. For example, the lawyer defending the action of protesters from extreme right to extreme left must try to identify an ethical equilibrium that may explain or mitigate actions that society has already presupposed as extreme by labeling the perpetrator as political dissident, a security threat or even a terrorist.

Second, lawyers' independence and professional privileges is not necessarily a particular liberal ideal in all contexts. Clients in liberal democracies are usually either educated or empowered or both. The know-how of the workings of the law is easily accessible even for the less resourceful clients, indicating that clients expect a more level field than the traditional archetypes call for. The hired gun may easily end up playing the championing role of the patriarch protector and the officer of the court may presume some exclusive insight that has no basis in reality vis-à-vis the client.

Third, it is not only a matter of clients having become empowered and knowledgeable of the law; it is also a matter that their claim for autonomy presents itself as legitimate. Orson Welles's version of Franz Kafka's *The Trial* (1962) describes the psychology of an outlandish asymmetry in the lawyer–client relationship. The dysfunctional over-sized, procrastinating lawyer, forever dormant in his dimly lit quarters, makes a strong case *against* professional autonomy even in more oppressed societies.

As a consequence, the two archetypes may not suffice as common denominators for the lawyer–client relationship. Clients assume greater autonomy in their meeting with their lawyers, and new archetypes should be created that recognize how the relationship is affected by its sociological and cultural backdrop. Present-day professional legal ethics should therefore dig deeper to find a way to describe the essentials of the lawyer-client relationship. Two types of theories may be needed: Social theories may properly describe both the dynamics of the relationship and possible *legitimate models* for the advocate, similar to that of Max Weber's ideal types. Cultural theories of a *narrative ethics* may provide a better alternative to the principled professional ethics, as it focuses on the persons and the context that is readily understandable. The possible use of social and cultural theories will be dealt with in the next sections below. In the last section, films as a potential source of knowledge about lawyer archetypes are discussed more in depth.

A social theory for three possible lawyer archetypes in the patron–client relationship

From a sociological standpoint, the lawyer's self-perception is not only shaped by the norms of the legal profession's ethical code or by the training from her education. Lawyers, as all other groups in society, operate in a social context that they become affected or indoctrinated by. The client's potential wealth, social influence and cultural references are all elements that may affect the dynamics of the relationship. History also informs of many such 'lop-sided' relationships of mutual obligations in all its phases, from the Roman Empire to contemporary academic analysis of power relations.[9] A social theory for lawyers' professional ethics should therefore include (i) an understanding of the *social structure* the lawyer operates in, (ii) a description of which *particular mutual obligations* that may appear, and (iii) a suggestion of *three possible legitimate archetypes* for how lawyers may shape their professional role.

The social structure invokes ambivalence towards the lawyer

Our social structure is perhaps more influential in shaping the relationship than the single actors themselves. In the words of Robert K. Merton, the social structure poses several and conflicting normative expectations towards a particular role-set. He describes the tension between the dynamic of a role-set (his examples are often doctor–patient) and the expectations of society to form a theory of sociological ambivalence towards for instance the medical profession.

The theory of sociological ambivalence observes that, on the one hand, a particular 'role' in society (like that of doctors or lawyers) must relate to the particular demands of the clients where 'each social status … involves an array of roles,' with observable conflicting demands by members of the same role-set.[10] On the other hand, the same doctors or lawyers must relate to the sociological ambivalence in the structures of society towards their particular role:

> ... sociological ambivalence refers to incompatible normative expectations incorporated in a single role of a single social status (for example, the therapist role of the physician as distinct from other roles of his or her status as researcher, administrator, professional colleague, participant in the professional association, etc.) ... the ambivalence is located in the social definition of roles and status, not in the feeling-state of one or another type of personality.[11]

Merton's theory of sociological ambivalence shows how lawyers may both have to address the particular and conflicting expectations of the clients, and the ambivalent attitudes they meet within the social structure. This suggests that a professional legal ethics must involve lawyers' archetypes that are sufficiently complex. In a social setting, it may quickly prove too extreme to base an ethics on a strong belief in individual anatomy, and it is too sterile and politically conservative to only refer to a narrow rule-of-law focus. Rather, archetypes in tune with the sociological ambivalence that surrounds them will acknowledge that the client's and society's expectations may not be coherent and logical. Furthermore, the archetype should reflect that the clients' and society's ambivalence is predisposed – not merely a reaction to the lawyer's type, particular personality or passion.

Some particular mutual obligations in the lawyer–client relationship

As the lawyer–client relationship presents itself as one of mutual obligations, it is necessary to describe this dependency in more detail. History's concept of the patron–client relationship describes the relationship as one where the parties have a mutual interest in each other's progress. One writer has aptly described the lawyer as a 'special purpose friend' to the client.[12]

The key function of the patron–lawyer will be to help the client progress in society in some way (get acquitted, earn more money, win on principle). In return the lawyer may expect her client to support the specific lawyer archetype she represents, speak well of her services to others and keep an ear to the ground on her behalf. Both have a mutual interest in that the lawyer increases her social status: the client's social status is affected positively if her lawyer has achieved public fame or recognition (i.e. by cultivating an image of the relentless, morally upright or shrewd attorney), if she takes on other clients belonging to the same group and brand herself as a lawyer fighting for a particular cause, or if she qualifies for prizes, ratings or titles (i.e. Human Rights prizes, unofficial 'most valuable' listings, appointments to committees influencing the law-making process, or receiving licences to appear before Regional or Supreme Courts).

These examples of 'co-dependence' resonate with the experience of legal practice. And to the extent that such aspects of the relationship are seen as the underpinning of the relationship in the mindset of the client, any abstract ideas of the lawyer as a hired gun or the officer of the court will lessen in importance.

Three possible lawyer archetypes

From the viewpoint of social theory, any exercise of power needs to be perceived as legitimate in order to expect to endure. A professional ethical code is the most important way of preserving the legitimacy of lawyers' position and their privileges, and the development of legitimate archetypes is the other. As already pointed out, if these codes and archetypes to too large an extent are constructed for and by the profession, the profession may experience loss of legitimacy. At the very least, lawyer archetypes should be able to meet the test of social theories akin to that of Max Weber.

A social theory of lawyer behaviour must be adapted to fit the function of the profession in society. Whereas Weber speaks of three ideal types of how state leaders legitimate their exercise of power that cover a specter of situations,[13] it seems more apt to describe lawyers' more limited function in our lives in terms of *archetypes*.[14] The value of working with three instead of a dual pair may be imported however. The dynamics that *three* archetypes provide may better attach to changes in society. The tendency of lawyers to think in opposites may better be reserved to the function of rules, not people.

How may one proceed to identify three archetypes that fulfil some criteria of legitimacy in social theory? Drawing on Weber, such archetypes may very well draw on philosophical and not empirical observations. The archetypes here suggested are also meant to meet a test of general experience which is not informed by any systematic collection of empirical data.

The present models of the 'hired gun' and 'officer of the court' both see the lawyer as one who defends and protects a legal principle. However, clients may not only and not always expect vindication of a legal principle, and not everyone is focused on the end result. Some are indifferent to or may even feel alienated by a lawyer who presents herself as 'a professional' whose only concern is the results that the letter of the law may provide. Some clients desire a lawyer to serve as an agent to rectify their moral or social status, regardless of whether that coincides with the legal outcome of the case. For instance, the battered wife may only want to live in peace from her husband, but in order to receive protection from the police she must press charges, and the focus of the system is to convict the perpetrating husband. The battered wife may expect her lawyer to 'fix' her legitimate problem and focus on living in peace, and she may even request that her lawyer works to avoid conviction.

Some client may not expect particular legal advice as she herself understands the law quite well, either through experience with the court system or by way of personal skills and access to legal material. The client may view the need for a lawyer as very narrow and merely as a means to access files or to give a professional approval to her own legal conclusions. In such lawyer–client relationships, the power of the lawyer lies in the licence and privileges given by law, and not so much in her legal expertise and know-how.

In yet another setting, the function of representation is not so much in the lawyer but in the law offices that serves as a meeting place (actual or in more abstract terms) for clients with same experiences and problems. To the group of clients to be represented by a particular law office may provide social standing within their group. Representation by the firm may in itself give some approval to the client's actions, and even convey a promise of victory or acquittal to their surroundings. The film *Chicago* by Rob Marshall from 2002 features the defence attorney

Billy Flynn (Richard Gere) whose representation entails guarantee of acquittal of even those rightly accused of murder. As the story unfolds it becomes clear that Billy Flynn's success has to do with many other skills than pure academic ones.

All these more or less legitimate expectations of the clients may point to the existence of a lawyer archetype as *the fixer*. The fixer is a type of lawyer that fulfils the client's desire for the lawyer rectifying her moral and social life, where the legal skill of the lawyer is of less importance.

*

The present archetype of the hired gun and the officer of the court are both based on a perception of the lawyer as finding solutions in the law. Whereas many clients are concerned with legal norms, not all of them are concerned with winning or losing on principle. Quite a few clients are not so concerned with how they win but whether they win. These clients expect the lawyer to know how to deal with informal power structures in the official institutions. The ethos or standing of the lawyer within the legal system and her ability to think strategically is of utmost importance in order for her to fulfil such expectations. They expect the lawyer to open new possibilities that do not merely have to do with reading the law, and presumes that the lawyer network, calculate the risks involved in choosing one strategy over the other and be aware of the preferences of the particular judge that presides over a case. As to the latter, the legal profession may want to deny that judges may decide a case based on personal value. Regardless, many clients will be inclined to think that they do.

These clients may also tend to evaluate the work of the lawyer and the functioning of the legal system according to such 'extra legal' criteria. The clients may accept a conviction or a loss on principle if the sentence is short or the loss is limited. Some clients may be affected by the lawyer representing the opposite party and the relationship to her own lawyer. A congenial relationship may offend some and be appreciated by others. And some clients may find a verdict more acceptable if the opposite representation had a decent behavior throughout the trial.

A second archetype may then be *the player* who is the realist agent who recognizes that law operates within the informal structures of the institutions of tradition.

*

The 'hired gun' and the 'officer of the court' both give powerful and illustrating descriptions of the relationship to the lawyer, the case and the judicial system. Many clients also identify their lawyer with the case, and expect the lawyer to function first and foremost as their legal representative. These clients may be of the opinion that their cases can only be won if they win 'on principle'. The doctor accused of mercy killing is convinced that her action is correct, and her issue with the authorities may only be solved if the court accepts the mercy killing as lawful. Such a client who has acted out of her beliefs would probably depend on the extent to which the lawyer would be willing to push the principles. Such clients would probably desire representation that can act both as the partisan 'hired gun' and the 'officer of the court' who also considers the interest of the legal system. It is somewhat presumptuous to remove clients from the principled ethical decision of the lawyer. Michael Gordon's *An Act of Murder* from 1947 makes a case in point. The hard-line judge Cook (Fredric March), who considers mercy killing of his terminally ill wife, is forced to reflect on the value of the different lawyer archetypes, as he himself may need one if he decides to end his beloved wife's misery. As a judge he has shown little sympathy for the accused and their partisan lawyers, but now he finds himself wishing for one if he himself becomes a client. The film allows the potential client to have these reflections, perhaps because he is a lawyer himself. A modern view of the client would accept that knowledge of the law or the court system should not be a prerequisite to be able to discuss the significance of choosing or alternating between the lawyer as a 'hired gun' or an 'officer of the court'.[15]

This third archetype may be termed *the idealist* whose focus on legal norms empower and legitimate the advocate's pursuit of winning on principle. The lawyer–client relationship allows for the discussion and alternation between the partisan role of the 'hired gun' and a paternal 'officer of the court'.

*

These three archetypes – the fixer, the player and the idealist – are informed by the sociological insights where the lawyer is seen to form a sociological pair with the client, and not an inwardly focused professional logic. The same sociological insights inform that the basic characteristics of the client's relationship to her or his lawyer are ambivalence and mutual dependence. The next step is now to discuss how this sociological basis for the lawyer–client relationship may blend with a narrative ethics for the use of analyzing films portraying lawyers.

A narrative ethics for the legal profession

The existing professional legal code is to be understood as a set of *universal principles*, disentangled from changes in the culture they operate in.[16] 'Principled ethics' is a tradition designed to respond to larger issues of good governance, such as John Rawls's exercise of the veil of ignorance.[17] Behind the veil of ignorance, we would probably want that each case and each client be cast with lawyers possessing the best possible knowledge about law, the highest integrity and an extra zeal for deserving clients in order to prevent miscarriages of justice in an otherwise trustworthy legal system. In short: if we do not know what is at stake and if we do not know which position we are put in, the advocate should fulfil the professional criteria whether the client is Hannibal Lecter or Dr Richard David Kimble.[18] Films' portrayal of lawyers may be analyzed with the aid of narrative ethics, first as it may supplement and contextualize the principled ethics and second as it can be applied in tune with the sociological and historical backdrop of the given case.

Universal principles often prove hard to apply in everyday practice, as they tend to be too opaque to be able to speak to the specific issues. Narrative ethics may serve as a supplement to principled ethics, or as a method for discussing whether there exists an absolute truth of a principle.[19] Narrative ethics focus on the moral in the stories and of the personas. It responds directly to issues that arise out of context, and universal principles become less interesting.

The storytelling in films is a viable primary source of narrative ethics. For instance, a film's narrative may puncture strong institutional beliefs, such as any court's ability to ascertain the facts of a case that from a principled standpoint too often is treated as a matter of fact. In Akari Kurosawa's *Rashomon*, the ability to find the truth in a criminal case is questioned by showing three different versions of an alleged rape. In addition to being able to raise an issue that escapes principled ethics, the focus of the narrative is not on finding the universal ethical principle that can guide us to the truth, but rather on the rhetorical situation that produces many possible truths. Nagisa Oshima's *Death by Hanging* (*Koshikei* 1968) probes in a similar manner whether the legal institution is able to discern the truth.[20] In *An Act of Murder* mentioned above, the conflict between the judge's preferred inclinations to apply a principled ethics conflicts with the narrative ethics presented to him by the destiny of his terminally ill wife. Also the narrative ethics do not search for a decisive answer but explores whether the principle in itself will affect the judge's decision to commit a mercy killing.

Universal principles may end up as being perceived as irrelevant if they do not manage to speak to the sociological and historical context of a given case. Narrative ethics consider the sociological backdrop as it becomes part of the story in a way that the opaque principled ethics cannot. This entails on the other hand that it may not provide decisive answers to an ethical dilemma. The focus is on the reflection and the transitions that the lawyer–client relationship will be exposed to as a case develops before the courts.

This supplement that the narrative ethics may provide is illustrated in Otto Preminger's *Anatomy of a Murder* (1959), where it is the personal qualities of the defence attorney Pauly Biegler (James Stewart) and not abstract principles of professional ethics that end up resolving the issue of whether Biegler should take on the case of the accused Lt. Manion.

In one of the first scenes the antagonist and lower-class client Lt. Manion (Ben Gazzara) meets the protagonist and humble small-town

Pauly Biegler, who has just turned to the defence after serving many years as district attorney. While in custody on the suspicion of murder of Barney Quill, whom he alleges raped his wife, Lt. Manion questions Biegler's legal knowledge as to figure out which defence may lead to acquittal:

Lt. Manion:	How do I know you can handle my case?
P. Biegler:	I guess you don't know. Shall we talk about it?
Lt. Manion:	I suppose so.
P. Biegler:	Come on, Lt. Don't be so bored. You know it might very well be that no lawyer can 'handle' your case … if you mean getting off scot-free.
Lt. Manion:	You seem to be forgetting: Barney Quill raped my wife. I have the unwritten law on my side.
P. Biegler:	The unwritten law is a myth. There is no such thing as the unwritten law. Anyone who commits murder on the theory it does exist has just bought himself room and board in the state penitentiary. Maybe for life. With that in mind, perhaps we can proceed with a few questions and answers … that might be of some help in your defence. But probably won't be.

Pauly Biegler then finds out that it took an hour from when Lt. Manion learned about the rape until he shot Barney Quill. At lunch, Biegler tells his long-time friend and colleague, Parnell, that he declined from coaching Lt. Manion into a phoney story. Parnell responds by telling Biegler that he is 'too pure for the natural impurities of the law.' According to the professional legal ethics, lawyers should not construct the client's statement. However, in Parnell's opinion, this principle is purely academic. Back in the jail, Biegler starts up again with the difficult task of telling Lt. Manion the four ways he can defend a murder without putting the words in his mouth. Biegler sets himself on a table slightly above Lt. Manion, leans forward while patting on his cigar:

P. Biegler: Number 1: It wasn't a murder. It was suicide or accidental. Number 2: You didn't do it. Number 3: You were legally justified. Like protecting your home or self-defense. Number 4: The killing was excusable.

Lt. Manion: Where do I fit in to this rosy picture?

P. Biegler: I'll tell you where you don't fit. You don't fit in any of the first three.

Lt. Manion: Why wouldn't I be legally justified in killing the man who raped my wife?

P. Biegler: The time element. If you caught him in the act, the shooting might be justified. But you didn't. You had time to bring in the police. You didn't do that, either. You're guilty of murder, premeditated and with vengeance. That's first degree murder in any court of law.

Lt. Manion: So you are advising me to plead guilty?

P. Biegler: When I advise you to cop out, you'll know.

…

Lt. Manion: If you're not telling me to cop out, what are you telling me to do?

P. Biegler: I am not telling you to do anything. I just want you to understand the letter of the law.

Lt. Manion: Go on.

P. Biegler: Go on with what?

Lt. Manion: Whatever it is you are getting at.

P. Biegler: You are very bright, Lieutenant. Now, let's see how bright you can be. Because your wife was raped, you'll have a favorable atmosphere in the courtroom. The sympathy will be with you if all the facts are true. What you need is a legal peg so the jury can hang up their sympathy on your behalf. You follow me?

Lt. Manion: Mm.

P. Biegler: What's your legal excuse, Lieutenant?

Lt. Manion: Not justification, huh?

P. Biegler: Not justification.

Lt. Manion: Excuse. Just excuse, huh? What excuses are there?

P. Biegler: How should I know? You're the one that plugged Quill.
Lt. Manion: I must have been mad.
P. Biegler: How's that?
Lt. Manion: I said I must've been mad.
P. Biegler: A bad temper is no excuse.
Lt. Manion: I mean, I must've been crazy. Am I getting warmer?

The dialogue obviously makes the viewer anticipate that Pauly Biegler now must make the choice whether to fill in the last pieces for his only possible defence or discontinue the relationship with the client. When Pauly Biegler gets up to leave it seems like Lt. Manion does not get his way. The lieutenant stops him at the door and asks again if he is getting warmer. We do not expect that Pauly Biegler will accept the case. However, his answer indicates ambivalence.

P. Biegler: I'll tell you that after I've talked to your wife. In the meantime, see if you can remember just how crazy you were.

During the meeting with the supposed raped wife, we find out that the doctor exam did not support that she had been raped. This piece of information should presume that Pauly Biegler is less inclined to take on the case. Back in the cell, Lt. Manion has arrived at the conclusion that he cannot remember the act. He can remember hearing the shots, but the shots didn't seem to connect with him:

Lt. Manion: They seemed far away, like someone else was doing the shooting.

Surprisingly, Pauly Biegler then smiles and tells the Lieutenant that he'll take the case. When Pauly Biegler asks for a fee of 3,000 dollars, it appears that Lt. Manion does not want to pay more than 150 dollars, at the most:

P. Biegler: Suppose I don't go along with you unless you pay me half the fee?

Lt. Manion: Well I'll have to take a lawyer the court appoints. I got my defense now. Right? Insanity?

It is difficult to make sense of his decision from the perspective of the principled professional ethics. Pauly Biegler's advice seems to have come close to constructing the client's statement. He provided detailed information, leaving it to the client to draw the necessary conclusions. With the added information that his wife was not raped, Lt. Manion comes across as particularly cunning when fishing around for the right defence.

Still, there is no doubt that the director presents Pauly Biegler as the film's hero and protagonist, even at the conclusion of the scene. The ethical narrative may show that the lawyer's professional code and principled convictions may alter upon meeting the client. The principled ethics of the professional code becomes more a moral starting point and less the factor that determines the premises for the relationship, and surprisingly so, as one of the said strengths of principled ethics is its ability to determine ethical dilemmas. The narrative ethics of Otto Preminger's *Anatomy of a Murder* suggests otherwise.

Another point may be made about the narrative ethics that these scenes inform of the mutual dependence in the lawyer–client relationship. Whereas the specific reasons for why Pauly Biegler decides to take on the case is not explicitly stated, we may nevertheless conclude that it is the wit of the lower-class client that affects the lawyer's advice, demeanor and final decision to take on the case. The lawyer's exclusive knowledge of the law ends up at the hands of the client at the end of the scene, giving a strong case for the existence of a patron–client relationship of mutual dependence. At the end of the scene, they both have entered into a relationship of mutual obligations, where they both share an interest in acquittal in a case where the evidence is strong against the accused. It may be said that Pauly Biegler walked into the police station as an 'idealist', but had a change of heart when Lt Manion clearly expected a 'player' who was willing to draw up different strategies for an acquittal regardless of whether the cost was to plead insanity.[21]

Before turning to a more systematic discussion of the portrayal of the lawyer–client relationship in films, one final note shall be made on how narrative ethics may blend with the aim of finding lawyer archetypes that are perceived as legitimate in society.

One important observation is how filmmakers' portrayals of lawyers may affect the way the latter behave towards clients and in courts. Lawyers are of course not forced to recognize any cultural critique of their behaviour. However, art inescapably relates to power in the ways that it talks to those who are affected by power.[22] So, not surprisingly, the clients upon whom lawyers depend will to some extent base their expectations of their legal representation on what they have seen in films (or television series).

Criminal law practice in Norway may give an example of how clients use (mostly American or British) films and television series as a source of their expectations of the client–lawyer relationship, ranging from the personal qualities of the lawyer to having specific understanding of legal norms that do not exist in Norway. Merely referring to my own experiences as a defence attorney, clients have made reference to the energy and dedication of Julia Roberts in *Erin Brockovich* and to the empathetic qualities of Amy Brenneman in *Judging Amy*. That Brenneman plays a judge and not a lawyer is of less consequence to the client's desire to make a parallel, which may indicate that the client expects all the officers of the court to hold certain qualities.

Clients have also referred to their expectations of the material content of Norwegian law that can only stem from American films, even if the film itself is not mentioned as a source by the client. For example, even if Norwegian criminal procedure does not know any Miranda rights, clients are quite often abashed that their rights are being read to them when they are brought in by the police. They expect that I rectify this perceived injustice, an expectation that can only be derived from American films. In another example, even if Norwegian tort law and professional legal ethics do not allow for the lawyer taking percentages of the client's compensation if winning the case, some clients have present the US principle of 'contingency fee' as the desired premises for me taking on the case.[23] Even if Norwegian rules of evidence do not recognize the principle of hearsay, clients have expected of me to throw out such evidence. Upon explaining that there is no such rule in

Norway, the client may still think that it is *just* if such evidence were thrown out, probably because films convincingly have visualized this element of justice.

The expectations of the clients may also be purely visual: Norwegian courts are designed in such a way that the accused and the witnesses give their statement in a box placed in the centre of the courtroom standing face to face and about ten feet away from the judge. Some clients question and are dismayed at the fact that the Norwegian courtrooms are designed this way ('will I not get closer to the judge?'). The expectation is obviously derived from films, where they in the US and in England sit next to the judge facing both of the advocates.

In addition to films affecting the client's expectations of the lawyer-client relationship, it should also be presumed that films affect how lawyers behave independently of the client's demands. In the writings of art's relation to politics, it is recognized that politicians may make references to popular art in order to legitimize their actions. The next section will explore the many ways that films have captured the behaviour of lawyers in ways that are likely to affect lawyers' understanding of themselves.

Lawyer archetypes in film history

Some methodological points of misrepresentation of law and law as metaphor

Lawyers and lawyer-movies have been part of film history since its beginning with D. W. Griffith's first movie *Falsely Accused* from 1907. The following analysis of lawyers in film takes into account that filmmakers may (intentionally or not) misrepresent the law or facts, that lawyers (and the courts) have been portrayed so many times that they have become part of film's language in the same manner categories such as 'man', 'woman' or 'child' have particular symbolic status.

*

As in other sciences, filmmakers frequently interpret and misinterpret legal science.[24] In a formal sense, films are clearly an unorthodox 'source of law.' Nevertheless they may affect our perception of the law and even influence the outcome of actual cases. Errol Morris's drama-documentary *The Thin Blue Line* serves as an example that there is no correlation between the lack of scientific accuracy in a movie and its potential impact on real cases. The film contains several errors regarding criminal procedure, but nevertheless its (partly erroneous) portrayal of the legal aspects of the case triggered the formal reopening of the case and release of the flesh-and-blood Randall Dale Adams.[25]

Any analysis of film's visualization of the law should therefore indicate whether the portrayal is at odds with the logic of legal science. However, the filmmaker's poetic license may also be of importance as the legal system is not autonomous and may prove more concerned with its own professional or personal interests. 'Misrepresentations' of the law in film may therefore very well be an intended expression with the purpose of challenging the hegemony of the professional expertise. Filmmakers' own interpretation of how the legal system works should also be welcomed as important to the workings of democratic society. A film may therefore also be analyzed in terms of how it defines and understands the basic reasons for the existence of the legal system.[26] Even if a 'misrepresentation' of the filmmaker may affect public opinion, the more valuable contribution is that such films have a great potential of making people interested in law and its institutions, precisely because the filmmakers are not being exacting.

USA is the dominant country of filmmaking, and it has also produced many films that give examples of lawyer archetypes. Its filmmakers have treated the role of the lawyer so many times that it may be argued that some lawyer stereotypes, as well as the institution of the court, has become part of film's 'language'.[27] Like all art, films rely on conventions. In order to be able to tell stories efficiently, a man, woman, child and material things symbolize on some level a convention in society. This is also true for lawyers and law's institutions. They may also be introduced in a story as a metaphor of something else.

One such example is George Cuckor's *Adam's Rib* (1949) where the marital relationship is the main issue of the film about prosecutor Adam Bonner (Spencer Tracy) and his wife and defence attorney Amanda

Bonner (Katharine Hepburn) who have ended up opposing each other in a high profile criminal case. Much of the film is spent in the courtroom, but the story is clearly not about lawyer archetypes or law's institution *per se*. The lawyers and the court rather serve as a metaphor of the battleground of the marital institution and the principle of equality of arms. Similarly, there is a slew of TV series about lawyers that address almost all other issues than the law.[28] Such films and TV series where lawyers become the windowdressing to tell other stories will usually end up as less relevant as sources to legitimate lawyer archetypes.[29]

*

Of the still *many* films that present themselves as particularly relevant to describe the sociological portrayal of the lawyer-client relationship, the portrayal of lawyer archetypes clearly changes depending on the social and historical backdrop of the times. The first historical trend in the early days of cinema is the establishment of the unscrupulous and tragic lawyer that is used by many filmmakers and that lasts until the 1940s. In the 1950s a new role of the heroic lawyer as a pillar of civil society appears on film. In the latter part of the twentieth century a diverse set of characters visualize the lawyer as the vindicator of legal principle.

The unscrupulous or ingenious lawyer

D. W. Griffith struck a note in 1908 with his portrait of the unscrupulous and tragic lawyer in *Falsely Accused* that has persisted in US cinema in the 1930s and 1940s. Lawyers tend to be portrayed as dubious or tragic characters, sometimes running with the mob. In William Wyler's *Counselor at Law* (1933) the attorney (John Barrymore) who has fashionable offices in the new Empire State Building is a lawyer who faces disbarment. This lawyer lacks all qualities of the idealist. To the extent he cares about his clients, he presents himself as a player, but his life on the periphery of society makes him an illegitimate version of the fixer.

Clarence Brown's *A Free Soul* (1931) tells the story of an alcoholic defence attorney who must defend his daughter's respectable ex-boyfriend on a charge of murdering the mobster she had started a relationship with, a mobster whom her father had previously gotten an acquittal for on a murder charge. The defence attorney Stephen Ashe (Lionel Barrymore) delivers a 14-minute monologue that was said to earn him the Oscar for Best Actor that year.

This lawyer trades his perceived professional autonomy for the desire to win a case that he perhaps for his daughter's sake should not take on. The client – and the director – expect a lawyer that can get an acquittal not by tactics, but by the passion of his defence for the moral side of the act of his client. Stephen Ashe may therefore also be seen as a fixer, a lawyer that is expected to vindicate the client's moral and social status.

Lawyers who serve other purposes than arguing the law are also found in the character of Tom Hagen (Robert Duvall) in Francis Ford Coppola's *The Godfather II* (1974). In Germany, the director Stefan Aust's *Der Baader-Meinhof Komplex* (1985) shows lawyers who smuggle messages back and forth between the RAF prisoners and RAF members on the outside, and smuggling guns hidden inside legal briefing books to the prisoners.

Of the several portraits of the villain lawyer who fixes things for his clients, filmmakers have also drawn positive archetypes of the lawyer who aids the client in other ways than on the point of law. In the heroic tale of Steven Soderbergh's *Erin Brockovich* (2000) the clients approach the law firm where Erin Brockovich (Julia Roberts) works as a secretary with personal and emotional demands. As her boss the lawyer does not meet the clients' expectations, she takes on the case without legal education or expertise. Her 'representation' lies in her dedication to the lives of her clients (and in her exceptional ability to remember names and numbers). Her defiance of the 'said' authority of the lawyers and capitalists who stand in her way makes for a positive variant of the villain who fixes the clients' problems in less amicable ways. 'Representation' is in this case about knowing as much as possible about the clients' lives.

In Tony Gilroy's *Michael Clayton* (2007) the lawyer (George Clooney) is known as the 'in-house fixer' who rectifies difficult situations, often through unconventional or expedient methods. The film is one of several that portrays lawyers in the context of the disturbing structure of the law firm.[30]

These very different films illustrate that the fixer is an archetype – for better or for worse – that takes on cases where it is necessary to have a close understanding of the clients' lives. The lawyer is on a quest or a journey with the client.

Lawyers get results – often as they rise from the ashes

Filmmakers frequently depict lawyers as artistic and free individuals with flaws (often a dependency on alcohol), who pick themselves up at the chance of representing a client where they can make a difference. These lawyers are good at law but even better at strategy. Most of all, the blows of life have taught them to expect unfair play from their opponents (usually a district attorney).

In James Flood and Elliott Nugent's *The Mouthpiece* (1932) a hot young prosecutor learns that a man he got convicted and executed was in fact innocent; he quits his district attorney job and becomes a defence attorney. He grows rich and powerful defending guilty racketeers, but eventually sees the errors of his ways.

In *Anatomy of a Murder*, the idealist-turned-realist Pauly Biegler is portrayed as a lawyer who likes his odd drink. In Joel Schumacher's notable film *The Client* (1994), a street-wise kid needs the assistance of a lawyer after having become a witness in a mobster murder case. He approaches the dried up alcoholic Reggie Love (Susan Sarandon) who despite her modest accomplishments as a lawyer manages to outplay aggressive FBI agents who want to push the kid into the witness stand with little regard for the risk of him being murdered by the mob. Another example is Carl Franklin's *High Crimes* (2002) where Morgan Freeman plays a drunken and unconventional Charlie Grimes. In the unfamiliar world of military courts, Grimes's shrewdness is worth more than academic knowledge of the law.

Substance abuse among lawyers is a problem, but one that filmmakers seem to view in a slightly positive light: the lawyers' personal experiences of tragedy somehow make them *more* qualified to take on the client's case.[31]

A more problematic portrayal is that of the cynical and alcoholic Frank Galvin (Paul Newman) in Sidney Lumet's accomplished *The Verdict* (1982). On one level Galvin is a hopeless drunk who ignores his cases and his clients. He is ready to accept a small settlement to avoid a trial against a Boston defence firm, but slowly realizes how he can win the case. Although Galvin's resources as a one-man law firm are inferior to the corporate Boston law firm, the director seems to presume that there exists an intellectual 'equality of arms' between the two parties. Although wholly unrealistic, the director points to a reoccurring stereotype of any protagonist on film where personal defeat is turned into victory when the individual applies himself, which is also true for the lawyer Galvin and the destiny of his client's case.

A reminder of the fact that individual will to succeed may not be enough is Joel Schumacher's *A Time to Kill* (1996). A young inexperienced defence attorney, Ellen Roark (Sandra Bullock), faces deeply embedded racism as her black client is on charge for murder of two men who raped his 10-year-old daughter. This time, the district attorney, Lucien Wilbanks (Donald Sutherland), who has been disbarred for alcoholism, wanders around his estate with his bottle as he advises Jake Brigance on tactics in the upcoming trial of the accused.

In a French-Isreali drama from 1983, Costa Gavras's *Hanna K.* portrays a lawyer (Jill Clayburgh), the child of Holocaust survivors, who is assigned to defend Salim Bakri, a Palestinian man accused of terrorism and infiltration. Hanna frees him, and soon another problem, that of reclaiming his family house in Palestine, appears. The film provides a Palestine perspective of Israeli injustice by looking at the case through the eyes of the lawyer. Law is more than its letters, and its institutions offer Hanna to agree to drop proceedings in exchange for Bakri being offered South African citizenship, with which he could legally claim land in Israel.

A different portrayal of the lawyer as a cultivator of norms is offered in Federico Fellini's *Amacord* (1973). The town lawyer (Luigi Rossi) appears at night. With charming pedantry he tries to explain the tradition and limitations of the people in the fictional town Borgo. This lawyer may also fit as a realist, as he in a comical sense sees himself as the carrier of tradition and institutional knowledge. However, on the streets he has no particular status, and in his attempt of storytelling he is hushed off by a woman cleaning her house.

The lawyer as a vindicator of rights – portrayals of the idealist in Europe and the US

In the 1950s and 1960s the ardent qualities of the lawyer became more positive, and in the success of the Hollywood system, the lawyer became an undeniable pillar of society. However, in European cinema, there is a much stronger ambivalence to the capabilities of lawyers to turn a case around.

A partly admirable partly critical portrayal of lawyers is found in the French director Henri-Georges Clouzot's *La Vérité* (1960). Dominique Marceau (Brigitte Bardot) is on trial for the murder of her lover Gilbert Tellier, but in the bigoted atmosphere of the court, Marceau's promiscuous lifestyle also comes under attack.[32] Marceau's defence lawyer becomes her *idealist* lawyer that is her 'hired gun' in the battle for her privacy, and an 'officer of the court' in the defence against the murder charge. In an exchange with the prosecutor (René Blancard) on her seduction of the murder victim, her right to a modern lifestyle is reduced to a battle of words between the lawyers. Both lawyers are so dead set on winning their case that the client becomes an object of the fight:

The prosecutor:	You spent weeks seducing him, didn't you? Weeks!
Defence attorney:	Objection! What length of time should she have spent? Is there any legal limit on how long a seduction ought to take?

A notable Italian example of the European ambivalence of the lawyer's capabilities is Vittorio De Sica's *Shoeshine* (*Sciuscià* 1946)[33] where Guiseppe's defence lawyer forces him to falsely put all the blame for a fortune-teller incident on his childhood friend Pasquale. The type of lawyer De Sica portrays is not an opportunistic one, but one who is unscrupulous in the defence of the client. The ardent defence of the client puts him in line with the idealist whose first priority is to win on principle. But his lack of consideration for the old friendship between the boys makes for a distorted kind of idealism that on a closer look seems to be more about his own vanity and desire to 'win' the case.

The unequivocally positive portrayal of lawyers battling over the 'truth' in a legal principle is predominant in the many accomplished US court movies of the 1950s and early 1960s. With the optimism of post World War II, these films celebrate the legal system, and some critics count these legal films as the best of the era.[34] The lawyers are usually morally balanced, virtuous representatives of their profession, and the judges are non-partisan.[35] Still, as shown above with the example of Pauly Biegler, not all of them are lawyers who aim to win on principle. These portrayals of lawyers must also be understood in light of the arrival of Hollywood's second technological revolution. In the 1950s almost all films were for the first time made in colour, it was the advent of the zoom lens and the innovation of deep focus.[36] These technological advancements allowed for the directors to focus on making aesthetically pleasing narratives and masterful characters.[37]

In the 1970s US film portrayals of lawyers' idealism became more complex. In Norman Jewison's … *And Justice for All* (1979), an ethical Baltimore defence lawyer, Arthur Kirkland (Al Pacino), is forced to defend a corrupt judge accused – and guilty – of rape. Despite having a real chance of being barred, Kirkland ends up shouting his own client's guilt at the court hearing. The film, although rather unrealistic in its plot, received two Oscars, one for Best Actor in a leading role (Pacino) and one for Original Screen Play. The film is a rare example of the lawyer-protagonist asserting his professional autonomy vis-à-vis the client.[38]

The difference between European (contintental) and US portrayal of the capable, driven and principled lawyer continues today. Laurent Herbiet's *The Betrayal* (*La Trahison* 2005) is about the French/Algerian wash-up of the 1960 Algerian war of independence. In the film, a French lawyer, Rossi, turns into a torturer. Rossi's torture is not stopped, due to the resignation, blindness and cowardice of those in power, and the film reminds us of the lesson of personal responsibility in Hannah Arendt's theories on the banality of evil.[39]

Another French film, Barbet Schroeder's *Terror's Advocate* (2007), is a docudrama portraying the real life attorney Jacques Vergés, whose clients include Klaus Barbie, the Jackal and Slobodan Milosevic.[40] The film portrays a lawyer who joined the French resistance in the 1960s and found himself defending bombers of the Algerian independence movement a decade later. The director attempts to disclose an enigmatic and compelling lawyer with personal links to terrorism. The lawyer is arguably an idealist, but an idealist that many would say has gone wrong.

In Finland, Ari Kaurismäki provided a fresh version of the principled lawyer in *The Man Without A Past* (2003). The real life defence attorney, Human Rights lawyer and founder of Amnesty Finland Matti Wuori appears in a captivating scene midway in the movie. The client, 'M' (Markku Peltola), has lost his memory and is held in custody on a vagrancy charge. The defence attorney enters the police station as a voice of humanity in the 'bureaucratic machine's legal abracadabra.'[41] Without even exchanging a word with the client, this *omnipresent* lawyer brings about resolve in perhaps the briefest lawyer–client relationship accounted for in film: Matti Wuori understands the client's wishes (get out of jail now) without having talked to him, and he effectively defeats the opponent (the police lawyer on duty is quick to argue but has to admit he is not in the right) with skill and principle (in contrast to the prosecutor, the defence attorney knows the law by heart and does not need to consult the books). Safely out on the street Matti Wuori seals their victory by giving 'M', who up to this point has not said a word, a cigar.

Kaurismäki's lawyer archetype is a positive and unassuming force, and a highly artistic visualization of the idealist. When Matti Wuori died in 2005, Kaurismäki stated in an interview in the newspaper *Voima*:

> 50 % of Finland's intelligence disappeared at once when Wuori died, and the remaining 50 % is just a hypothesis. Of the fighting humanism 80 % disappeared, and anarchy vanished completely. Matti was a good example of how one individual can make a difference.

Kaurismäki's high esteem of the commitment of Matti Wuori to use his knowledge of the law to the betterment of the desolate and impoverished shows the humanist face of the idealist archetype that few other accomplished films have managed to portray.[42]

Conclusion

The narrative ethics of films informs us that the principled professional ethics of lawyers only serve as a starting point of a moral dilemma that finds its solution in the meeting with the client. It is people – often the client – who shape the lawyers' ethics. The client furthermore carries expectations of how justice can be served and films may prove to be an important source of information to the client. Due to the impact of film as a mass media, it should also be expected that lawyers themselves are influenced by how they are portrayed. To filmmakers, the portrayal of lawyers is not an open playing field. Certain conventions are attached to the use of lawyers and the court, as they are portrayed so often and in many of the most important films in the history of cinema that they have become part of film's language. These elements give reason to the relevance and importance of films as a source to legal science in its research on professional ethics and lawyer archetypes.

On film, the description of the lawyer–client relationship is usually one of mutual dependence (Orson Welles's *The Trial* providing the notable exception). The lawyer is also usually presented as 'a special purpose friend'. Films fully confirm that the social structures carry a considerable ambivalence to the role of the lawyer. This ambivalence is at its most interesting in films where the destiny of the client depends on the lawyer's heroism. Sometimes it seems as if filmmakers desire to portray lawyer's capabilities as somewhat overstated or at least in need of precision.

Filmmakers may challenge the very reasons society has given for having lawyers and courts. 'Misrepresentation' of the law should not merely be discarded as irrelevant to law's institutions and lawyers. Importantly to the formulation of lawyer archetypes, filmmakers' portrayals take place in the context of a sociological backdrop of the times, either by anticipating or by commenting on events. Film history show that there have been changing trends in how to portray lawyers depending on changes in society. In these terms, the claim of the existing professional code as being universal is hard pressed.

The three suggested lawyer archetypes – the fixer, the player and the idealist – may all be found in important and widespread films. Film history also provides a 'positive' and a 'negative' expression of the different archetypes. The fixer may appear as a protagonist in romantic films, like that of the character of Erin Brockovich, or a villain like any lawyer subjugated by the mob, by personal bias or by corporate firms. In both versions, the fixer tends to be on a quest with the client. The player is usually portrayed as both a human being and a lawyer. The moral core of the lawyer is usually illustrated by the existence of some vice, such as alcohol or drugs that makes the lawyer sensitive to the client's exposure to the legal system. The idealist may be identified as the lawyer who poses questions such as 'what is true?' or 'what is right?' in the context of a specific case. As a protagonist the idealist tends to appear in realistic and technically accomplished movies. In the not so sympathetic versions, the idealist tends not to come across as 'real to life' but appears in thrillers where she or he collapses in a desire to win the case at all costs.

The narrative of films, then, tends to depict a lawyer's ethics not unlike the premises of the hero in Greek tragedy. To a large degree the lawyer on film make choices in accordance with some pre-designed alternatives. Only some films provide examples of lawyers making choices out of individual passions where they only obey their own nature (*A Free Soul*, *Terror's Advocate*). The extent to which this holds true for the entire catalogue of films, at this point the distance between the narrative ethics of films and the principled ethics of the professional ethics is at the greatest.

Notes

1 The International Code of Ethics for advocates was first adopted in 1956 by the International Bar Association (founded in New York in 1947). Regional organizations, such as The Council of Bars and Law Societies of Europe (CCBE founded in 1960), adopted a not identical but harmonized Code of Conduct for European Lawyers in 1988 (renamed and last amended to the Charter of Core Principles of the European Legal Profession in 2006). Neither the Inter-Pacific Bar Association (IPBA founded in 1991) nor the Inter-American Bar Association (IABA founded in 1940) have separate ethical codes.

2 Charles W. Wolfram, *Modern Legal Ethics* (St. Paul, MN: West Publishing Group, 1986), p. 581. The IBA Code of Ethics was inspired by, and is in content similar to, the American Bar Association's (ABA) Canons of Professional Ethics (1908), which in turn were borrowed from the Canons of the Alabama State Bar (1887), which in turn were inspired by several sources such as ethics resolutions in an 1830s legal textbook.

3 Geoffrey C. Hazard, Jr. and Angelo Dondi, *Legal Ethics: A Comparative Study* (Stanford: Stanford University Press, 2004). The early modern value given to the independence of the legal profession under monarchical, non-democratic governments originated with the privileges of self-government that constituted numerous social groups – and not just lawyers and other proto-professionals – of that era. The lawyers have kept some of the privileges, as their independence is perceived as key to the rule of law and thus to modern constitutional government. Promotion of rule of law and democratic government and human rights are the central aims of IPBA (http://www.iaba.org/indexEnglish.htm), ABA (http://www.abanet.org/about/history.html), CCBE (http://www.ccbe.eu/index.php?id=16&L=0) and the Japan Federation of Bar Association (founded in 1949 http://www.nichibenren.or.jp/en/about/index.html).

4 The two archetypes developed in US academic writing essentially differ where 'the hired gun' tends not to make moral choices for the client's position on guilt or innocence and tends not to decline the acceptance of a case due to moral or political convictions. 'The officer of the court', on the other hand, differs by claiming autonomy over the client by presuming

the liberty to decline the assignment if the client does not follow advice that is in the interest of justice, and presuming the liberty not to have to accept an assignment if defence of a client's act runs counter to her moral or political convictions.

5 This 'pure-client model' sees the free exercise of the client's autonomy as essential to her dignity. The reflection of the archetype's ideals are found in the ethical codes principles that the advocate is obliged to promote the best interests of the client (CCBE para 2.7). Some systems, as the Norwegian, explicitly protect the right of the lawyer not to be identified with her client's position, Norwegian Bar Association Code of Conduct for Defence Attorneys section 2.2.

6 CCBE section 1.1 prescribes that the lawyer must serve the interests of justice, the ABA Model Rules para 4 states that instigation of proceedings must have a legitimate aim and in para 1.6 (b) (I) a lawyer may be required to alert the public in order to prevent the client from committing a serious crime. The officer of the court is seen as a protector or guardian of the client, as it is not possible to achieve moral neutrality.

7 The examples are many, one of them being *To Kill a Mockingbird* (1962), where the respected town lawyer Atticus Finch (Gregory Peck) adheres to representing his black client despite pressure from the racial bigotry of the town's local mob, and defends him in the social context of racism in the court of a small town in Alabama.

8 Satyajit Ray, *An Enemy of the People (Ganashatru* 1989), with his portrayal of the lawyer Dr Stockman.

9 Richard P. Saller, *Personal Patronage under the Early Empire* (Cambridge: Cambridge University Press, 1982); Andrew Wallace-Hadrill (ed.), *Patronage in Ancient Society* (London and New York: Routledge, 1988).

10 Robert K. Merton, *On Social Structure and Science* (Chicago: University of Chicago Press, 1986), pp. 113–122.

11 Ibid., p. 123.

12 Charles Fried, 'The Lawyer as Friend: The Moral Foundations of the Lawyer–Client Relationship', 85 *Yale L. J.* 1060 (1976).

13 Weber's ideal types consist of the *charismatic leader* whose legitimacy to rule is not unlike the monarch who draws it from his personality, the *traditionalist* whose legitimacy is ensured by his consistency and continuity,

and the *legalist* whose legitimacy to wield power must be tied to the rule of law.

14 Lena Ebervall writes that she is inspired by Weber's ideal types in her *Försvararens roll: Ideologier och gällande rätt* (Stockholm: Norstedts Juridik, 2002). However, it is difficult to discover the link between Weber's theories and her discussion, which is based on the 'hired gun' and 'officer of the court' shaped in US academic debate. She does not reflect on whether Weber's theories need to be modified in order to be applied to the role of lawyers, or how the two archetypes from the US academic debate relate to the three ideal types of Weber's theory.

15 By considering mercy killing he, as a judge, is confronted with his own hatred towards defendants and his daughter's (Geraldine Brooks) love for defence attorney David Douglas (Edmond O'Brien).

16 Sir Thomas Lund, *The Professional Conduct and Etiquette of Solicitors* (London: Law Society, 1960), p. 18, as referred to in Ebervall, *Försvarens roll*, section 1.4.2.

17 John Rawls, *Theory of Justice* (Cambridge, MA: Belknap Press of Harvard University Press, 1971).

18 In Jonathan Demme's *Silence of the Lambs* (1991) Hannibal Lecter (Anthony Hopkins) is a serial murderer. In Andrew Davis's *The Fugitive* (1993) Dr Richard David Kimble (Harrison Ford) is unjustly convicted of murdering his wife.

19 A theory of a narrative ethics is proposed by John D. Arras in his article 'Nice Story, But So What?: Narrative and Justifications in Ethics', in Nancy S. Jecker, Albert R. Jonsen and Robert A. Pearlman (eds.), *Bioethics: An Introduction to History, Methods, and Practice* (New York: Jones and Bartlett Publishers, 1997), pp. 206–225. The narrative ethics is presented as a communitarian alternative to universal principles. Arras presents three different types of narrative ethics: the supplemental approach, the historical narrative approach and the postmodern approach. In the supplemental approach, the narrative functions as an illustrator of principles which otherwise may be difficult to understand or apply.

20 Chin'u Ri, a poor 22-year-old, born in Japan to Korean parents, had been arrested, tried, and executed for raping and killing a Japanese schoolgirl. Ri's case made headlines, particularly after a journalist published a book

of Ri's letters showing him to be, in Oshima's words, 'the most intelligent and sensitive youth produced by post-war Japan'. Ri's defence team had argued that his actions must be understood in the context of his second-class social status. Oshima voices in this film his opposition to both the death penalty and the systemic prejudice against ethnic Koreans in Japan. He also calls into question our very notions of reality and identity.

21 An infamous example of strategic-lawyer-advice-going-bad from pop culture is the case of The 13th Floor Elevators vocalist Rocky Erickson who, faced with charges on possession of marijuana, went along with the lawyer's risky strategy of pleading insanity, claiming that repeated use of LSD had affected his mind. As a result, although he was acquitted of possession, he was declared to be insane and was sent to Rusk State Mental Hospital in northeast Texas. There he was to remain for three years, being subjected to brutal electric-shock therapy. Although being declared sane upon leaving the mental hospital, he emerged in arguably worse shape than when he first went in; see John Collis 'The Psychedelic World of The 13th Floor Elevators', *Liner Notes*, Charly Records Ltd (2002).

22 The dynamics between art and politics are since long acknowledged with the reception of Murray Edelman's classic *From Art to Politics: How Artistic Creations Shape Political Conceptions* (Chicago: University of Chicago Press, 1995), where he convincingly argues that art influences politics.

23 The Norwegian Bar Association, *Etiske regler – Salærpolicy* (Ethical Rules – Fee Policy) no. 60 (1994), p. 32.

24 Some of US filmmakers' 'mistakes' are accounted for in Paul Bergman and Michael Asimow, *Reel Justice: The Courtroom Goes to the Movies* (Kansas City: Andrews McMeel Publishing, 1996). History is another science which frequently has to relate to filmmakers' misrepresentation of events, from D. W. Griffith's obviously wrong portrayal of black's behaviour as elected politicians (blacks did not place their feet on the tables or play with their shoes in parliament) in the stunning *Birth of a Nation* (1915), to the provoking rewrite of others' history in Clint Eastwood's *Letters from Iwo Jima* (2006).

25 Bergman and Asimow, *Reel Justice*, pp. 49–54; Richard K. Sherwin, *When Law Goes Pop: The Vanishing Line between Law and Popular Culture* (Chicago: University of Chicago Press, 2000), p. 3.

26 David Ray Papke made an elegant and precise link between films' heralding of the jury and Alexis de Tocqueville's reasoning on the importance of the jury in constitutional democracies in '12 Angry Men Is Not an Archetype: Reflections on the Jury in Contemporary Popular Culture, *Chicago Kent Law Reivew* 2 (2007), p. 747. His citation of Tocqueville's *Democracy in America* (Garden City, N.Y.: Doubleday, 1969 [1835]), p. 271, seems particularly relevant: '[T]he jury is above all a political institution; it should be regarded as one form of the sovereignty of the people; when the sovereignty of the people is discarded, it too should be completely rejected ...'; and on page 276: 'The jury ... is both the most effective way of establishing the people's rule and the most efficient way of teaching them how to rule.' One may also add that Tocqueville believed that unless the citizens engaged in society's many informal and formal organizations of civil society, democracy would end with absolute atomized individuals wholly unsuited to protect and carry on with democratic rule.

27 David Ray Papke, 'Law, Cinema, and Ideology: Hollywood Legal Films of the 1950s', *UCLA Law Review* 48, no. 6 (2001); Roy M. Mersky, 'Law and Popular Culture in the Film Collection at the Tarlton Law Library', *Legal Studies Forum*, no. 1–3 (1998); Michael Asimow, 'Bad Lawyers in the Movies', *Nova Law Review*, no. 2 (2000); Michael Asimow, 'Embodiment of Evil: Law Firms in the Movies', *UCLA Law Review* 48, no. 6 (2001).

28 i.e. David E. Kelley's *Ally McBeal* (1997) and *Boston Legal* (2004). Lawyers and the legal institution are not alone in being deployed. Hospitals, doctors and perhaps in particular nurses find themselves included in the film's plot for wholly other reasons than medicine; see i.e. B. Kalisch, P. Kalisch and M. McHugh, 'The Nurse as a Sex Object in Motion Pictures, 1930 to 1980', *Research in Nursing and Health*, no. 3 (1982).

29 Court comedy was not particular to the US. In the 1930s Swedish studio system lawyers were often an integral part of the many comedies and 'light' movies, such as *När rosorna slå ut* (1930), *Kärlek måste vi ha* (1931), *Ungkarlspappan* (1935), *Äventyr i pyjamas* (1935) *Flickornas Alfred* (1935), *Släkten är värst* (1936). The lawyer is also the butt of the joke in Ingmar Bergman's *Smiles of a Summer Night*.

30 Michael Asimov, 'Embodiment of Evil: Law Firms in the Movies', *UCLA Law Review* 48, no. 6 (2001).

31 In some European countries, the defence profession grew out of the local bars or pubs, as in England. In Sweden, a disparaging 'title' for defence attorneys was 'liquor lawyers' (*brennvinsadvokatene*), Ebervall, *Försvararens roll*, p. 46.

32 Clouzot's notable films, like *La Vérité*, contain a gloomy strand of poetic realism, presenting characters who are not only doomed, but live dismal and often evil lives. This is also true of *Quai des Orfevres* (1974), *Wages of Fear* (*Le Salaire de la peur* 1953) and *The Devilish Ones* (*Les Diaboliques* 1955).

33 The first of this neo-realist director's four most notable films, the other three being *Bicycle Thieves* (*Ladri di biciclette* 1948), *Miracle in Milan* (*Miraclo a Milano* 1950) and *Umberto D* (1952).

34 David Ray Papke, 'Law, Cinema, and Ideology'. The notable films are: *A Place in the Sun* (1951), *The Caine Mutiny* (1954), *Trial* (1955), *12 Angry Men* (1957), *Witness for the Prosecution* (1957), *I Want to Live!* (1958), *Anatomy of a Murder* (1959), *Compulsion* (1959), *The Young Philadelphians* (1959), *Inherit the Wind (The Monkey Trial)* (1960) *Judgment at Nuremberg* (1961), *To Kill a Mockingbird* (1962), *Billy Budd* (1962).

35 Anthony Chase, 'Lawyers and Popular Culture: A Review of Mass Media Portrayals of American Attorney', *Law & Social Inquiry*, no. 2 (2006).

36 John Belton,'Technology and Innovation', in Geoffrey Nowell-Smith (ed.), *The Oxford History of World Cinema* (Oxford: Oxford University Press, 1997), p. 259.

37 To portray strong and accomplished protagonists was not exclusive to films with lawyers, but part of a general trend of storytelling of genre film in the 1950s. Westerns (especially those of John Ford) had a similar plot development in the 1950s. Crime movies turned from having protagonists with a strong element of cultural dissident in the film noir of the 1940s, to protagonists that were a more pleasing product of the middle class in the 1950s (in particular with the success of Alfred Hitchcock).

38 Other examples are the two versions of *Cape Fear*, J. Lee Thompson's from 1962 and Martin Scorcese's remake from 1991.

39 Hannah Arendt, *Eichmann in Jerusalem: A Report on the Banality of Evil* (1963). She coined the phrase 'the banality of evil' to describe the jurist Rudolf Eichmann who claimed as his defence that he just followed orders

when deporting Jews to the concentration camps. She raised the question of whether evil is radical or simply a function of banality – the tendency of ordinary people to obey orders and conform to mass opinion without critically thinking about the results of their action or inaction.

40 Barbet Schroeder has previously directed the film *Reversal of Fortune* on the Claus von Bülow case, and the docudrama *General Idi Amin Dada*, where Idi Amin plays himself.

41 Peter von Bagh, *Aki om Kaurismäki* (Stockholm: Alfabeta, 2006), p. 186.

42 The use of real life defence attorneys to play 'themselves' has also been used by other Scandinavian directors, and this practice may warrant a separate discussion in another paper of why the lawyer role is given this sense of 'reality' whereas for instance doctors or priests are not cast in the same way. Some examples from other Scandinavian films may be given, however: Norwegian cinema, modest in its impact on the world stage, provides three examples of films using real life defence attorneys: Olav Hestenes in Anja Breien's *Voldtekt* (1971), Alf Nordhus in Rolf Clemens's *Operasjon V for vanvidd* (1970) and Oddvar Bull Tuhus's *Angst* (1976).

8

The Menace of Venice, Or Reading and Performing the Law in/of *The Merchant of Venice*

Leif Dahlberg

There's his period—
To sheathe his knife in us. He is attached.
Call him to present trial. If he may
Find mercy in the law, 'tis his; if none,
Let him not seek't of us.
(William Shakespeare and John Fletcher, *All Is True* (*Henry VIII*), I.ii.210–214)

Introduction

The textual situation of William Shakespeare's *The Merchant of Venice* (1598) is unusually good compared with many of his other plays, since the three principal sources conform with each other and also presumably conform with the author's manuscript (rather than a prompt book).[1] Yet it is not easy to know how to read the text of the play, nor is it a simple matter to stage and perform it. Although the play is presented as a comedy both paratextually[2] and in most theatrical performances,[3] and contains plenty of jest, good humour and verbal wit, the play also has darker sides. The ending of the trial scene in the fourth act in particular has been viewed by many critics as troubling and difficult to accommodate with our sense of a happy resolution.[4] However, I will argue that the play strongly conforms to the laws of genre and of comedy. The principal support for this claim is that the strengthening of community presented and enacted in *The Merchant of Venice* operates by way of social inclusion, whereas in tragedy the strengthening of social bonds typically would take the form of exclusion and/or symbolic sacrifice of the protagonist in the form of a victim or scapegoat.

The difficulty of 'reading aright' is itself a recurring topos in the play, connected with the reading of character (Antonio's, but also the suitors' and Shylock's), executing a will (the will of Portia's dead father), solving riddles (the texts on the three caskets), reading legal documents (the bond and Venetian law), but also more generally with perceiving and understanding the difference between appearance and reality. In fact, one could argue that one of the central issues of the play is about the fate of reading. It should also be noted that the figure of reading appears in other, less topicalized places in the play, as when Lorenzo reads a letter in Jessica's 'fair hand' (II.iv.12), when Bassanio (in Belmont) reads Antonio's letter (III.ii.314–320),[5] and when the Duke (in the court of justice in Venice) reads the letter from Bellario recommending Balthazar (IV.i.150–162).[6]

I will approach the question of reading – and of performing a reading – in and of the play by discussing in turn the problematics of reading Antonio's character; the execution of the will of Portia's father; the reading and solving of the riddles of the three caskets and choosing the right one; and the reading of the bond between Shylock and Antonio both in terms of contract (civil law) and criminal act (criminal law). This will open the way for a critical discussion of how to read the terms 'Christian' and 'Jew' in the play, and also of the meaning of the double conversion enacted in the play, which is the most difficult part of the play to appreciate for a modern audience. In this way I will try to both enact and problematize the law of genre in and of the play.

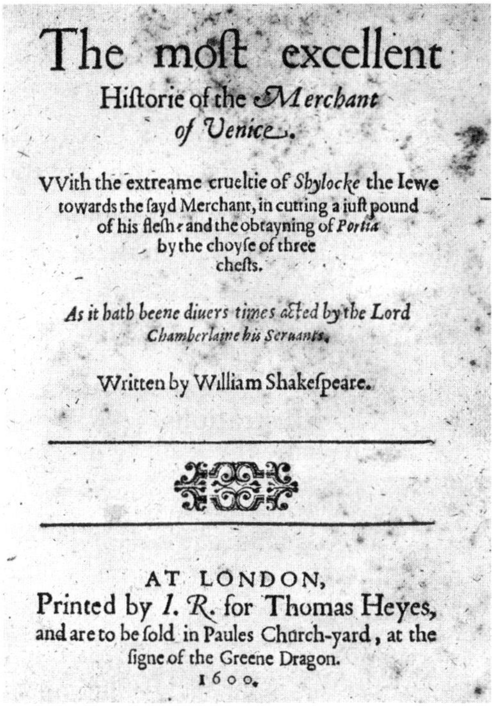

The moſt excellent
Hiſtorie of the *Merchant*
of Venice.

VVith the extreame crueltie of *Shylocke* the Iewe
towards the ſayd Merchant, in cutting a iuſt pound
of his fleſhe: and the obtayning of *Portia*
by the choyſe of three
cheſts.

As it hath beene diuers times acted by the Lord
Chamberlaine his Seruants.

Written by William Shakeſpeare.

AT LONDON,
Printed by *I. R.* for Thomas Heyes,
and are to be ſold in Paules Church-yard, at the
ſigne of the Greene Dragon.
1600.

Figure 1: Title page of the First Quarto of *The Merchant of Venice.*

Plot construction and place

Before we venture on this reading exercise, it is necessary to present the plot lines and to sketch the geography or topography of the play. The play has a double plot – the romance plot with Bassanio and Portia as main characters, and the bond/revenge plot with Antonio and Shylock as protagonists – that Shakespeare took over from his probable primary source, the first story of the fourth day in Ser Giovanni's *Il Pecorone.*[7] To this story Shakespeare has added both the casket scenes (which replaces the three journeys to Belmont in *Il Pecorone*) and the Lorenzo-Jessica sub-plot. The two main plots are interlaced in the play according to a regular and logical pattern so that, for instance, complications in the romance plot in the first act naturally motivate and lead over to the bond/revenge plot where Antonio secures Bassanio's romantic venture; and when in the third act it is revealed that Antonio's own ventures 'have miscarried', this inversely motivates Portia's intervention in the bond/ revenge plot in the fourth act in order to rescue Antonio.[8]

In a similar way, the play moves between the two locations Venice and Belmont in a regular back-and-forth motion in the first three acts, whereas the fourth act entirely takes place in Venice (primarily in the court of justice) and the fifth act brings the story back to Belmont.[9] The movements between these locations – which take place on water – are not represented in the play and neither is the time it takes to travel. In fact, although time in some respects is crucial for the interlacing of the plots (Shylock's loan to Antonio is for three months), the representation of time is neither realistic nor well measured, but rather indicates the order of events.[10] Another way of perceiving the absence of travel time in the play is to say that Venice and Belmont are floating on water (which in a way is factually true of Venice): at times they appear separate and distant, at other times adjacent and connected. In contrast to the minor role played by time in the play, the construction and production of place is of utmost importance.

The first thing to notice about the construction of place is the apparent differences and contrasts between the city of Venice and the (seemingly) rural Belmont.[11] Whereas Venice appears to be a place for (male) friendship, commerce and positive law, Belmont is the realm of love, romance, and patriarchal law (law of the father). Venice is furthermore characterized by trade economy and capitalism, whereas the economy of Belmont appears to be based rather on agriculture and landed property. Venice is a place of heterogeneity and conflict, whereas Belmont is a place of homogeneity, harmony and music. Venice represents modern, urban reality, whereas Belmont is a foreign and perhaps even imaginary place, representing both past times and a possible happier future. Whereas Venice is a place for the regulated – but also irregular – use of (male) force, Belmont is a place where the strict (but virtuous) rule of patriarchal law appears open to subtle (female) manipulation. Although the two locations in these (and other) respects are constructed as each other's opposites, it is possible to move between them – though for women the transition should be made in male disguise – making the differences more nuanced and the contrasts less absolute. The transition between the two places also involves an element of risk, since in the play water, apart from serving as a means of transportation, signifies danger.

The second thing to note about the construction of place in the play is that there are a number of correspondences between the two realms. Although Venice appears to be a place marked by risk and the need for financial security, in the stable agricultural economy of Belmont the will of the father sets up a veritable 'lottery' where Portia neither can choose between her suitors nor refuse anyone of them. In the play, the risk characteristic of Venice therefore corresponds to chance in Belmont. In this way Venice and Belmont at times appear not so much as separate and opposite, but as connected and even folded into each other. Related to the logic of contrast and correspondence between Venice and Belmont are the analogies with Elizabethan London and the English countryside, where you on the one hand find an urban economy based on trade and venture capital (corresponding to Venice) and on the other a rural economy based on agriculture and landed property (corresponding to Belmont), as well as growing conflicts between these economies. These analogies may be set up in the following matrix:

	'There'	*'Here'*
Urban (etc.)	Venice (diegetic)	London
Rural (etc.)	Belmont (diegetic)	English countryside

The representation of the opposition between Venice and Belmont on the Elizabethan theatrical stage hence has the function of ideologizing the opposition and conflict between town and country, between trade economy and agricultural economy, etc. In this respect one may compare Shakespeare's Venetian comedy with the *fabula palliata*, which is the name given to the adaptations of Greek comedies on the Roman stage (its literal meaning is 'play in Greek dress'). The *fabula palliata* of Plautus and Terence simultaneously presented a distant and exotic reality (Greece) and represented local (Latin) moral problems in an 'other place' (heterotopia) where all similarities to real people, locations and events are accidental or coincidental. This way of constructing the diegetic space and place is of course also found in Shakespeare's other

Italian plays – *The Two Gentlemen of Verona* (1580s), *Romeo and Juliet* (1594–95) and *Othello* (1604) – and in his other plays situated in faraway places or distant times.[12] In this way, one can say of Shakespeare's plays in general and of *The Merchant of Venice* in particular that by simultaneously representing foreign countries and peoples and representing contemporary English society, it was possible both to superimpose and blend these realms ('here' and 'there') and to comment on them indiscriminately. Hence, in a similar way in which Venice and Belmont at times are made to connect and fold into each other in the play, the foreign places represented in the play are enfolded by the theatrical representation. The representations of 'here' and 'there' simultaneously implicate and complicate each other in ways reminiscent of representations and understanding of space in Baroque art and philosophy.[13]

It has often been suggested that the legal proceedings in the play are informed by local (English) affairs, such as the trial and public execution of the Portuguese Jew Roderigo Lopez in London in 1594[14] – an event that is said to have spurred the restaging of Christopher Marlowe's *The Jew of Malta* (1589), a play that contains additional source material for Shakespeare's play.[15] It has been argued, furthermore, that the legal proceedings in the play are informed by the historical and in Shakespeare's own time aggravated conflict between the traditional and independent common law system and the Court of Chancery.[16] The Court of Chancery constituted a court of appeal that tried the equity or fairness of sentences (but not questions of guilt). However, the Court of Chancery was also closer to the royal court and the perceived conflict between the rigidity of positive law and equity may to some extent be seen as a political struggle over control over the legal system. Although the correspondences with local events in England are suggestive and in some ways appear convincing, it is important to stress that they may be as obfuscated as the representation of Venice in the play. In Shakespeare and John Fletcher's play *All Is True* (*Henry VIII*) (1613), great liberties are taken with recent English history.[17] In other words, perceived similarities with historical and local events and with legal affairs in England are not sufficient in themselves to establish factual or causal relations with diegetic elements.

Furthermore, the interweaving and implication of Venice and London may not always have been intentional, but may also be due to lack of knowledge of actual Venice, both among the audience and in the writer. It should not be surprising, then, that since there were only a limited number of Jews in London in Shakespeare's time and their abodes and movements were not regulated by law as they were in historical Venice, there is no mention in the play of the regulations that stipulated that Jews in Venice were to remain in their ghetto after sundown (nor is there any mention of the ghetto in the play) and it is possible for the Jew Shylock to be invited to Bassanio's house for dinner (I.iii; II.v).[18] In a similar way, although in historical Venice the Doge had not presided over criminal proceedings since the fourteenth century (and magnificoes did not act as judges), in Shakespeare's play the 'Duke' is both present at the court of justice and presiding over the proceedings (IV.i). There are also occasional inconsistencies in the play, for instance that the sovereign city state of Venice is described both as a 'state' (III.iii.29) and as a town with a 'charter' that may be revoked (IV.i.39).

Here I would like to make a note on the construction of place when staging the play in later times and in other places – for instance in contemporary Stockholm – creating a double-layered 'there' according to the following matrix:

	'There' (1)	*'There' (2)*	*'Here'*
Urban (etc.)	Venice (diegetic)	Elizabethan London	Stockholm
Rural (etc.)	Belmont (diegetic)	Elizabethan countryside	Swedish countryside

The second or intermediary 'There' is not represented on stage (although it could be represented in the form of an Elizabethan stage), but rather serves as a mirror of or point of perspective on Venice. In other words, the audience should be well aware that the representation of Venice in the play is tainted by Elizabethan worldviews and that the presentation of actions and persons is governed by the theatre conventions of Shakespeare's time, and so on. This may be seen as a refraction or as another fold in the representation of the play. Likewise, contemporary stagings of the play may want to stress the distance to Elizabethan views by adding new elements to the plot. For instance, in a recent mise en scène of the play at the Royal Dramatic Theatre in Stockholm (2004), the trial scene in the fourth act contained a supplement in which the conversion of Shylock was staged.[19] However, the conversion was not presented as a joyful and socially inclusive event, but as a degrading and humiliating act.

This refraction or folding of representational space can be enacted yet another time in film adaptations of the play. For instance, in the film adaptation by Michael Radford (2004), there is, in contrast to the text of the play, an explicit and topicalized mention and representation of the Jewish ghetto in Venice, which creates a sub-place within the urban space. Although this is an addition to the play much like the conversion scene just mentioned, it can also be seen as a correction of the unhistorical representation of Venice in Shakespeare's play. The spatial matrix of this film adaptation would look something like this:

	'There' (1)	*'There' (2)*	*'There' (3)*	*'Here'*
Urban (etc.)	Venice (diegetic) Jewish ghetto (diegetic)	Elizabethan London	Contemporary metropolitan USA ('Hollywood')	Stockholm
Rural (etc.)	Belmont (diegetic)	Elizabethan countryside	Rural USA	Swedish countryside

Depending on what value one would understand as invested in the third 'There', the ideological construction of space and place will be quite different. The insertion of the Jewish ghetto in the diegesis together with the explicit show of anti-semitism (neither of which is found in the play) are in any case not innocent amendations. It is not obvious where to situate the ghetto in the matrix: Does it belong to the diegesis (There (1)) or to the representation (There (3))? Perhaps it should be placed in the space created by folding the different 'Theres' into each other?

Although I have presented the construction of space in and of the play in terms of folds – both in the diegesis and in the staging – it should be noted that in the text of the play, the making of space is often a function of turning: both literally in terms of 'turning' and figuratively as turns of phrase. We will return to these matrices, folds, and turns in the concluding discussion. But now, after having presented the plot and the construction of diegetic place and discursive space, it is time to try to read the script.

Reading in Venice

The text of the play – though not necessarily the play itself[20] – begins by Antonio speaking of his unexplainable 'want-wit sadness' that wearies both himself and his friends. Both Salerio and Solanio offer suggestions of how he has 'caught it, found it, or came by it' (I.i.3), but these are all refused by Antonio. Although it appears to be a recent affliction rather than a 'humour' in the sense of a character trait or medical diagnosis, Antonio professes to Bassanio that it is a more permanent condition: he famously says that the world is but a 'stage, where every man must play a part, / And mine a sad one' (I.i.78–79). In response to this Gratiano suggests that it should be his own role to 'play the fool' (I.i.79). Gratiano certainly is both a merry and talkative character in the play, but the role of the fool or clown – an obligatory character in Elizabethan comedy[21] – is played by Launcelot. However, when Antonio and Bassanio are left alone on the stage, Antonio immediately asks about the lady that Bassanio has 'sworn a secret pilgrimage' (I.i.119), and the reader is made to believe that it may indeed be this venture that is the cause of Antonio's sadness.[22] Regardless of the nature of Antonio's sadness and its possible causes, more significant in the play is the importance placed on 'knowing' oneself and revealing one's true character. This is indeed the central issue in the trial of character that the riddles of the three caskets perform on Portia's suitors.

The will or testament of Portia's dead father is first introduced in the play in the second scene of the first act by Portia herself in connection with a discussion of the difficulty of following good council:

> If to do were as easy as to know what were good to do, chapels had been churches, and poor men's cottages princes' palaces,—it is a good divine that follows his own instructions,—I can easier teach twenty what were good to be done, than be one of the twenty to follow mine own teaching: the brain may devise laws for the blood, but a hot temper leaps o'er a cold decree,—such a hare is madness the youth, to skip o'er the meshes of good counsel the cripple; but this reasoning is not in the fashion to choose me a husband,—O me the word "choose"! I may neither choose who I would, nor refuse who I dislike, so is the will of a living daughter curb'd by the will of a dead father: [...] (I.ii.12–25)

What Portia says here is indeed true for most of us – it is all too easy to disregard both good council and one's own better judgment when the mind is tempted by what it desires – but it is not for Portia to choose by her own will, she must follow the will of her dead father. In his testament he has devised a sophisticated machinery that will ensure the selection of a true husband for his daughter. It consists of 'three chests of gold, silver, and lead' (I.ii.29–30) and the suitor 'who chooses his meaning chooses' Portia (I.ii.30–31). To Nerissa, Portia's maid, this deontological system appears more as 'lott'ry' (I.ii.28) than as good sense, but as is revealed in the second act, each chest or casket is provided with a verse that suggests its content and reveals the character of the 'chooser' (II.vii). Hence, when the suitors read and interpret the riddles of the caskets, they are as much reading as being read, and in performing a choice of one casket they are revealing their own true character. The reward promised by choosing the father's 'meaning' is to find Portia's portrait – as well as possessing the original. The punishment for not reading aright and choosing the wrong 'meaning' is either a carrion (the figure of vanity) or a fool's head – and each of these are provided with verses that relay their meaning, but also to fulfil the promise not to woo another woman.

It is certainly called for to ask what it means to read the verses and to choose between the caskets. Is there indeed a 'right' reading and a 'right' choice? Is there an explicit rule that one may follow and that determines the right choice? Perhaps all choices are equally 'right' in that they reveal the truth of the suitor's character? And the issue would then not so much be a question of finding Portia's portrait but of knowing oneself and of knowing if one is (or will be) a good husband for Portia. In other words, we would find the same issue in the casket scenes as in the opening of the play, when we found Antonio having 'much ado to know' himself (I.i.7). One should also note that these tests of character are indeed obligatory ingredients in the traditional romance plot, where it is necessary to exhibit both the virtue of love and the love of virtue.[23] But the insistence on character and on virtue in the romance plot carries over to the other plot line in the play, and in the same way as Antonio and Bassanio (among others) have had their true characters read and tested, so will Shylock's character be read and tested in the trial in the fourth act.

I will not dwell on the readings that the princes of Arragon and Morocco perform in terms of the verses and how they reveal their characters. They are after all minor figures in the play. There is reason, however, to tarry a little on Bassanio's performance and on his character. It has often been noted that although Bassanio in comparison with the princes is neither vain nor a fool, he is not really presented as a catch for Portia nor as an ideal male heir for Belmont. However, as Filomena Mesquita points out, Bassanio does personify the ideal of venture capitalism: using other people's money for his own ends.[24] Hence the marriage between Bassanio and Portia signifies the fruitful union of trade economy and agricultural economy.

In his interpretation of the riddle, Bassanio shows proof of good judgement not only in discerning appearance and reality (III.ii.73–105), but also insight into the workings of the law:

> The world is still deceiv'd with ornament,
> In law, what plea so tainted and corrupt,
> But being season'd with gracious voice,
> Obscures the show of evil?
> (III.ii.73–77)

Within the context of the play, and in particular in relation to the trial scene in the fourth act, these lines can take on an ambiguous meaning either as a prolepsis of Shylock's use of the bond to get revenge on Antonio or as undermining Portia's graceful and technical legal argumentation – or both.

In contrast to the three riddles on the caskets and the verses inside them, the reader is not given the opportunity to read the bond between Antonio and Shylock. Instead we are offered a number of contesting and conflicting interpretations of its meaning and value. The primary meaning is that it is a contract stipulating the terms for Antonio's loan of three thousand ducats for three months from Shylock. In contrast to his usual habit, Shylock agrees to lend the money 'gratis', that is, without interest. The suggested meaning of this in the play is that one lends money to friends without interest but to strangers and enemies with interest. Since Antonio and Shylock are anything but friends, it would seem natural for Shylock to take interest, but instead he offers a loan without interest as an offer of friendship to Antonio. The sincerity of this offer is strongly questionable, both in regard to Shylock's aside upon the entry of Antonio (I.iii.36–47) and in view of Antonio's previous hostile behaviour towards Shylock and other Jews (I.iii.101–124). Similarly one may question what it means that Antonio seemingly accepts this gesture of friendship and says not only that 'there is much kindness in the Jew' (I.iii.149), but speaks of Shylock as a 'gentle Jew. / The Hebrew will turn Christian, he grows kind' (I.iii.173–174). One should remember that Antonio has said that he would 'call thee [a dog] again, / To spet on thee again, to spurn thee too' (I.iii.125–126). But disregarding the sincerity of their gestures of friendship, this is the 'meaning' of the act of lending money without interest given in the play. It would be intriguing to pursue the role of friendship in this and other plays by Shakespeare, but I will have to leave that for another occasion.

It is equally open for questioning that the stipulation in the contract that 'the forfeit / Be nominated for an equal pound / Of your fair flesh, to be cut off and taken / In what part of your body pleaseth me' (I.iii.144–147) is said to be a 'merry sport' (I.iii.141) – and hence not meant to be taken literally.[25] Indeed, Bassanio immediately protests against Antonio signing such a bond. In other words, the meaning of the bond in the play is uncertain already before it has been signed. But the uncertainty of its meaning troubles Antonio little since he expects to receive 'thrice three times the value of this bond' (I.i.155) a month before the forfeiture.

It is only when all his ventures have miscarried that the meaning of the bond becomes a serious issue for Antonio and indeed in the play itself, and it is only then that the issue of literal meaning and legal readings will arise. In the academic literature on the play there has been a long debate about the (positive) legal value of this bond, and one often finds cited reference to the ancient Roman law (the Law of the Twelve Tables) that creditors could under certain circumstances divide the body of a debtor among themselves, but already Hegel noted that there is no historical evidence that this law ever was enacted.[26] One may also note that there are equally ancient laws that prohibit signing a contract that constitutes a threat to one's person or personal freedom.[27] As has already been mentioned, there are critics (both legal and literary) that want to place the play in the legal situation of Elizabethan England. It could also be mentioned that there have been many attempts to situate – or even retry – the case in modern legal systems.[28] On the question of the relevance of positive law, either Venetian or English, either ancient, early modern or modern, I would side with those who argue that it is not possible to judge or evaluate the events in the play based on historical law, whether canonical or secular, or other legal systems. However, the play certainly is informed by historical law and contemporary legal praxis, by conceptions of old law and new law (Hebrew and Christian law), as well as by thinking about natural law. The play can perhaps also be seen to make comments on the nature of law.[29] This does not necessarily mean that law and legal proceedings in the play are to be seen as literary and the justice of the play as poetic justice. Rather, what it means is that we cannot simply short-cut the argumentation by saying that since the bond in the real world would be illegal and invalid, it would neither automatically nor necessarily imply that the bond is illegal or invalid in the play.

The first reading of the bond presented in the play is that of Shylock, whose desire for revenge has been maddened by anger at the loss of his daughter and of his ducats, and who argues that the 'merry sport' should be read literally.[30] The second reading is that of the Duke, who expresses his hope that Shylock will 'show [...] mercy' (IV.i.20) and withdraw his plea and 'Forgive a moiety of the principal' (IV.i.26). The third reading is that of Portia (appearing in the guise of man and with the symbolical name Balthazar),[31] who first maintains that the bond indeed is legally valid, but that there is another 'law' which demands of us to show mercy. The fourth reading is also performed by Portia: when Shylock has rejected the claim of mercy in this case, Portia on the one hand presents a hyper-literal reading of the bond – 'no jot of blood' (IV.i.302) – and on the other hand invokes the 'alien statute' of Venetian law and without notification turns the civil proceedings into a criminal trial (so-called cross-action), accusing Shylock of having made an attempt on the life of a Venetian citizen. The penalty for this crime is execution by hanging.[32]

Although from a legal point of view it is quite reasonable to argue that the bond is invalid, this is not because it does not allow the letting of blood (that should be understood as part of taking flesh, since you can hardly take one without the other),[33] but because it would be invalid (and therefore not legally binding) to sign a deed that constitutes a threat to one's own or somebody else's life.[34] It could also be argued, as has been done by several critics, that moving from one case to another is not according to due process, in particular moving from a civil case to a criminal case.[35] In other words, the court would have had to present a formal accusation that Shylock had made an attempt on Antonio's life, and allowed Shylock to defend himself against this allegation.[36] However, in Shakespeare's play the action moves directly from Portia's invalidation of the bond (which is a judgement in the civil proceedings) to the judgement that Shylock has tried to kill Antonio (which would be a judgement in a criminal trial). But since what is presented is not a real trial, one should not hasten to judge it by the same standards as in real life.

Moreover, the bond does not only have a literal legal meaning in the play. The bond between Antonio and Shylock can also be taken to signify the primordiality of contract in law, as the law of law, as well as the foundation for civil society in a 'social contract'. In other words, the freedom to enter into voluntary and legally binding transactions is seen as fundamental to civil society.[37] In this way the bond can also be read as a symbol (an iteration) of social bonds between citizens. Hence, the invalidation of the bond in the play suggests, among other things, that the social bond uniting and constituting Venice is not so much a legal bond (a contract) as a moral bond, and that Shylock does not belong to this community until he has given up his bond and accepted the primacy of moral community over law.

I would suggest that when the tables are turned on Shylock, when the accuser becomes the accused, this is rather a figure – or a prefiguring – of the conversion that will be part of the sentence (or rather of the conditions for pardon). Not only are the civil proceedings converted to criminal proceedings, but the man who refused to give mercy to his enemy is forced to accept mercy by his new accusers. Before proceeding with this argument it is necessary to engage with the allegation that the mercy shown by the Court and by Antonio is hardly worth its name.

In order to save his life, Shylock not only has to give up all his property, he also has to give legitimacy to his daughter's union with Lorenzo, and finally also to convert to Christianity. Indeed, how could this sentence be considered 'mercy', let alone 'Christian' mercy? There have been voiced very strong opinions on this point, and many perceive the talk of mercy as mere hypocrisy.[38] Thus, some critics have argued that the sentence is primarily ideological in that it allows the Christians to punish Shylock for pursuing an activity that their economic and financial system is dependent on, in other words using Shylock as a scapegoat.[39] It is hardly possible to seriously argue for the legality of the sentence and it is also difficult to argue what terms of mercy would be just in these circumstances. But in the poetic situation in the play, there is one bankrupt man, Antonio, whose life has been threatened by Shylock. In this respect it is not entirely unjust that part of the property of the one is given to the other as penance for having threatened his life. The fact that the property will be transferred to Lorenzo and Jessica at Shylock's death can both be seen as 'kind' and as a way of forcing Shylock to accept their union, including Jessica's (voluntary) conversion to Christianity.

However, the issue that appears to have provoked most critical controversy in recent times is the condition that Shylock must convert to Christianity lest the Duke should 'recant / The pardon that [he] late pronounced' (IV.i.387–388). Although it can be argued that a formal pardon may not be revoked – just as one may not 'unsign' documents or treaties once they have been signed[40] – what has disturbed both critics and audiences is the violence against the modern conception of freedom of religious creed as an inalienable human right.[41] In our secular times, questions of religious faith tend to be considered to be private and a matter of personal choice, and it certainly would be offensive today to force religious conversion, especially under threat of death. But the situation is quite different both in the play and in Shakespeare's time. After all, the play is written some two hundred years prior to the French revolution and the declaration of universal human rights. One should also remember that in the view of Shakespeare's time, forcing Shylock to convert to Christianity not only made him part and member of the social body, it also enacted the salvation of his soul. But there is more in the conversion than meets the eye.

Reading conversion

As suggested already in the introduction, I would argue that the proper and legitimate mode of reading the conversion in the play – and also in Shakespeare's time – is as a figure of social inclusion rather than as a serious punishment or as a form of exclusion. It is possible to argue for this reading along several lines. Perhaps the most forceful argument – but to some extent a circular one – is to apply the law of genre. Although comedy may end by chastizing and socially excluding the immoral personage – as in several of Molière's plays – the 'meaning' of comedy in Shakespeare's time tended to be to reinforce social community by inclusion, not by exclusion. Hence we find in the play the achievement of a union of men with women, of Venice with Belmont,

Figure 2: Court scene in Doge's Palace, Venice. Engraving by Giacomo Franco, *Questa e' la Real Sala del Collegio …* (1610). National Library of St Mark's, Venice.

and of the Jews with the Christians. Indeed, if Shylock's conversion was an actual punishment, it would imply a stigmatization. But in the context of the play, the conversion would inversely remove the markings of being an outsider.

Although this fits well with our understanding of a happy ending proper to comedy, there is also the issue of style and tone of the play, both in form and content. And indeed, the play mixes high and low elements (character, language, topics) in ways that befit classical comedy.[42] However, this aspect of comedy—which it shares with satire and (later) with the novel—has always been problematic for literary theorists that posit that one should not mix genres.[43] In the case of comedy it is not possible to define exactly what kind of elements belong to the genre or delimit a place in a system that belongs to it alone: comedy is by definition a mixed genre – impure, parasitic, contaminated, inverted, invaginated.[44] Rather, since comedy as a literary genre defines a certain mixture, a certain way of mixing elements, which may be found in narrative and drama as well as in film and interactive media, one may say of *The Merchant of Venice* that it participates in comedy without exclusively belonging to this genre. It is therefore not a violation of the genre to emphasize the more serious or darker sides in the play, as is done in several recent stagings and adaptations. In fact, the play may be said to participate in several genres, not all of which may be literary.[45] This inclusive schema is both an inherent part of comedy and part of the description of the genre – and it is natural that modern drama (Beaumarchais, Diderot, Büchner, Strindberg) develops from comedy and not from tragedy. As we will see, there is an analogy of sorts between the issue of literary genre and the question of religious and national identity.

At the time in history when Shakespeare lived and work, as James Shapiro has shown in an excellent study, both English national identity and Christian religious identity were being questioned and reconstructed.[46] In the former case it was a response to changes in English society such as increasing mobility and trade, in the latter it was in response to the Reformation which divided the country. Obviously the two questions were intertwined. According to Shapiro, the question 'What is a Jew?' (or 'What makes a Jew a Jew?') is the reverse (or mirror image) of the question what is an Englishman and a Christian. In other words, the issue of conversion has a peculiar meaning both in relation to these times of religious turmoil and in relation to a growing presence and awareness of foreigners. Although in Elizabethan England one had limited contact with and knowledge of Jews (converted or not), according to Shapiro there nevertheless existed an understanding that Jews, in contrast to other peoples, did not blend with or dissolve in other peoples.[47] This may be contrasted with a conception of English self-identity common at the time – that the English constituted a mix of different peoples (Celts, Saxons, Normans, etc.).[48] It would appear, then, that the English were a mixed genre of people, albeit not always and not necessarily of a humorous kind.

The literal meaning of religious conversion is about turning to and following the 'right' path, but reading the conversion in the play is also a question of reading the terms 'Christian' and 'Jew', both in a historical context and in view of our own times. As just mentioned, the meanings of these terms were not fixed, but were being unsettled, questioned and reposited. The issue of forced conversion and persecution of Jews also take on a different meaning in relation to contemporary historical events in Portugal and Spain and in other places, and is also related to the persecution of other religious and ethnic groups.[49] Without wanting to bracket or put aside these issues, I would like to venture on a reading of the conversion in the play as a rhetorical schema – a figure of thought – for solving legal and social conflicts and for conceiving community. In this light, conversion does not (or not only) signify a change of religious faith, turning from one religion to another, nor moving from one genre of belief to another. It is not a question of turning things about or inside-out (inversion) in ways that will change their nature (perversion). Rather, in conversion we meet a figure of turning around or turning-with, of 'with-turning', as in dance when turning together with each other (and with the music). In *The Merchant of Venice*, the site of the conversion coincides with the place of law, and this spatial convergence suggests that the space of law in the play is defined by the conversion. In this light, the ultimate end or telos of a legal trial is neither punishment (or revenge) nor reconciliation between parties, but that the parties perceive or understand that there is another ('higher') interest than their own particular or individual interests. In other words, conversion is a figure producing a certain legal space that shapes and defines the discursive activity of the courtroom, either virtual or real.

There are a number of questions that arise from this view of the conversion as producing a certain kind of legal space, but we can only touch upon a few of them here. First, the suggestion that legal court practice imitates the conceptual schema of religious conversion should be simultaneously intriguing and disturbing for a legal system that tries to keep out the specter of religion from law – as any positivist legal system would – and this may in turn invite comparisons between how legal systems deal with those who do not conform to their standards and how religious institutions handle moral issues. Second, it invites questions regarding mediatization and spectacle: Are legal trials to be considered as a primarily closed – even private – space or are they open and public? And what is the current understanding of 'public space' in law? If the legal space of the courtroom is defined by a certain closure and a highly limited access for media – which is the case in most Western societies today – then what is the meaning of the term open and public trial? In other words, where is the place of law in contemporary society? In what discursive and social folds do legal conversions take place?

A third series of questions concern the relation between society and the trial as a place of law. It is easy to see that the court of law represents society in the sense that it acts on behalf of society. However, the court of law also represents society as a re-presentation or image of society, and in this way it constitutes what Michel Foucault called a 'heterotopia', an 'other place' that constitutes society in providing us with a structural representation of society.[50] In what ways does the court of law constitute society in terms of the conversion? I believe one could view the legal conversion as the enactment or pronunciation of community in the sense that particular interests are articulated within the fold(s) of law. This should not be taken to mean that it is the individuals who constitute the community, but obversely that it is the conversion that constitutes them as singular members of a community. In this way the legal conversion could perhaps be seen as a version of what Jean-Luc Nancy calls the 'co-appearance' or 'com-pearence' (*com-paraissance*) of the finitude of the singular being.[51] In other words, it is in the legal space of the conversion, enacted in the court of law, that the legal subject is made visible, becomes 'ex-posed', by the community. This line of thought obviously needs to be elaborated, but this is not the place for that venture.

It is time to conclude. Perhaps there is no other – or more proper – way to end but by returning to the scene of the conversion, which after all is not represented in the text of the play. It is imperative that we read and re-read this critical point, this turning point in the play. The meaning of the conversion is indeed the spinning movement that it sets in motion at the centre of the legal and theatrical stage.

Notes

1 See the introduction to William Shakespeare, *The Merchant of Venice*, ed. John Russell Brown (1955) (London: Thomson Learning, 2003), pp. xiv–xx. All citations of and references to the text of the play are to this edition. Citations of and references to other plays by Shakespeare are to *The Complete Works: Compact Edition*, ed. Stanley Wells et al. (Oxford: Oxford University Press, 1998).

2 The title page of the first Quarto edition (1600) reads: 'The most excellent / Historie of the *Merchant / of Venice.* / VVith the extreame crueltie of *Shylocke* the Iewe / towards the sayd Merchant, in cutting a iust pound of his flesh: and the obtaining of *Portia* / by the choyse of three / chests. [....]' On the running head of each page the title is both abbreviated and transformed: 'The comicall History of / the Merchant of Venice'. The second Quarto edition (1619) slightly amends the title to 'The Excellent History of the Merchant of Venice', but retains the running heads of the first Quarto. The Folio edition (1623) has simply the 'The Merchant of Venice'. The published adaptation of George Granville (Lord Lansdowne) from 1701 uses an alternative title, 'The Jew of Venice. A Comedy', which may have as its source the 1598 record in the Stationer's Register: 'a booke of the Marchaunt of Venyce or otherwise called the Iewe of Venyce'.

3 Linda Rozmovits describes how *The Merchant of Venice* under Henry Irving's direction (1879) was transformed into a tragedy. See her *Shakespeare and the Politics of Culture in Late Victorian England* (Baltimore: The Johns Hopkins University Press, 1998), pp. 62–63.

4 See for instance Nicholas Rowe, 'Some Account of the Life etc of Mr. William Shakespeare', in *Works*, 6 vols. (1709), I, pp. xix–xx (quoted in R. F. Hill, '*The Merchant of Venice* and the Pattern of Romantic Comedy', *Shakespeare Survey* 28 (1975), p. 75); W. H. Auden, 'Brothers & Others', in *The Dyer's Hand and Other Essays* (New York: Random House, 1963), p. 221; Sarah Kofman, *Conversions. Le Marchand de Venise sous le signe de Saturne* (Paris: Galilée, 1987), pp. 68–69. Daniel Kornstein argues that although the play formally is a comedy, it should be termed a 'legal parable', *Kill All the Lawyers? Shakespeare's Legal Appeal* (Princeton: Princeton University Press, 1994), pp. 88–89.

5 Antonio's letter (read by Bassanio): '*Sweet Bassanio, my ships have all miscarried, my creditors grow cruel, my estate is very low, my bond to the Jew is forfeit, and (since in paying it, it is impossible I should live), all debts are clear'd between you and I, if I might but see you at my death: notwithstanding, use your pleasure,—if your love do not persuade you to come, let not my letter*' (III.ii).

6 Bellario's letter (read by the Duke): '*Your grace shall understand, that at the receipt of your letter I am very sick, but in the instant that your messenger came, in loving visitation with me was a young doctor of Rome, his name is Balthazar: I acquainted him with the cause in controversy between the Jew and Antonio the merchant, we turn'd o'er many books together, he is furnished with my opinion, which (bettered with his own learning, the greatness whereof I cannot enough commend), comes with him at my importunity, to fill up your grace's request in my stead. I beseech you let his lack of years be no impediment to let him lack a reverend estimation, for I never knew so young a body with so old a head: I leave him to your gracious acceptance, whose trial shall better publish his commendation*' (IV.ii).

7 Ser Giovanni's *Il Pecorone* was written (in Italian) in the late fourteenth century and first printed in Milan in 1558.

8 The interlacing of the plots can be graphically represented in the following diagram:

Time	Plot 1 (Romance plot)	Plot 2 (Bond/revenge plot)	Sub-plot (Lorenzo-Jessica)
Act 1, scene 1	X	(X)	
Act 1, scene 2	X		
Act 1, scene 3		X	
Act 2, scene 1	X		
Act 2, scene 2			(X)
Act 2, scene 3			X
Act 2, scene 4			X
Act 2, scene 5		X	

Act 2, scene 6			X
Act 2, scene 7	X		
Act 2, scene 8		(X)	(X)
Act 2, scene 9	X		
Act 3, scene 1		X	
Act 3, scene 2	X		
Act 3, scene 3		X	
Act 3, scene 4	X	X	X
Act 3, scene 5			X
Act 4, scene 1		X	
Act 4, scene 2	(X)	X	
Act 5, scene 1	X		X

9 The movements between Venice and Belmont are represented in the following diagram:

Time	Place 1 (Venice)	Place 2 (Belmont)
Act 1, scene 1	X	
Act 1, scene 2		X
Act 1, scene 3	X	
Act 2, scene 1		X
Act 2, scene 2	X	
Act 2, scene 3	X	
Act 2, scene 4	X	
Act 2, scene 5	X	
Act 2, scene 6	X	
Act 2, scene 7		X
Act 2, scene 8	X	
Act 2, scene 9		X
Act 3, scene 1	X	

Time	Place 1 (Venice)	Place 2 (Belmont)
Act 3, scene 2		X
Act 3, scene 3	X	
Act 3, scene 4		X
Act 3, scene 5		X
Act 4, scene 1	X	
Act 4, scene 2	X	
Act 5, scene 1		X

10 For example, Bassanio has been in Belmont less than 24 hours when a messenger arrives to announce not only that Antonio's ships are wrecked, but also that the time period of the loan (three months) has passed and that the loan is forfeit (III.ii.219 f.); similarly, Lorenzo and Jessica appear to travel around in Italy with the speed of modern day transportation (III.i.72–120).

11 Leonard Tennenhouse, 'The Counterfeit order of *The Merchant of Venice*', in *The Merchant of Venice. Critical Essays*, ed. T. Wheeler (New York: Garland Publishing, 1991), pp. 198–202.

12 For an interesting discussion of the 'meaning' of Venice in Shakespeare's *Othello*, see Peter G. Platt, '"The Meruailous Site": Shakespeare, Venice and Paradoxical Stages', *Renaissance Quarterly* 54, no. 1 (Spring 2001), pp. 121–154.

13 See Gilles Deleuze, *Le Pli. Leibniz et le Baroque* (Paris: Minuit, 1988), pp. 38–54.

14 The connection between Shylock and the legal case of the Jewish physician Roderigo Lopez was first made by Sidney Lee in the article 'The Original of Shylock', *Gentleman's Magazine* 268 (January–June 1880), pp. 185–200. See Richard Halpern, *Shakespeare Among the Moderns* (Ithaca: Cornell University Press 1997), pp. 167–168.

15 James Shapiro, *Shakespeare and the Jews* (New York: Columbia University Press, 1996), pp. 184–187 *et passim.*

16 See e.g. Mark Edwin Andrews, *Law versus Equity in The Merchant of Venice. A Legalization of Act IV, Scene I* (Boulder: University of Colorado Press, 1965); George W. Keeton, *Shakepeare's Legal and Political Background*

(London: Pitman, 1967); O. Hood Phillips, *Shakespeare and the Lawyers* (London: Methuen, 1972); Nicholas W. Knight, *Shakespeare's Hidden Life: Shakespeare at the Law* (New York: Mason & Lipscomb, 1973), pp. 178–190, pp. 280–286; Theodore Ziolkowski, *The Mirror of Justice* (Princeton: Princeton University Press, 1997), pp. 168–172. For attempts to apply the distinction between positive law and equity to the present times, see e.g. Kornstein, *Kill All the Lawyers?*, pp. 83–85 *et passim*; Daniela Carpi, 'Law, Discretion, Equity in *The Merchant of Venice* and *Measure for Measure*', *Cardozo Law Review* (May 2005), pp. 2317–2329.

17 See Gerard B. Wegemer, 'Henry VIII on Trial: Confronting Malice and Conscience in Shakespeare's *All Is True*', in S. W. Smith and T. Curtright (eds.), *Shakespeare's Last Plays: Essays in Literature and Politics* (Lanham: Lexington Books, 2002), pp. 73–90.

18 Riccardo Calimani, *Histoire du ghetto de Venise*, trans. S. Rotolo (Paris: Stock, 1988). For a critical discussion of the presence of Jews in England in Shakespeare's time, see Shapiro, *Shakespeare and the Jews*, pp. 13–88.

19 *Köpmannen i Venedig*, directed by Mats Ek, Royal Dramatic Theatre, Stockholm, 2004.

20 In many stagings of the play one finds an elaborate presentation of the city of Venice, as mentioned by John Russell Brown in his introduction to the Arden edition (p. xxxiv). This is also the case in the recent film adaptation by Michael Radford (2004), which begins by depicting the city as strongly anti-semitic (voice over) and in a scene on the Rialto is shown how Antonio unprovoked spits on Shylock. But it is not only the beginning of the play that may be transformed: in a discussion of nineteenth-century representations of the play, Linda Rozmovits describes how on some occasions the play ended with the closing of the trial in the fourth act, leaving Shylock alone on the stage. (See her *Shakespeare and the Politics of Culture in Late Victorian England*, p. 78.)

21 Martin Wiggins, *Shakespeare and the Drama of his Time* (Oxford: Oxford University Press, 2000), p. 63, p. 70.

22 Steve Patterson, 'The Bankruptcy of Homoerotic Amity in Shakespeare's *Merchant of Venice*', *Shakespeare Quarterly* 50, no. 1 (Spring 1999), pp. 9–32.

23 Whereas in the romance plot the virtue of love and the love of virtue are equally true and confirm each other, in the epic – a more serious literary

genre – they are frequently opposed chiastically. For instance, in Virgil's *Aeneid* Aeneas proves his virtue (*pietas*) by giving up his love for Dido.

24 See Filomena Mesquita, "Travesties of Justice: Portia in the Courtroom', in D. Carpi (ed.), *Shakespeare and the Law* (Ravenna: Longo Editore, 2003), p. 122.

25 Kornstein, *Kill All the Lawyers?*, p. 72. For a suggestive reading of the meaning of 'an equal pound / Of your fair flesh', see Shapiro, *Shakespeare and the Jews*, pp. 113–128.

26 G. W. F. Hegel, *Grundlinien der Philosophie des Rechts* #3, ed. J. Hoffmeister (Hamburg: Verl. Felix Meiner, 1955), p. 26.

27 For instance in Solon's *seisachtheia* ('removal of burden'), as described in Aristotle, *The Athenian Constitution*, 6.

28 Part V, 'The Case of *The Merchant of Venice*: Shylock v. Antonio on appeal', in Susan Tiefenbrun (ed.), *Law and the Arts* (Westport: Greenwood Press, 1999), pp. 149–235.

29 R. S. White, *Natural Law in English Renaissance Literature* (Cambridge: Cambridge University Press, 1996), pp. 159–184.

30 For a discussion of representations of revenge in Elizabethan drama, see Ronald Broude, 'Revenge and Revenge Tragedy in Renaissance England', *Renaissance Quarterly* 28, no. 1 (Spring 1975), pp. 38–58.

31 Barbara Lewalski has argued that the name Balthazar contains an allusion to the Book of Daniel (where the prophet is called Balthazar). In the apocryphal Book of Susanna, the young Daniel – the name means 'the Judge of the Lord' – 'confounded the accusers of Susanna, upholding thereby the justice of the Law' ('Biblical Allusion and Allegory in *The Merchant of Venice*', *Shakespeare Quarterly* 13, no. 3 (Summer 1962), p. 340).

32 In historical Venice, the execution of death sentence followed an elaborate ritual, see Guido Ruggiero, *Violence in Early Renaissance Venice* (New Brunswick: Rutgers University Press, 1980), pp. 1–2 *et passim*.

33 Anthony Hecht, 'The Merchant of Venice: A Venture in Hermeneutics', in *Obligati: Essays in Criticism* (New York: Atheneum, 1986), pp. 186–187; Christopher Colmo, 'Law and Love in Shakespeare's *The Merchant of Venice*', *Oklahoma City University Law Review* 26, no. 1 (2001), p. 319.

34 Hegel, *Grundlinien der Philosophie des Rechts* #66, p. 73.

35 See e.g. 'The Case of *The Merchant of Venice*'.

36 An example from modern cinema that illustrates this is Rob Reiner's *A Few Good Men* (1992). A similar move is found at the end of the film *The General's Daughter* (directed by Simon West, 1999).

37 Hegel objected strongly both to the idea of social contract as the foundation of civil society and to the view that a contract could be regarded 'as a contract of all with all, or as a contract of all with the sovereign and the government' ('als ein Vertrag aller mit allen, oder als ein Vertrag deiser aller mit dem Fürsten und der Regierung') (Hegel, *Grundlinien der Philosophie des Rechts* # 75, p. 80). See also the extended discussion of social contract in his *Über die wissenschaftlichen Behandlungsarten des Naturrechts* (1802–1803).

38 Richard H. Weisberg, 'Antonio's Legalistic Cruelty', *College Literature* 25, no. 1 (Winter 1998), pp. 12–34.

39 See A. D. Moody, 'The Letter of the Law (III.iii–v; IV.i)', in *The Merchant of Venice: Critical Essays*, ed. T. Wheeler (New York: Garland Publishing, 1991), p. 86; René Girard, 'To Entrap the Wisest: Sacrificial Ambivalence in *The Merchant of Venice* and *Richard III*', in *A Theater of Envy. William Shakespeare* (New York: Oxford University Press, 1980), pp. 243–255; Richard Halpern, *Shakespeare Among the Moderns*, pp. 176–184 *et passim*.

40 Edward T. Swaine, 'Unsigning', *Stanford Law Review* 55 (May 2003). See also Jim Lobe, "Bush Mulls 'Unsigning' Treaty for International Criminal Court', *OneWorld.net*, 5 April 2002 (http://www.commondreams.org/headlines02/0405-02.htm); John B. Anderson, 'Unsigning the ICC', *The Nation*, 29 April 2002, (http://www.thenation.com/doc/20020429/anderson).

41 As formulated in the (French) Declaration of the Rights of Man and of the Citizen, article 10 (1789); the Constitution of the United States of America, first amendment (1791); the United Nations Universal Declaration of Human Rights (1948), article 18; the Charter of Fundamental Rights of the European Union, article 10 (2000).

42 Aristotle, *Poetics* 1447b24–48a27, 1449a33–37; see also the more extensive definition of tragedy at 1449b25–50a14.

43 Horace, *Ars poetica*, 1–13; Nicolas Boileau-Despréaux, *Art poétique* (1674).

44 Jacques Derrida, 'La Loi du genre' (1979), *Parages* (Paris: Galilée, 2003), p. 237. This implies that there is no single statute that governs or rules over genres. See Leif Dahlberg, 'Namnet på det fantastiska', in *Tre romantiska berättelser* (Stockholm: Symposion, 1999), pp. 325–361.

45 Derrida, 'La Loi du genre', p. 245.

46 Shapiro, *Shakespeare and the Jews*, pp. 13–88.

47 Ibid., pp. 165–173.

48 Ibid., pp. 43–45 *et passim.*

49 Ibid., pp. 5–6, 14–20, 131–165.

50 Michel Foucault, 'Des Espaces autres' (1984 [1967]), in Michel Foucault, *Dits et écrits II, 1976–1988*, ed. D. Defert and F. Ewald (Paris: Gallimard, 2001), pp. 1571–1581.

51 Jean-Luc Nancy, *La Communauté désœuvrée* (Paris: Bourgois, 1986), pp. 68–78.

9

Man and Dog

The Modernity of Law – Jurists, Violence, Poetries, and a Photograph

Rainer Maria Kiesow

It is really bizarre. This thing with the law. Desperately seeking justice, we ended up with law. From the beginning onwards. Thousands of years ago. There is a radical and brutal separation of an imagined world (justice) and the world of that which happens (laying down the law by judges). This separation, alienation, autonomy has not had any consequences on the functionality of the latter. Revolutions (dreams) are not so much concerned about law, and in the end the utopian struggle for justice reaches its dénouement not only in a Code civil, but also in a Code de procedure civile. So law always wins out over justice. But despite this sad fact – a fact that would require a new revolution for the just cause, with the same mundane effect – law remains intangible. All projects of justices and justifications touch the law like water on an oily surface. There is no attachment. It is slippery and oily in the world of jurists. Watch your step! Really bizarre. Really bizarre to imagine that justice – and such celestial ideas – could enlighten a well oiled machine that functions in a radical and exclusive mode: the one could be right – or the other. You never know when you are in a courtroom. The machine spits out always one decision – or another decision. The machine of law is perhaps the greatest producer of uncertainty. And this – not justice – is its most obvious secret. And this is its modernity. Since the old days. It is really bizarre. Because law, in its old way of judging cases between parties, because law, in its endless power of the one or the other interpretation, because law at the end is the result of the imagination, the constructions, the poetries of the legal-workers. In this sense, man, the character of man, returns into the discourse about jurisprudence and into the jurisprudential discourses themselves. And that is why, at the end of the following fragmentary reflections and stories on the fragmentary world of modern law, there is a photograph, a photograph of a jurist.

Questions and answers, ideas and aperçus

Is law our only hope? Is law a means towards creating a better community? What is law? Constitution, constituted, mediation, proceedings, solution …

Is law simply just law? A distinction like other distinctions in society? This would not exclude fulfilling hopes, but that just would not be part of the agenda.

Is law also injustice? Is law still law when injustice is involved? The death penalty, torture, racial laws, international criminal courts….

Is law modern? If law is just law, this question is meaningless.

Questions upon questions. And no answers. Instead of answers, which cannot be answers, especially not to universal questions, the following will provide some observations, readings, ideas. It's about blacks, courts, violence, the media, secrets, Jesus, poetry, lemons, milk, Roman law, irrationality, photographs. But one thing should not be forgotten in the process: there is nothing worse than ideas that always have something modern about them, having just occurred to someone. Louis-Ferdinand Céline said in his *Entretiens avec le Professeur Y*: 'I have no ideas! Not a single one! And I find nothing more vulgar, common, repulsive than ideas! The libraries are full of them! And café terraces! … and the philosophers! … That is their business, the ideas … the syntheses! And the cerebral mutations!' So, no ideas, just aperçus.

The black guy was lucky

An ideal guilty party. Brenton Butler. Black, young, male. A couple was holidaying in Jacksonville, Florida. White, of retirement age. Husband and wife were returning – with a muffin, coffee and a newspaper in their hands – from their motel reception area to their room to have their breakfast. It was 7.30 in the morning on a summer's day in the year 2000. In front of their motel room a man suddenly appeared, demanding the handbag and the wallet. He was given these and then he shot the woman. The husband provided the police with a description of the person. Three hours later, Brenton Butler was picked up by the police on his way to an interview for a job in a video store. Nothing about Brenton tallied with the description given: he was young, a 15-year-old school boy, his T-shirt had a conspicuous logo, he was wearing glasses and didn't have a fisherman's cap on – he was simply the only black guy to cross the police's path. Sitting on the back seat of the police car, he was presented to the husband of the murdered victim, who immediately identified the school boy as the murderer.

A trial took place. The husband, the only eyewitness of the murder, stuck to his statement: Brenton was the person he saw. The two assigned counsels uncovered one scandal after another regarding the police investigations. Brenton was hit, a confession forced out of him, evidence not secured, witnesses for an alibi – Brenton repeated that he was at home at the time of the crime – were not questioned, etc. In the end, the jury acquitted Brenton. The husband could not understand this. Four months later, a prisoner told his cell mate that he had killed the white woman. His fingerprints were taken and they were the same as those on the handbag. The murderer had been caught!

Media of violence, the violence of the media

And the media? The murder in Jacksonville was a huge media event. Young black man shoots elderly white tourist – in the sun state. But the case was also dealt with in another medium, in a French documentary film by Jean-Xavier de Lestrade called *Un coupable idéal*. No accusation, no apotheosis of truth, no presentation of the grimace of the evil old white man, no explanations, no, just a recording of the events of the trial with a few commentaries by those involved. The viewer had to form his own image. The film was awarded an Oscar for the best documentary of the year 2002.

Violence is omnipresent: among white people, black people, on television, among the police, among state prosecutors, at court. The documentary film shows this – and offers no explanations. How is this to be understood? Until the question of understanding is answered, it must be ascertained, historically and currently: violence is immortal. Yes, violence is the mother of law. There is no state philosopher of the European modern era who has not tried to prevent the war of everyone against everyone else and of each individual against each individual by means of a contract and the law. But violence has remained. Violence has been met with violence: state violence, the separation of powers with legislating violence, the monopoly of violence. *Vis* and *ius* – just by shifting the letters around, violence and law even become interchangeable.

Law?

Law as the preventer of violence is therefore itself violent. The greatest violence of law – even before jails, death row, compulsory executions – is the power of interpretation. Justice is a theatre of interpretation. This or that interpretation. You never know when the curtain will drop and this or that interpretation remains, victorious. The power of words and their impact on people's lives – that is the uncanny violence of the legal constitution of social community. There is no end to violence.

Yet the violence of the law is invisible. It is not to be seen in the media, nowhere. The clever constructions of law and the myth of justice have disguised the fact that the blood of people is oozing from the cylinders of the modern machinery of law, not just in the United States of America. The discussion about torture in the police headquarters in Frankfurt is just one example.[1] May torture be used in order (as the case may be) to save a life? But the concrete conflict (of values?) in the head of the policeman, and in the heads of the criminal law professors, is by no means the most interesting aspect of this debate. It is not just a question of what a modern state based on the rule of law may do, how much force it may use. One way or the other, the state is the most violent actor ever to have arrived on the scene. No, the real question is that of truth. The question of how much blood truth costs. It is a question of the truth of violence, and the violence of truth. Torture was conceived as a modern factory of truth towards the end of the Middle Ages and the beginning of the modern era. That still works today: Brenton Butler confessed. Whether truth is right – that is another question altogether.

Secret

The violence of the word, of the interpretation, the violence of the law has no author, no cause, no mover any more – since the death of reason and the death of God. This old way of viewing the world essentially has fallen to pieces. Violence and the understanding of violence can only be regarded as fragments. This fragmentation – and this also means duplication, unfolding – of the phenomena is itself an act of violence. The dissection of man by modern science, the showing of the human heart on television, the proud presentation of a brain in science-shows, the organ transplantation observed from people's living-room couches – here metaphors and imagination are being murdered. This violence exists. It is the violence of the explanation. It is the violence of modern science. It is presented on TV not as violence but as salvation – and as truth. Life is not permitted to be a secret.

Violence in the media. Here Europe is very much behind the times – there is not much violence to be seen on TV, even if the opposite is often claimed when violence breaks out somewhere. Bowling for Columbine? The US American, the white woman's husband, sees a lot of violence in the media – and becomes anxious and wants to protect himself from violence and buys weapons and encounters violence with violence, and shoots, and shoots, and shoots. Violence becomes violence through violence. Behind this is fear. Fear sells. Are the media responsible for this? The media want to sell. They cannot be reproached for this. Values (which values?) are hard to sell. Values are always just values. And law is just law. That's its secret.

Violence!

Violence is a scandal. Evil is a scandal. Can evil violence be understood? How it breaks out, is expressed? Perhaps the time has come to stop trying to understand, to renounce the violence of truth, and to recognize what can be read in the literature of violence and of evil since Romanticism, that modern factory of the subjective: violence eschews meaning. It is astonishing, frightening, sudden. In this particular form it resists rationality. It is free. It is Baudelaire's 'dream of bloody scaffolds', a 'nightmare full of unknown things' of the kind to be seen in Goya's paintings – but not to be understood. Modern? Unmodern? No, it is not a battle between the modern and the old, as was the case centuries ago. The butchery of wars, the massacres at schools, the murders committed by perverts – these remain a universal mystery which, as mysteries, cannot be solved. The media try to track down this mystery, in a paradoxical mixture of showing and discussing violence. The discussion about showing violence, about violence in the media, has not got very far. It can only be hoped that this remains the case.

For the solution to the mystery of violence would not mean, for example, the end, or the condition of the possibility of the end of violence, but would itself be the sublimation of violence. Explanations, findings, are acts of violence – restrictions on freedom. What is to be feared is the power of the right interpretation – a rightness, a truth, a justice for the achievement of which torture is always to hand. Violence in the media is always better than the violence of the media. As long as this and that opinion exists, as long as the mystery stands up to the blather of the interpretation, as long as the media do not disseminate

THE one and only opinion, as long as science only produces precarious truths, so long as meaning-giving does not reign supreme, knowledge will not itself become a frightening, violent knowledge. The diversity of opinions will not be able to impinge on violence. Nothing will ever happen to violence. But something would happen to the world, if it were exempt from thinking. Of thinking about the abyss of violence. The abyss of man. An abyss that is itself without end.

Jesus

Did the murderers of Jesus do badly at school? Were they good class mates? Had they watched too many gladiator fights? Did they spend too much time in taverns – and too little talking and thinking? Childish questions.

Art

Is violence not an excess of signs? Violence as artwork. To look at. Especially in the (old and new) media. A matter of taste.

Self-reference

The evil images are silent.
The evil deeds are not rooted in words.
Violence rests in itself.

A short history of modern law

It often seems that law is the main focus of the New Modern Europe. Legal guarantees and procedures are primary conditions for accession states; the European Constitution is imminent; without democracy and a constitutional state nothing is possible in Europe, in our hypermodern Europe which, over a decade and a half, has seen a reunification (for example, in Germany) and at the same time a new fragmentation (for example, in the Balkans). The New Europe is being driven not just by economic (wealth), political (participation), and touristic (mobility) hopes, but also by legal ambitions. These concern justice, or at least legal procedures, i.e., the dual achievement of 'democracy and law', in brief, the constitutional state. This is where history, more precisely, an old history of law, comes to the minds of the propagandists of the modern European constitutional state. In the opinion of these eager and highly educated legal-culture Europeans, it is above all old Roman law, or rather the Ius Commune of the modern era that is based on it, which forms the (peaceful, cultural, civic, economic, constitutional) basis of the modern, and especially of the New Europe – a specific form of (legal) memory culture.

But which law, which kind of law, do the optimistic and historically minded legal-culture-Europeans (not only jurists and historians, but also politicians and publicists everywhere) imagine or remember? A law that is established, that acts as a guarantee, one could almost say a friendly and tangible law. A law which people can have, on which they can rely. But is this idyll of the law, this positive image of the law, this hope in the law – nurtured by history – not a deception, a cobbled-together memory, a fabrication which fails to recognize the real aspect of modern (and in particular of ancient) law? In order to question this willing deception, this almost folkloric idea of an established European law, it may be useful to reflect on the foundations of the law, its theory and its history in Europe.

There were (at least) three fields of Modern Law: the natural law of law, the alphabet of law, and the positive law. The examination of past notions of a scientifically based and developed law as well as the past and present attempt to order legal knowledge in Europe as well as the rise of positive law are, though not only, a story of the failure of modern law. On the one hand, the failed attempt to give law a secure foundation comparable to natural laws; on the other hand, the failed effort to tame a jurisprudence already perceived by the ancients as a collection of fragments and to offer at least a reliable arrangement of the eternally antagonistic laws, jurisdictions and doctrines; on the third hand (history and theory and law are many-handed monsters), the failed effort to put the diverse jurisprudences into the prison of the LAW, given by a state.

The long history of law is one of a law which is ambiguous, uncertain, disorderly and fragmentary. Law has never been modern (because modernity cannot be the subject of an every-hour-spectacle, given by the theatre of law). One observation repeatedly made in the context of analyses of the law as based on natural law and order still remains surprising and in need of (impossible) explanation: since antiquity the law has been perceived as something precarious, for which reason it has been divided and collected (digests), rearranged and set into a whole (pandects), confined in the margins in (medieval) glosses and commentaries and at the same time fixed as text. In the modern era it has been built up successively on concepts either of God, nature, or reason, and finally bounded by systems, science, and new laws. Yet the numerous attempts to secure this precarious law have always ended in the contemporary ascertainment that the law remained precarious and so had to continue to be secured: a process of uncertainty, certainty, uncertainty, certainty, and so on, that continues to this very day. The following is also surprising: why has the law not long since lost its function of rendering the expectations of society members towards one another calculable, of allaying conflicts or exerting power 'in a civic manner', especially as the law is obviously a very dubious fly-by-night? Why is the law still highly regarded in society, although contrary to what people expect of it and it expects of itself, it is perhaps the functional system that is most strongly based on uncertainty? Why is it that the constitutional state is regarded as the apotheosis of the historical development of society – as can be observed yet again in recent European history and as expressed not least in the demands made of EU accession candidates in terms of (not just human) rights – despite the fact that uncertainty is thus even installed as a fundamental principle of the modern, just, social state?

Perhaps these interrogative paradoxes can be unpicked if the poetic constitution of the law is focused on. A Poetry of Law could perhaps observe this from a historical, philosophical, and theoretical viewpoint. In the law itself and at its core, namely in jurisprudence, both the facts and the norm are constantly being newly produced. This takes place in the argumentative strategies of the parties in a legal battle and in the final decision of the judge, meaning that in the law decisions are made, and reality is not recognized as such but recognized only as lawful. In this sense, the law constantly exhibits uncertainty and ambiguity, that is, not the application of a fixed rule and thus the extraction of a clandestinely fixed meaning, but its construction, its poiesis.

This poietic principle of the law rests on the art of those jurists who 'make' the law also to tame it. The triad of doctrine, jurisdiction and legislation tries to tame the huge surplus of (different and contradictory) meanings and possibilities. This produces another meaning which further feeds the surplus; what comes out of this legal business in the end is always a newly made addition.

The Eternal Poetry of Law lies in the thesis whether it is not the poetry written into law, whether it is not the equivocal meanings of the law, whether it is not the law's rhetorical qualities that make the law so attractive, so fungible, and so readily instrumentalized in many different historical and contemporary societies. And is it not least this fungible aspect of the law which, in the European history of the last 200 years, runs quite contrary to the hopes that have been, and still are, placed in that law? And so it is precisely the non-modernity of law, this eternal everyday business, which makes law possible. Law is, because law has never been modern.

Law and order or the liberal imagination

Law is, because violence is. *Ius* and *vis*. That at least is the view of the law held by the man on the street. Law is condemnatory. Law is criminal law. The public has always only been interested in the theatre of terror and the concomitant comedy of law. See the Brenton Butler case. No one (almost) is interested in the legal chronicle of the civic sphere. What fascinates is the right to punish, the duty to punish, which in short is the punishment that mirrors the evil act (abstract or concrete). The game with life and death – on the side of crime, on the side of law. Criticism – is pointless. Violence rules. Is that modern? Can anything else be imagined? Law and order are on the agenda. Still. Again. As in the pre-modern era, tired of liberal, libertine postmodernism, the demand is for: law and order!

Criticism – both of legal omnipotence and of the violence of the legal order – would presuppose a standpoint. But this is exactly what we are missing. At most, a political opinion can be mustered in order to criticize the state of the law. One can no longer believe what one says, or better, one can only *believe* what one says.

What does 'politics and law' mean, both of which are often being critically questioned with reference to something that lies beyond, beyond the liberal (neo-liberal?) power of imagination? Having visited the field of violence in law and through law, the field of violence in society, the field of the violence of opinions and interpretations, the field of violence in and through poetry, we briefly take a quick look at the ghetto of legality, the ghetto of the law. This ghetto is populated by jurists, professors, commentators, judges. The judges are the ones who count. The courts have always exerted the power of the civil sphere. Inconspicuous, yes, invisible. Civil law is hardly appropriate for great theatre. Fragmentary, contradictory, situative and case-related, it never had and still does not have the mordant edge of a criminal law that has to do with life and death. Michel Foucault once spoke about the 'silent functioning' of civil jurisdiction, which, by being disorderly, fragmented, non-uniform, is reminiscent of a tortuous and confusing work by the artist Tinguely. In this confusion there are not even (system theoretical) irritations. Foucault speaks of 'disturbances', but only mechanisms of functioning. All the cogs and wheels of the machine seem to smile at us: all these things that do not work ultimately result in its working. A game of disorder. And Foucault is perfectly right when he says: 'Our jurisdiction is not dishonoured when it is compared to that of the Ancien Régime'. Exactly: neither the new modern law book nor the new modern science or doctrine of law have been able to call a halt to the maelstrom of wild judgements. The *application* of the law is always 'limping' behind. On the side of norms, and on the side of facts.

Lemon or milk

Foucault published a short text with a puzzling title in an October 1978 issue of the daily newspaper *Le monde*: 'Le citron et le lait'. Lemon and milk. And yet: milk *and* lemon are impossible. Disgusting! Astonishingly enough, the article is about the law. The administration of justice, to a certain extent law in short, has to apply the laws, however much it may have to support itself on crutches and limp. The administration of justice, the law, is not there to reinstate the social order. Foucault says this in the newspaper more clearly than anywhere else: he has no time for demands for the politicization of justice, whereby of course he did realize that justice is political. That is the old distinction between prescription and description. The eighteenth century wanted to drain the ocean of laws and the many judgements, the nineteenth century finally produced the one, unified law, but the expectation people had of it was not fulfilled. Or as Foucault writes: 'The architecture of law cannot at the same time be a mechanism of order'. During the tea ceremony the question asked is: milk or lemon. In the context of a theory of society therefore, the question must be: law *or* order. For the laws will not bring about order, because of the legal system's own logic, and order by means of laws is not only the motto of a global conservatism, but above all a monstrous hybrid: law *and* order.

Law and order is the ghost which is always lurking when you look beyond the liberal imagination of politics and law. For example, in the much-lauded international criminal court, which was nothing other than luck late in life for Slobodan Milosevic. The stake of the (not quite) international community is high. The coin is global justice. Beccaria already dreamed of being able to finally prosecute criminals in every corner of the land with a modern criminal code: 'Inside the borders of a country there should be no place that is beyond the law. Its power must follow every citizen like the shadow the body'. Beccaria the liberal?

Justice

'I dont know what meaning work has in our time, but I think that skill is a weakness, knowledge a dangerous trump, and I am satisfied to have genius and no talent whatsoever, allowing me not to work, and to play like a child: for work loves pomp and splendour, is ugly and false like justice'. This is how the artist Kees van Dongen replied in a survey carried out by an art magazine in 1929: 'What does it mean: to work?' So justice is ugly and false – and in love with pomp. An astonishing statement. Yet 'justice' is surely one of the top ten universal super good-words, along with peace, nature, health. But all these universal goods have an 'other' side to them, they are all not to be had 'easily', they have all long since been deconstructed, destroyed, demystified. Sometimes (perhaps even always) peace needs discord in order to become or remain peace. Nature kills. Health is expensive and a social construct that brings about sickness, as otherwise it, health, would not exist (a wonderful book on this is the study by Georges Canguilhem, Foucault's teacher, *The Normal and the Pathological*). And justice also has another side, other sides, fabricated, intemperate, wistful. *Fiat justitia, pereat mundus*. Exactly: loving pomp, ugly and false. A word, weak-willed and dangerous, a weapon for anyone who would like to suggest something to people. A word that troubles one's own conscience, a word, a written word that kills, that even kills the person who may say it: Surely you remember the report:

The machine

The machine leads to death. It inscribes the law that has been broken on the body of the condemned person. For hours on end. Dozens of steel nails inscribe the letters into the skin. Water is sprayed from tiny jets onto the streaming blood and washes it off their back. Yes, you could decipher the writing, even though at first you saw 'only labyrinthine, criss-crossing lines'. You just had to read carefully. And for a time. It was not supposed to be 'a simple script'; it was not supposed to kill immediately, but only after a period of twelve hours, on average. Furthermore, the script was not intended to be deciphered visually. The condemned person deciphered the script 'with his wounds'.

However, this time the machine did not kill the condemned man. Although everything was as it had always been. The condemned person did not know why he had been condemned, he did not know the judgement, it was not announced to him, he had 'had no opportunity to defend himself'. No, he did not even know 'that he had been condemned in the first place'. Why should he? He would 'find out through his body'. And the machine – it functioned. The officer operating it knew it 'best'. He adjusted it carefully and cleaned it: 'Up to this point manual work is required, but from now on the machine works all on its own'. Yes, everything was as before, like in the days of the 'former Commandant' who was 'soldier, judge, constructor, chemist, designer' and invented the machine. But now, in these new times, many regarded the machine as an 'outdated installation'. There were no more 'sincere supporters'. 'The injustice of the procedure and the inhumanity of the execution were beyond doubt'. The explorer saw things that way, too, and thus disappointed the officer's hopes that he would recommend the old procedure to the new Commandant, by saying: 'No'.

The machine did not kill the condemned man, for the officer realized: 'the time has come', and set him free. The condemned man left the machine and then witnessed a 'great change'. The officer undressed himself – 'Now he stood there naked' – re-adjusted the 'machine', and 'now it was almost staggering to see how he managed it and how it obeyed him'. Then he himself lay down on the 'bed'. The 'Harrow' steered by the 'Designer' descended and pushed the needles into his skin. The machine began its 'silent work' in order to write 'be just' on the body of the non-condemned officer. But suddenly a cog fell down from the Designer, then a second and a third. More and more wheels fell into the sand. 'The machine was obviously falling to pieces; its silent working was a delusion'. The needles of the Harrow were no longer writing, they were just pricking. Finally the Harrow shifted the impaled body aside. 'Blood was flowing in a hundred streams, not mingled with water, the water jets too had failed to function'. The explorer wanted to help, but nothing more could be done. The face of the officer was 'as it had been in life … the lips were firmly pressed together, the eyes were open, with the same expression as in life, the look was calm and convinced, through the forehead went the point of the great iron spike'. The machine of justice leads to death. Its own included.

You can read this in Kafka's story *In the Penal Colony*. The 'doubtless' unjust procedure prescribes: 'Be just'. Justice – ugly and false, brutal and deadly!

The black image of justice

The concern here is to question justice, to relativize it, perhaps even to take leave of it. Justice is the justice of the victor, and even the just victory has hateful features. Justice is not THE one and only justice. Justice is something that is made, fabricated, a product of man's labour and mind. And what man makes is, then as now, often ugly and false, precarious and never unambiguous. Often it would be better for justice to remain in the dark, invisible, absent – so that man can live (and kill).

Yes, Roman law is no longer alive.

Le droit romain n'est plus

We now have to speak about Louis Aragon. Louis Aragon was born in Paris in 1897, was an assistant doctor in the First World War, discovered Dadaism and Surrealism in the 1920s, became a friend of André Breton, wrote poems, his great panorama of Paris, *Le paysan de Paris*, appeared in 1926, the city discovered and seen with the eyes of a peasant. In 1928 he got to know a young Russian emigré, Elsa Triolet, the love of his life and his companion during his resistance to fascism. He was imprisoned, broke out, and with a weapon in his hand continued to write – novels, poems, short stories. In 1944 he published his *Aurélien*, perhaps the most beautiful novel about justice and love, impossible justice and impossible love. After the Second World War Aragon became something akin to the incarnation of the communist intellectual, writing essays, articles, and poems. In 1970, after the death of Elsa, he distanced himself from the world, wrote only one more text, and died in 1982 – a life full of passion and dedication.

During the German occupation of France in the early 1940s, Aragon, who was in the Resistance, wrote several short stories, including *Le droit romain n'est plus* (Roman law no longer exists). The plot is simple: from different narrative perspectives, as it were, prismatically, we read about the dominance of a German regime in a small French town. The story has two main figures. First there's Lotte Müller, stenographer in the law court. Her friend Bubi is fighting on the eastern front. She is a party member and thinks that the only well-brought-up, cultivated man in that boring little town, with neither shops nor music, is the Gestapo head, a first lieutenant and a man of letters. She wouldn't mind being involved with him, but he's so busy, and she's surely not his type, his 'thing'; the Jews are his 'thing', he sees them everywhere and finds them everywhere. 'One could say he makes them, he also kills them'. The only good point in the day is when the court convenes. The judge, the military judge, is called von Lüttwitz-Randau. Not good-looking, like Bubi, her generally attractive friend (how boring), no intellectual, like the Gestapo head, older, not breathtaking, but he has something. Lotte is his secretary – and he has designs on her, so why not, as far as women are concerned looks are not everything. Men, when the time comes, you just have to close your eyes.

The second main figure is the judge, von Lüttwitz-Randau. Below a portrait of Hitler, in a massive, misshapen building – beside him Lotte, his little kitten, takes the minutes – he administers the law. How boring, only two death sentences today, only two executions. The fellows were planning something against the Germans. Von Lüttwitz-Randau – who, once he takes off his glasses, can't see that Lotte doesn't want to see him – recently read a very interesting article in the *Völkische Beobachter* about the development of German law. He himself once wrote about it, in his doctorate, in 1925: *De jure germanico*. And how right the Führer is. Roman law, the law of the Jews, this Non-German law must be eradicated and a new, German law created so as to serve the German cause, not just with the means of power and violence, but also with words. The concept of justice that prevailed at the time of Siegmund und Sieglinde, when incest was imperative to save the race, yes, that justice must be reinstalled. All for the success of the Germans, for the German cause.

Lotte's only source of amusement was at court sittings; even a completely banal session with one, two death sentences, quite boring really, was better than the rendezvous with the judge that followed. But what of it? What else was there!

Von Lüttwitz-Randau dreamt of the law, of good law. He had been professor of Roman law, then, when Hitler was still on the streets. And he, the professor, already anticipated that nothing could become of Roman law, a new justice had to be created, with a new law, but not even that was really the case. True German law did not need a code, a statute book, paragraphs. There could not be a Code Hitler, like formerly the Code Napoleon. Hitler's thoughts, the thoughts of the Führer, were not codifiable. And yet new lawyers were required, for everywhere in Europe a new start had to be made, with a new German, a modern law.

For von Lüttwitz-Randau the dream soon came to an end. During a jaunt through the countryside with his lady friend Lotte, the two were captured and kidnapped by resistance fighters. The judge was put on trial, by terrorists, as he described them, after which he was asked: WHO are the terrorists? He thought he would have rights by law, after all, had he not administered the law. And law is law? He had applied his law. The German law against terrorists. He couldn't remember how many people he had condemned to death. 'That many?' Justice took its course. The tribunal ended. They put him in a car and drove through the night on lonely mountain roads to the places where Germans had thrown children against a wall, raped women, and killed men. They did not find inner peace, neither the drivers, nor the person being driven. In the end they shot him, at dawn. The pastor, one of the resistance fighters, 'laughed nastily', the leader said: 'No, not there. Your blood is not to desecrate the soil on which the blood of our heroes flowed'. They shot at him in the gutter, like at 'a chicken'.

The resistance fighters implemented their kind of justice. That justice was followed by death. Aragon, himself a resistance fighter, sees the other side of justice precisely. Nasty laughter, court procedures, the gestures of the victors, people become animals. What is the face of justice?

Foucault again

When Foucault wrote 'Le citron et le lait' in 1978 he was in the middle of giving lectures at the Collège de France about governmentality, i.e., a theme that is being scrutinized today in the globalization debate, which latter is as modern as the Marx of *The Communist Manifesto* was once modern. This debate is taking place in the dwellings of professors and in cafes. Much, much too much, has been written about the ideas of the French master thinker on the themes of power, violence, government and bio-politics. Foucault himself was no longer interested in that after his lectures from 1977 to 1979. The paradoxical superpower of an irrational rationality of a modern capitalist kind, i.e. the observation already formulated by Max Weber that modernism just about functions by not functioning – the lines, spots and dots from Tinguely and Pollock: all this swallowed the myth of the general principle of law, the myth of power, the myth of steering and controlling society.

Was Foucault a liberal? A Neo-liberal? What of it! In 1978 he received Soviet dissidents, on the same evening when the Soviet secretary general was dining with the French president in Paris. His lectures were about the history of liberalism. About the seductive power of the liberal idea. About a thinking that could imagine that better government perhaps meant less government. A paradox. A paradox that taps into, even unlocks, contractual relations, relations based on distance, self-made men, i.e. the whole varied panorama of private practices. A paradox which, like all paradoxes, with its explanations that explain nothing, refers man back to himself. Regret has repeatedly been expressed that Foucault did not continue his governmentality studies. There has just been one Foucault Effect, without Foucault himself.[2] Agamben is the youngest and most prominent mourner at the grave of French theory. But Foucault did not take his leave. He continued. At another point. When, in the modern world, the old paradoxes fully unfold, when the government of liberal thinking has taken over the powerless power, through its complete self-elimination, then it is again time to take a look at man, to analyze the techniques of the self, the care for oneself. When in the old Greek story the Cretan lies, does not lie, lies, all that remains is the Cretan. Not the Cretan as such, but the Cretan himself.

Photographic finish

In 1924 August Sander photographed a notary in Cologne. The man is posing in front of the steps to his house or office. A hat, sharp edged, like a kind of horizontal guillotine, buttoned coat from which a high stiff white shirt collar protrudes, in his right hand a walking stick, in his left a leash; the black thoroughbred greyhound shines like his master's heavy leather shoes. Self-assured, important, stiff as a post. Law and order. Snappy brutality. Later, the photographer was censored by the Nazis. Whether the notary was permitted to continue working as before? Reflections on modern law, on the modernity of law – that would mean creating a science of the unique being, an impossible science of man.

A photograph is like a rubbing of reality, to use a formulation by Roland Barthes in his autobiographical fragment *La chambre claire*. Herein lies the sadness unleashed by observing a photograph. A photograph always says: 'That is what it was like'. A photograph does not bear any future within it. History and photography were invented in the same century, the nineteenth. A photograph always says – nothing more. It cannot say anything. Time is crushed. It was as it is. Chance. And it is as it is, not just at the end of *The Buddenbrooks*. However banal, simple, mad that is. What does it mean? A photograph says nothing about that. Nothing at all. A photograph is as indifferent as nature. More will not remain. Of our hopes about the law. That has something to do with people. Foucault suspected this and turned his attention to his history. To the history of man. In a totally melancholic way.

Notes

1 In 2002 the police arrested the kidnapper of the youngest son of a well-known banking family in Frankfurt am Main and threatened him with ill-treatment in order to make him confess to the whereabouts of the child. A series of court decisions on different levels were given concerning this 'use of torture', the last from the European Court of Human Rights on 1 June 2010 – Grand Chamber, Gäfgen v. Germany (22978/05).

2 *The Foucault Effect: Studies in Governmentality*, ed. Colin Godon, Graham Burchell and Peter Miller (Chicago: University of Chicago Press, 1991).

IV.

COURTS OF LAW: THEIR BUILDINGS, ROOMS AND ACTORS

10

Images of Finnish Justice

Pia Letto-Vanamo

How things used to be: Images from the 1970s

The Finnish court system and judicial procedure underwent significant reforms during the 1990s. The separation of urban and rural courts, deriving from the times of estate-based society, was abolished. An independent prosecution service was established, and also the Courts of Appeal began to arrange oral hearings. In effect, the reforms that had been advocated ever since the beginning of the century were implemented during that one decade. In international comparison, the rate of modernization of judicial proceedings was very slow indeed; the reasons for this were mainly historical. However, today's legal policy, and even the everyday work of the courts, are marked by integration into Europe: Finland's membership in the European Union and Finland's obligations under the European Human Rights Convention.

So many things being different today, it is interesting to take a new look at some photographs taken thirty years ago.[1] Timo Honkanen, a third-year law student and serious amateur photographer, had in 1974 been assigned by the Finnish Lawyers' Association to travel around the country and take photos of Finnish courts. The images were shown in an exhibition attached to a lawyers' event arranged in Kuopio in October of that same year. The exhibition was used to draw the attention of political decision-makers to the sorry state of Finnish courthouses and to the scarcity of the resources allocated to the court system.

However, the images are not merely about buildings and the external trappings of judicial proceedings. At that time, the construction of courthouses with state funds had not yet begun, but Finland was also otherwise quite attached to the old. The images reflect the long traditions of Finnish administration of justice: the traditions and the attitudes of the Code of 1734, an enactment from the days of Swedish rule. The images are interesting also owing to the time when they were taken. The legal policy debates of the 1970s gave rise to many of the reforms that took effect over the following decades, and some reforms, such as the nationalization of the courts, were in fact in progress just at that time. The images have been taken in the summer of 1974 – a time when it was known or at least anticipated that the Finnish court system would change: the images still show how things used to be.

First and foremost, the images published in this article are intended as an illustration of the history of Finnish judicial procedure, and the exceptionally slow disappearance of the archaic forms of adjudication. Elsewhere in Europe, procedural rules had been reformed already in the nineteenth century or in the early twentieth century, as was the case in Sweden. The images show also how little the public purse was opened for purposes of local administration of justice. From the earliest sessions in farmer houses the local *ting* moved to parish halls, community halls, fire stations, etc.

When one looks at images of summary court sessions today, the distance and the passage of time are startling. This is not merely a matter of appearances. Even in improvised premises, the atmosphere in the sessions is often devout and dignified, with the community spirit apparent. In contrast, today's court system, only thirty years younger, is just another set of cogs in the administrative machinery. Notwithstanding the trends of democratization and lower hierarchies, the modern courtroom is marked by the offices and roles of those working there. Legal disputes have become more complex, and the parties almost always speak through experts, that is, their attorneys.

It can also be said that the images relate to a time when the legitimacy

Figure 1: Waiting room with a painting by Albert Edelfelt: 'Governor Vibelius defending the Finnish Law', Espoo Judicial Circuit 1.8.1974.

of justice and judgements arose from the conviction, or at least the assumption, that the courts obeyed the law (laws) and that the law was an expression of the will of the people. Popular control and the common sense of justice were brought into the proceedings by the panel of laymen (in Swedish *nämnd*). In today's 'late-modern society' the legitimacy of legal decisions is more and more often sought elsewhere, *inter alia* from the alternatives to traditional dispute resolution in court.

Most of the themes affecting the court system during the 1970s had in fact been subject to discussion all through the twentieth century. For instance, the 1901 report of the Commission chaired by Professor Rabbe Axel Wrede already contained all of the main ideas that were

Figure 2: *Ting* session 19.8.1974, Iitti Judicial Circuit: judge, two apprentices and seven laymen. Sessions were held in a youth association house.

finally implemented in the 1990s. Moreover, they were also the same ideas that had been put into effect in Sweden in the 1940s, when that court system was reformed, and already during the preceding century in many other European countries.

Starting from the Wrede Commission, almost every decade saw another commission or working group in action – sometimes more than one – pondering the reform needs and models for a court system and procedure that still were based on the Code of 1734. The early proposals were usually the fruit of joint efforts by academics and judges, and largely based on foreign influences. The backlash came in 1939, when harsh criticism was directed against the proposals that far too much emphasis was given to the 'considerable virtues of our domestic tradition'; it was argued that Finland should model itself after Sweden and Norway rather than after Denmark or Central Europe. There was support for the retention of two different forms of court of first instance and for the collective vote exercised by the laymen *(nämnd)* on the *ting*.

Figure 3: *Ting* session 30.7.1974, Halikko Judicial Circuit.

Also at later stages, the comments on, and attitudes towards, the Finnish court system have stressed the importance of holding on to the peasant tradition and national customs. Even in the 1970s, the proposed reforms were not markedly based on international examples. In contrast, in the 1990s many of the reforms, especially on the procedural side, were justified by reference to international developments. More often than not the impetus came from the obligation to Europeanize the domestic system.

Finland has a three-tier court system. In the main, all cases are first heard in the District Courts (Swedish *tingsrätt*). The second instance is the Court of Appeal (Swedish *hovrätt*); at the moment there are six such courts in Finland. The Supreme Court is the highest instance.

The District Courts were established as late as in 1993. The designation derives from Sweden, and is an example of continuity and of change at the same time. In the past, the Swedish rural areas had their *ting* and the towns their local courts (*rådhus-/rådstugurätt*), which after the reforms of the 1960s and 1970s were unified into District Courts (*tingsrätt*). Moreover, this is not merely a lexical matter. The term – like many other legal and political terms – is a conscious reference to a long Nordic tradition, the settlement of disputes by free and independent farmers.

Hence, the *ting* pertains specifically to rural dispute settlement and the self-determination of the peasant communities. Historical sources indicate that already very early the able-bodied and tax-paying men convened to local assemblies (*ting*) to deal with mutual concerns (=things). At first, these assemblies took place outdoors. But no later than in the mid-sixteenth century the meetings had moved indoors, to the house of one of the more wealthy members, offered for this purpose for the duration of the session.

In the towns, the administration of justice was originally a task for the Town Court (*rådhusrätt*). The inhabitants of the town, more precisely its burghers, were represented by a council, which was charged also with adjudicative tasks at the council house or town hall. The town clerk's office took care of administrative matters and the Town Court of adjudication. The latter became professionalized relatively early, with the activities of the Town Court becoming established and regular.

The history of the Courts of Appeal began in the times when Sweden was a great power, and there was a need to make the administration of the realm more effective and more centralized. Administrative reform was pushed forward with the establishment of a number of centralized colleges for various administrative matters and judicial reform with the creation of a set court hierarchy. In 1614, a Court of Appeal (*hovrätt*) was established in Stockholm to see to the king's adjudicative tasks. At the same time, it was ordered that recourse to the Court of Appeal was dependent on the case having first been heard in the lower instance. Before long, there were more Courts of Appeal established in Sweden, for example – as a result of the then prevailing policy of Swedification – in Turku in 1623 and in Tartu in 1630. As appellate instances, the Courts of Appeal were able to monitor and to unify the administration of justice at the local level.

Figure 4: Helsinki Town Court, 1st department session 30.5.1974; three judges (magistrates) and attorneys.

At the same time as the Courts of Appeal were formed as appellate instances, they were formed also as a special forum (*forum privilegiatum*) for the nobility. For the noble born, they were the court of first instance. No less than one half of the members of the court had likewise to be noblemen, the rest being persons learned in the law.

It is generally believed that the establishment of the Courts of Appeal was the first impetus also for the law being approached as a professional pursuit. Even though it took 200 years from the establishment of the Courts of Appeal before a law degree was in fact made a required qualification for judicial office, already the earliest court records contain complex legal arguments and conclusions. The language of the court differed considerably from everyday speech, containing numerous Latin terms and quotations.

The proceedings in the Court of Appeal were in writing; more and more parties found it necessary to retain the services of attorneys. The preliminary drafting of decisions was entrusted to referendaries, and already in the 1630s an apprenticeship system was established in the Courts of Appeal, the system that is in use even today. Young men aspiring to the judiciary, especially as substitute local judges in the countryside, were encouraged to enrol as trainees of a Court of Appeal.

Thus, in addition to its estate-based history, the adjudication of the Courts of Appeal represents a professionalized form of justice. Its history is also that of a civil service culture, with decisions being made on a collegiate basis, albeit under the constraints of rigid bureaucracy and seniority rankings, as well as many other indicators of the internal hierarchy of the members of the courts.

The Royal Supreme Court was established in the Kingdom of Sweden in 1789. During the period of Russian rule (1809–1917), supreme jurisdiction in Finland was exercised by the Governing Council, later renamed as the Senate. Judicial affairs were dealt with by one of the senate divisions, the Judicial Division, which indicates that there was no clear separation of powers in effect in Finland at that time. The independent highest instance, that is, the Supreme Court, was established in 1918.

The power of tradition

It is clear that tradition has constituted one of the barriers to court reform; it has not been at all easy to achieve change in the long history and peculiar characteristics of the Finnish court system.

Early court records show that the focus of the legal process was on the local peasant community. The communities dealt with matters together, in local assemblies (*ting*). The community operated on the basis of oral communication, with documents, or indeed writing, hardly ever being used. All affairs thus became public knowledge as soon as they were introduced in a court session. This is not to say, however, that the community for the consideration of matters of mutual interest and for the dissemination of information would have comprised every person in the locality. Instead, the early *ting* was composed solely of able-bodied and tax-paying males.

The *ting* sessions, held twice or three times annually, were the main

Figure 5: Helsinki Court of Appeal. Working premises for presenting officials 18.6.1974.

Figure 6: Supreme Court of Finland, a chamber session 21.8.1974.

events of the year, and people wished to be present when their affairs, and those of their neighbours, were considered. It was normal that people arrived in numbers to the session – to the *ting* house, its yard or other nearby houses. At the same time, it was evident that being present made a difference. The head of the assembly (Swedish *häradshövding*), or his substitute, the 'law reader' (*lagläsare*), would put questions to the audience, for example on the drawing of property boundaries or the paternity of a child out of wedlock, or inquired into the views of the public, for example on the severity of a criminal penalty or the form in which a penalty should be enforced.

In the mid-sixteenth century, at the latest, a panel of laymen (Swedish *nämnde män, nämnd.* Finnish *lautamies, lautakunta*) had been drawn from among the greater *ting* community. It can be said that these men followed the *häradshövding* from the outdoor '*ting* stones' indoors, around a table on the bench. In early Finnish, *lauta* (plank) means the same as *pöytä* (table), hence *lautamies* could be translated as 'table man'. However, *lauta* is also the same as *penkki* (bench), and the early laymen 'bench men' – referring to the German tradition with the term *Schöffenbank*. The direct translation of the Swedish term *nämndeman* into English would be a man nominated by name.

At first, the panel of laymen (*nämnd*) was used only in the consideration of given types of cases, but later it was designated for the duration of the whole *ting*. At the same time, the composition of the *nämnd* became more established, so that some of the laymen sat on the panel also during the next sessions in the same *ting* district. It is also known that the laymen on the court were normally selected from among the most respected and wealthiest farmers.

The cases in *ting* sessions were either simple criminal cases or civil disputes (relating to the use and ownership of land). Criminal law was act-oriented, with little regard to the motives of the offender. Hence, every misdeed came with a price: A bruise cost three marks, a wound six marks, and the price of manslaughter was forty marks. In most cases, convictions were based on eyewitness reports or confessions. In the absence of a witness or confession, oath taking was the normal procedure. A person suspected and accused (by the plaintiff) of a given

Figure 7: The panel of laymen at the *ting* 1.8.1974, Espoo Judicial Circuit.

act was given the opportunity to deny any responsibility by swearing an oath.

Civil disputes concerned land, that is, the very basis of all economic activity. The disputes were normally decided with the support of assayers or laymen, i.e. by reference to the community. The participation of community representatives in the decision could also legitimize decisions adverse to the parties, and hence make it more likely that the decision would also be observed as good law. Only later would the legitimacy of a judgement become linked to the law and to an independent judiciary applying the law. But during the millennium just started, legitimacy is (again) being sought in the procedure, its appropriateness and 'fairness', as well as in various alternatives to regular court procedure.

Thus, justice in the rural areas was administered by the head of the assembly (Swedish *häradshövding*; circuit judge), who was solely in charge of his jurisdiction, the judicial circuit. In the towns, adjudication was a task for the mayor (Swedish *borgmästare*) and the councillors or magistrates, and more recently the judicial councillors and the municipal councillors in the Town Court. A judicial circuit consisted of several *ting* districts, that is, units where the *ting* sessions were held. Each of the districts also had its panel of laymen, sitting in the *ting* with the judge.

In the larger judicial areas, the judge did in fact embark on a *ting* journey, by loading family, apprentices and paperwork on a sleigh in the beginning of the winter sessions and setting out on a *ting* round. The stay at each of the localities, at the house assigned for the *ting* and for the accommodation of the judge, continued until all the cases had been dealt with. This was the practice well into the twentieth century. The centre point of the judicial circuit was the Registry, located in the municipality where the judge resided, which was where the land law matters of registration of title and mortgages were dealt with.

That the Finnish *häradshövding* system lasted for such a long time is a relative rarity in international comparison. The considerable changes in the system occurred only after the judicial circuits were nationalized, the fee-for-service regime was abolished and the number of judges was increased through the establishment of the positions of district judge. These reforms took place at the end of the 1970s and in the beginning of the 1980s. The final elimination of the differences between urban and rural administration of justice took place as late as in 1993.

It was usual that persons appointed as *häradshövding* had already served for a long time as justices in a Court of Appeal and/or the Supreme Court. Hence, the position as *häradshövding* was the pinnacle of a judicial career. The foremost reason for seasoned judges moving to the countryside to administer justice there was money, more precisely the fees-for-service paid directly to the judges. The income of a circuit judge, even in a small judicial circuit, easily surpassed the income of a justice of the Supreme Court. This remuneration system had the advantage of merited and respected judges seeking positions in the courts of first instance, but there was also a flip side to this particular coin: justices of the Supreme Court, and even presidents of Courts of Appeal, resigned their positions and took on a Circuit Judgeship for lucre, normally to deal with relatively simple cases and to issue land registrations and mortgages.

Figure 8: Registry of the Espoo Judicial Circuit 1.8.1974.

Even though the distanced and patriarchal status of the circuit judge and the formality of judicial procedure were emphasized, there was a lot of variation in the physical circumstances of adjudication. This is because Finland has hardly any courthouse tradition to speak of, and even the courthouses of the City Courts often left much to be desired. In this sense, Finland and Sweden have adopted very different approaches, even though a rule in the 1734 Code of Buildings provided for the construction, financed by the peasants, of court buildings in every circuit. Only with the tradition of office buildings since the 1970s and with the courthouse projects of recent years has Finland begun to approach the Swedish standard.

According to the 1734 Code of Buildings, the courtroom must be a 'houseroom of an adequate size'. Under a Decree issued in 1956, a courtroom was to be designated for each *ting* district, with the location being decided by the ministry of justice. The courtroom was normally in a state office building or in rented premises. Sessions could be held in farmhouses, spas, community halls, farmer's association premises, fire stations and municipal offices – or in one of the few designated courthouses, which normally were in poor condition. Thus, hearings were often arranged in premises that could not be set up so that they looked 'more dignified than usually'. Both seats and tables could be lacking, and parties might have to remain standing for hours on end. The waiting rooms, where everyone arrived in the beginning of the day in court, were often crowded and badly ventilated, with the attorneys conferring with their clients within earshot of everyone else.

The circuit judges were responsible for the rent payable as well as the other costs of operating the Registry, including all wages and salaries other than the salary of the apprentices, who were paid by the state. In addition, the *häradshövding* was obliged to remit a given amount of the fees collected by him to the state. Most of the income of the judge, often more than eighty per cent of it, accrued from real estate matters, that is, registrations of titles and mortgages. The costs and the income varied greatly from one judicial circuit to the other, with the financial result often dependent on how efficiently the judge could organize the work and how much he and his family members participated in the work.

In 1971, the legislation governing the management of judicial circuits was amended so that the transfer of circuit judges to salaried positions became possible. Gradually, the system where the income of the circuit judge was based on fees-for-service was abolished, with all of his salary being paid by the state. The fees were now payable to the state, which undertook to pay for the overhead costs of the judicial circuit and for the wages and salaries of court staff, such as clerks and typists. In a decree issued in 1976, it was expressly provided that state funds could be used for the procurement of office equipment and other goods essential for the appropriate operations of a judicial circuit. That same year, legislation was passed on the nationalization of the City Courts and the city prosecution services. The system of fees payable for court documents was abolished towards the end of the following decade.

The changeover to a salary system was a ten-year process. It brought telephones and copiers, paid for by the state, to the judicial circuits.

Figure 9: Entrance to session rooms, Hollola Judicial Circuit, 26.7.1974.

Figure 10: Room for *ting* sessions, Juva Judicial Circuit 24.7.1974.

The growth in the number of clerical staff began at the same time, followed by unionization and increased training. The process led to the construction of new courthouses as well, but only towards the 1980s.

One of the main themes for the whole of the 1970s was the background of the members of the judiciary: judges were socially and politically distanced from the citizens, which gave rise to a lack of trust in the courts. Attempts to tackle this problem were made for example through reforms of legal education. The final and concrete changes in the recruitment base began with the changeover to a salary system and with the establishment of the positions of district judge (*tingsdomare*). Ever since the 1970s, the number of first instance judges has increased considerably, and at the same time, the proportion of women in the judiciary has begun to rise. In 1950, the Finnish judiciary consisted of 557 judges, 45 of whom were women. In 1970, the corresponding numbers were 699 and 84. And according to the statistics for 1990, the numbers had grown to 1,981 and 914.

However, there are no clear data about the differences of attitudes and conceptions among the current crop of first instance judges and their predecessors. In contrast, a study was carried out in 1995 where district judges were asked about what constitutes a good life and about their relationship to work, money, leisure and family. It was found that, in the main, judges are no different from anyone else in Finland. Also in more general terms, the symbolic self-differentiation of Finns – unlike that of for example the French – is not linked to the formation of social classes over time and to any concomitant values or conceptions. In contrast, the protestant working ethic, a kind of 'pioneer spirit', has indeed been important for the definition of commonly accepted and desired values.

This is not to say, however, that Finnish judges would not be clearly a part of the middle class, characterized by expertise gained through education, and enjoying a respected and legitimate status as a part of the community. It is not uncommon that the profession of the law is 'inherited'; it is only very seldom that a judge would have a working class background.

The many roles of laymen

The original function of the *nämnd* in the court was to represent the rural community and to participate in the settlement of the conflicts arising between members of that community. They were aware of local affairs and knew the local people; the legitimacy of the decision made in the *ting* was largely based on their existence and credibility. With the appreciation of the status of the local judges and the closer identification of the judge with the state judicial authority, the laymen lost some of their stature.

According to the provisions of the 1734 Code of Judicial Procedure, in force until the 1990s, there were seven laymen on the court (of whom at least five had to be present); the laymen had the authority to override the opinion of the professional judge, but only by unanimity. With the unification of the courts of first instance in 1993, laymen were introduced also in the towns. Thereafter, they were markedly lay *judges,* they were given individual votes and subjected to the responsibility of judges. At the same time, the scope of the cases in which the participation of lay judges was expected was narrowed.

As the collective vote of the laymen in the court was considered to make them passive, repeated calls were made for a changeover to individual votes and the subjecting of the laymen to the responsibility of judges. This was finally achieved in 1993. At the same time, it was provided that a lay judge must be a Finnish citizen resident within the jurisdiction of the District Court and between 25 and 62 years of age. The lay judges are elected by the municipal councils, and they should be as representative as possible of the population in the municipality in terms of age, profession, sex and mother tongue.

One peculiarity of the Finnish system is that the layman arrangement has survived for so long. In part, this is a result of the overall slow rate of change in the court system. Many of the reasons have been political, but finances have also played a part: A system composed of circuit judges and laymen did not put much demand on the public purse. Moreover, when discussing laymen, one should keep in mind that systematic judicial training and civil service training began in Finland

Figure 11: Laymen at the *ting* 22.7.1974, Kuopio Judicial Circuit.

in the 1820s and it was as late as 1900 before all of the circuit judges serving in Finland in fact had law degrees.

The growth in the provision of legal education and the growth in the number of lawyers are even more recent phenomena. In part, this is due to the small number of cities in Finland and, as a result, to the lack of urban culture and attitudes. Hence, the traditions and practices relating to justice have been rural in character. The same applies to the image people have of the administration of justice in general.

The communal way of conflict resolution in rural areas, as mentioned above, was of course also in use elsewhere in Europe. In the other European countries, however, the main rule was that a judiciary with an academic education gradually came to supersede the earlier modes of conflict resolution. It was only in the nineteenth century that laymen were again accepted as court members; this was a result of the French Revolution of 1789 and the concomitant dissolution of the Estates and democratization of the society, the courts included.

The same process also took place in Norway and Denmark, but not in Finland or Sweden.

In the latter countries, the participation of laymen in the administration of justice continued without interruptions. Only the justification for that participation changed from time to time. References to local knowledge became fewer, while democracy and popular control gained currency. In the debates of the 1970s, the prevailing arguments pertained precisely to democracy and popular control. In the 1990s, there was certain confusion of argumentation, and in the 2003 Report of the Commission for the Development of the Court System, which emphasized the need for judicial specialization and expert competence, it was proposed that the lay judge system be severely curtailed, and in fact it was only justified at all by reference to its very long traditions.

Folksy character of the procedure

For a very long time, judicial procedure at the local courts was characterized by archaism. The cases were usually not very challenging in terms of the law, and the layman institution emphasized the local character of adjudication. Nonetheless, the judge no longer donned tails in the 1970s, and the sermon preceding the opening of a local session was formally abolished in 1971. Nonetheless, this practice was continued in many judicial circuits on an informal basis. Besides various oaths, the sermon opening the local session was one of the last vestiges of the formalistic tradition in the administration of justice; the forms, as well as early adjudication also more generally, were closely connected to the practice of religion.

Another form of 'sanctimoniousness' was the culture, prevalent until the end of the 1970s, of not justifying court decisions at all or justifying them very pithily. In criminal cases, it was normal to state that 'the Court had looked into the matter and considered' that what had been put forward in the concise charge had (usually verbatim) been proven. Hence, the judiciary could with some justification be compared to the clergy, in the sense that the latter designate certain activities as sinful, but usually do not say why.

Figure 12: Oath of the witness, Iitti Judicial Circuit 19.8.1974.

Moreover, the procedure in the court of first instance was a blend of judicial interventionism and folksy informality. In a sense, the distant and strict 'old man judge' was *paterfamilias*. This status was reinforced both by the nature of the cases before the court and the structure of the decision-making there.

There is no reason to assume that the older generation of judges would not have known the law or for some reason chosen not to obey it. Until the 1970s, legislative changes occurred relatively slowly and the volume of legislation was but a fraction of what it is today. And, moreover, the written law is still today at the pinnacle of the hierarchy of the sources of law. Nevertheless, the issue was more of the dominant position of the ideal of one single correct solution. Nowadays no one believes – in theory or in practice – that there were any one single correct solution; with a number of possible outcomes, the emphasis has shifted to transparency and the supply of proper justification and reasons for the particular outcome reached by the court.

Even though the traditions and the 'folksy character' of Finnish first

Figure 13: *Ting* session 22.7.1974, Kuopio Judicial Circuit.

instance procedure were long a point of pride, the folksiness turned later into a barrier to development and, for instance, a reason for the long delays experienced in the processing of cases. The delays were evident especially in civil cases: Procedure in the courts of first instance had gradually turned into a routine where various briefs and other documents were read out aloud to the court, by persons with varying talents of delivery. It was also common that hearings were repeatedly postponed.

It has been noted above that calls for oral and direct procedure had been made already in the beginning of the twentieth century. One of the early arguments against this idea was the lack of qualified attorneys. At the same time, no effort was made to reform the provisions on attorneys and counsel. A law degree was not required; it sufficed that an attorney was of good character and capable of the task at hand.

The attitudes towards attorneys have been one of the barriers to procedural reform. Finland, together with Sweden, is among those few European countries where a legal qualification has not been required of trial attorneys. At the same time, the legal profession has not had any specific privileges: The professional title *asianajaja* (Swedish *advokat*) is reserved for the members of the Finnish Bar Association, but they have no monopoly of legal services, nor is it compulsory for the parties to retain the services of an attorney in the first place. The historical reasons for this state of affairs lie in the minor significance of the cities and city burghers and in the slow rate of modernization of justice, while the ideological reasons pertain to the emphasis of the yeoman tradition and to the general aversion to retain any sort of expert advisors (lawyers included).

Procedure in the first instance was finally reformed in the 1990s. An oral main hearing is now the norm. There is a specific provision to the effect that 'a party shall not read out or offer to the court any written statements, nor otherwise make his case in writing.' The case shall be dealt with in the main hearing without interruptions. In extensive cases, this has led to a situation where both the judges and the attorneys 'sit' one case for several weeks at a go. The judgement is normally to be pronounced at once after the hearing; there are also new, relatively detailed provisions on the statement of reasons to be supplied as a part of the judgement. In the Courts of Appeal, the procedure was from the beginning written and based on the referendary system. Repeated calls were made for a change to oral procedure. Nowadays, following legislative amendments in 1998, procedure is oral also in the Courts of Appeal.

Note

1 See further: Pia Letto-Vanamo and Timo Honkanen, *Lain nojalla ja kansan tuella/Moments of Finnish Justice in the 1970s* (Helsinki: Edita, 2005).

11

Imagining the Judge

A Case Study of Judicial Portraiture

Leslie Moran

Introduction: Why study images of judges?

It is perhaps a trite point to note the importance of the office of the judge and the significance of the individuals that hold judicial office in general and those in senior judicial positions in particular. Judges continue to play a key role in managing and resolving disputes.[1] Their decisions not only have importance for the individuals involved in the immediate dispute but also have a potential to impact upon wider social and institutional relations within their jurisdiction and beyond. The importance of the senior judiciary is well captured in the suggestion that they are the third branch of government. With these factors in mind why study portraits of judges?

The imagination, I want to suggest, plays a key role in encounters with the judiciary. Face-to-face meetings or observation of the judiciary is rare. Research suggests that when such encounters do take place, for the majority, they are of short duration.[2] Furthermore, in courtroom settings the geography and manners that shape encounters in that location tend to further limit the interaction, positioning the judge as a distant and remote figure. For a few, the imagination mediates the face-to-face encounters. For the majority the imagination is the whole of the encounter.

The written text (rules, books, reports, journals, etc.) and the literary imagination (literary conventions, genres and literacy skills) have long been privileged as the objects and techniques that generate and reproduce ideas of the judiciary.[3] Canonical legal and scholarly texts are largely an elite and a professional cultural form through which the imagination works to produce the encounter with the judge and the institution of judicial office. But they are not the only medium of encounter in that professional context. Various scholars have noted that a much wider range of cultural objects, practices and technologies of representation are used to generate and reproduce legal culture in its formal and professional settings. These include spaces, places and buildings and more specifically their architecture and spatial design, theatre, fashion or dress and sculpture.[4]

Scholarship on law and popular culture adds another dimension. Popular culture, these scholars suggest, plays a key role in the generation and dissemination of ideas and experiences of law and legal systems in general and I would add the judiciary in particular. In this context the cultural objects include novels, magazines, journals and newspapers, films, TV, photography, websites and so on.[5]

Of particular interest here is the growing body of work documenting the importance of visual culture in law.[6] The reasons for this growing interest in the visual image in law are various. Some associate it with a change in the significance of visual culture: the rise of a 'post-literate' society.[7] The impact of visual culture upon day-to-day legal practice, particularly in the courtroom, has been cited as a professionally focused factor influencing scholarly interest.[8] A connected pedagogic rationale aligns a growing interest in the visual image with a demand for visual education and visual literacy skills in legal education.[9] A rather different argument comes from those who have noted the long-standing iconoclastic tendencies within the Common Law that elevates the word while condemning and marginalizing the importance of the visual.[10] As Bruno Latour has noted, iconoclastic periods and projects devoted to the destruction of visual images and the marginalization of the visual have also been intimately associated with an explosion of image production and circulation.[11] But one effect of iconoclasm is not so much the eradication of the visual as an important medium of communication but the establishment and enforcement of a set of taboos that prohibit any formal acknowledgement of the importance of images. These taboos produce the institutional, professional and scholarly invisibility of the visual. While this is not a situation unique to law[12] it is something that has particular importance in law being an institutional, professional and scholarly context in which the written text occupies a dominant position.[13] With regard to this paper, Latour's insights warn against assumptions that legal and professional interest in visual culture is a new or a recent phenomenon. A study of judicial portraits is concerned not only with current preoccupations but also with the longer history of the role of visual culture in making and disseminating ideas about the judiciary.

The judicial pictures at the heart of this essay span the period from 1824 to 2010 and are a set of portraits of the sixteen Chief Justices of the Supreme Court of New South Wales, Australia. This data set includes fifteen painted portraits that represent all but the current Chief Justice displayed in or near the Banco Court,[14] on the 13th floor of the New South Wales Supreme Court building in Queen's Square, Sydney, Australia. It also includes pictures of sixteen Chief Justices found on the website of the Supreme Court.[15] The pictures of the first thirteen Chief Justices are digital photographic copies of the painted portraits. Different photographic portraits are used for the last three Chief Justices. Last but not least the case study includes a pdf file entitled 'Chief Justices of New South Wales' that is found on the Chief Justices website.[16] It contains images of all the office holders including some different images; in particular it includes a photographic portrait of Chief Justice Gleeson (1988–1998) that does not appear elsewhere. Burke suggests that a data set such as this (a series of portraits over a period of time) is particularly valuable.[17] It provides opportunities not only to study the features that the pictures have in common but also creates the possibility of identifying and examining differences between them. Minor changes, Burke suggests, may be indicative of changes of major significance.

Before examining these pictures in more detail my study begins with an examination of existing legal scholarship on visual images of judges.

To date most of this work focuses on images in film and television. My turn to judicial portraiture seeks to provide an antidote to some of the limitations of this scholarship. But only a small body of legal scholarship relates to judicial portraiture. In response to the insights and limitations of this work, I turn to a wider body of art historical scholarship on portraiture. The objective here is to identify some of the key themes of relevance to a study of images of judges. Two sub-genres of portraiture scholarship have particular significance. The first is concerned with portraits of members of particular professions or occupations. The second is a small body of work on 'state' and 'official' portraits. The remainder of the chapter then applies the insights drawn from this review of existing scholarship to the portraits of the Chief Justices of New South Wales.

Existing scholarship on the visual image of the judge

To date legal scholarship on the visual image of the judge is dominated by work on images of law in film and television drama.[18] Noting that 'legal cinema' is ubiquitous in American English-language cinema Ross Levi provides a thematic analysis of the online International Movie Database, using terms such as 'lawyer' and 'jury'.[19] He identified 251 titles with references to 'judge' in the plot line descriptions. While this is not quite equal to the number of 'hits' when using 'lawyers' (he identified 366 titles), it does suggest that judges are significant figures in the genre of 'legal cinema'.[20]

However, the apparent importance of the judge in cinematic plot lines is not reflected in scholarship on law and film. There is little scholarship devoted to the study of the image of the judge in this medium. And work that does address the issue suggests that the judge is a marginal figure.[21] This seems to be an effect of the dramatic and narrative structure of 'legal cinema'. Within courtroom drama (the dominant form of 'legal cinema') the moral dilemmas and the narrative are largely formed and driven by other figures in the drama, in particular those playing the role of the lawyer and the advocate. Character development is also associated with these figures.

Black argues that in courtroom drama the judge is spatially and visually marginal,[22] largely confined to the courtroom, and more specifically the bench, which tends to be in the background or on the edge of the drama. On the rare occasions when judges do stray to other locations, he explains, their institutional characteristics and attributes quickly disappear.[23]

Does this change when TV is added to the analysis? In general the answer appears to be 'no'. Lawyers remain the preoccupation.[24] One possible exception to this is reality TV and court TV in particular. Some scholars suggest that, as a general rule, judges also remain marginal characters in this new format.[25] However, there are some exceptions.[26] The example most frequently cited is *Judge Judy*.[27] Various factors seem to inform this repositioning of the judge. One factor that puts the judge at the centre of the show is the removal of lawyers from the TV courtroom. In *Judge Judy* the parties appear without lawyers. In the absence of lawyers the opportunity and need for judicial management of the proceedings and the parties grows. The character of the judge is a key part of the entertainment. Judge Judy's interventions allow not only for the articulation of the judge's professional and personal understandings of the legal rules and conventions that inform the dispute but also provide an opportunity for the judge to demonstrate her evaluation of the moral, social and political worth of the parties and their disputes. Another important feature of the *Judge Judy* court is that it appears to use a courtroom process that bears little resemblance to the adversarial trial. Christie suggests that the proceedings have been radically transformed and are substantially inquisitorial.[28] This shift is important as she argues that the adversarial courtroom format, which depends upon limiting the judicial interventions, would erase the opportunities for judicial entertainment. Another effect of the inquisitorial style of reality court shows appears to be that it has an impact upon the wider profile of the judge; upon what is 'known' about the judge. Christie explains:

> Unlike actual judicial officers, about whom the public knows very little, Judge Judy is a TV-star. Her private life is a matter of public record…

> Judge Judy as Jewish mother, wife and grandmother is also Judge Judy as decision maker.[29]

This overview of work on the image of the judge in film and on TV suggests that in general the judge is a 'bit part'.[30] As a general rule the popular cultural image of the judge is limited and limiting with little potential for development. Judge TV is a relatively rare exception. It repositions the judge, to the centre of the action and the image. But this appears to be a recent development and one that requires changes to the courtroom process traditionally associated with the Common Law. Are there other and earlier visual formats and other contexts in which the judge is at the centre of the picture?

On judicial portraiture

Judicial portraiture puts the judge at the centre of the visual image. What if anything does legal scholarship tell us about this type of judicial image?[31] The material that does exist is of two types. One is a small group of texts that take the form of short notes published in legal professional journals recording decisions to commission portraits, detailing unveiling ceremonies and the (re)hanging[32] of judicial portraits.[33] These provide some, albeit limited, evidence of the production and use of judicial portraits. Legal historical scholarship is the second type of work making reference to judicial visual images: sculpture, brasses and painting. Here images are used primarily as historical 'evidence' of something else such as judicial dress.[34] Little or no attention is paid to the history or purpose of the judicial image per se. Despite this limitation the work makes a small contribution to the history of images of identified individual holders of judicial office. It suggests that the production of judicial images of named or identifiable individuals is a long-established practice in the English Common Law with its origins in the fourteenth century,[35] probably beginning with effigies and other forms of funeral monument.[36] However, despite this long history little or no scholarship has examined its nature, history or significance. But this far from exhausts scholarship that is relevant to the study of judicial portraits. There is a large body of work on portraiture in general that may be relevant. It is to that literature that I now want to turn.

On portraiture

Various themes within scholarship on portraiture have relevance for the study of judicial portraits.[37] As a general rule the portrait is strongly associated with the empirical.[38] A key objective of portraiture is to produce a likeness of the sitter painted from life. Another key theme of portraiture is truth – the portrait being a true image of the sitter. This includes but is not reducible to the need to reproduce the visible, physical appearance accurately. It also extends to the representation of character and personality. Two particular bodies of work on portraiture have a closer substantive affinity with judicial portraiture. The first relates to portraits of members of professions. The second is concerned with state and official portraits.

Ludmilla Jordonova's work draws attention to the role portraiture plays in the (self) fashioning of professionals as members of a social elite.[39] With particular reference to scientific and medical portraits she demonstrates that a picture of a specified individual has a double function. Not only does the portrait play a role in the construction of the identity of the individual sitter, but it also plays an extremely important role in the composition and construction of a collective and institutional identity.[40] The portrait of the individual is shaped by the ideas, values and virtues associated with the institution and the collective. The portrait makes them visible, public, and accessible.[41] The study of these portraits, she suggests, can tell us much about the status and the values associated with specific groups and institutions and the particular values and virtues that the individual portrayed is identified with and embodies. But the application of Jordanova's insights to judges needs to be treated with some caution, as judges are not merely figures associated with the legal profession. They occupy a very particular position as officers of State. So what can work on 'state' and 'official' portraits add to Jordanova's insights?

Jenkins defines state portraits as 'representations of rulers or their deputies'.[42] Judges, by way of their historical connection with the Sovereign, as the embodiment of justice and more generally as the third branch of government, certainly have the clear potential to fall within the parameters of the phrase 'rulers and their deputies'.

Jenkins argues that state portraits have a specific purpose. It is a genre of portraiture that foregrounds the qualities and characteristics of the office rather than the personality and the character of the individual office holder. These images are not the portrayal of an individual as such but are 'the evocation through [the] image of those abstract principles for which he (sic) stands.'[43] It is also, she suggests, a form of portraiture that resorts to special methods of handling the sitter, using distinctive aesthetic codes designed to give visual form to a particular set of institutional attributes, characteristics, qualities particularly concerned with social and political rank. Charlotte Townsend-Gault notes that one of the effects of this is that these portraits often look 'bland … and so predictable that they are often dismissed as vacuous statements and indifferent art.'[44] But I would echo her suggestions that the former is untrue and the latter irrelevant.

Both Jenkins's and Townsend-Gault's insights suggest that state portraits are not only a highly stylized and formalized sub-genre of portraiture but also one that evidences little change over time. It has also been suggested that state and official portraits are (like all forms of portraiture) subject to change in response to social, political, philosophical and cultural transformations. Schama, for example, explores the impact of the emerging bourgeois model of the family life, respectability and good order upon the image of the British Royalty.[45] Others have tracked changes in the image of the figure of the ruler in the wake of bourgeois and communist revolutions.[46]

Scholarship on professional and official portraits both emphasize the importance of the institutional dimensions of the image. But Rosenblum argues that this should not detract us from the fact that these portraits are also of identified and identifiable individuals:

> However extreme the fictions of portraiture could become … the very idea of a portrait demanded the empirical record of the unique facts of each sitter, an individual to be mistaken for no one else.[47]

Thus while institutional imperatives may dominate these images, the individual is not totally erased. This begs a question about the balance between the institutional demands and the imperatives of likeness and truth strongly associated with portraiture at any one point in time and over time.

Pictures of 'Scarlet and ermine'

A glance at the judicial portraits that make up the case study conveniently collected together in the leaflet entitled *Chief Justices of New South Wales* suggests a considerable aesthetic consistency in the portraits of the sixteen Chief Justices of New South Wales.[48] At times it is difficult to differentiate one from another. These portraits seem to be produced not only according to a fairly rigid visual code but also one that has considerable durability. What are the recurring characteristics?

The repertoire of poses is limited. All, with one exception, are full or three-quarter body portraits. A majority (11) are shown standing. The body of the judge, not the face, dominates the surface of each image. But the preoccupation is not physical likeness – far from it. The sitter's body is largely obscured and overwhelmed. The painted surface is dominated by the robes and other paraphernalia of judicial dress: the voluminous full length scarlet robes, white fur trim, collar and thick cuffs, the white bands, black waist band and sash, white gloves.[49] The sitter's body lies hidden beneath and is little more than a device to hold and display the insignia of office. The striking similarities between the different portraits evidence an enduring preoccupation with the symbols of office.

It is a preoccupation that is enhanced by the representation of the sitter's face. The head and face of the sitter, the part of the body that perhaps most clearly differentiates one sitter from another and has well-established associations with the character and individuality of the sitter, makes up a relatively small part of the image. Furthermore, facial expressions are standardized; all express gravity, a sturdy tranquillity. In these pictures the overwhelming majority wear a judicial wig, for most it is the full bottom wig. This frames and limits the visible face and covers much of the head. Individual characteristics such as hair colour and style, the shape of the face, the ears and so on are largely obscured. These pictures are made using a visual language that negates the quixotic, the particular and the idiosyncratic.

Nor does this exhaust the similarities between the portraits. A majority set the figure of the judge against a dark background with little or no detail visible. It offers little to distract the eye away from the preoccupation with the signs of office. Props, if not absent altogether, are strictly limited. Again this works to orientate the viewer's gaze to the symbols of office that cover the body of the sitter. On the rare occasions when props do appear they invariably take the form of books (sometimes papers and a pen).[50] The book not only symbolizes law but it fashions the sitter's character as the virtue of subordination to the word of the law. This is a life that is shaped by way of its devotion to the letter of the law to the labour of writing the law. This sitter's particular character is made through this association with the word.

Various factors influence the aesthetics found in these portraits. First, the full body portrait is a style of representation associated with images of rulers and other social and political elites. In the first instance, it is a pose associated with the sovereign. The work of Kantorowicz shows that from medieval times any representation of the sovereign's body was not only a representation of the physical/natural body of the one who occupied that position but always also a symbolic representation. The sovereign's image is always an image of a double body.[51] As such the physical body is always also a body that is an image of the virtues and qualities of sovereignty and of the body politic. The full body is the image of the complete sovereign and the totality of the body politics. Pose, clothing/robes, background and props all play an important role in fashioning the meaning that is produced through the personification of power, authority, justice, good order. Scholars of portraiture have documented the way the aesthetic code that was devised for the representation of the sovereign was used in the production of images of other elites both old and new.[52] For the small number of people who made up the elite and who had the necessary economic, political, social and cultural power to commission the production of a portrait this code provided not only a means of fashioning and expressing their own self-image but also a means of displaying their position in society for others to recognize.

The enduring use of these aesthetic codes to depict the judiciary also has another significance. It visualizes the qualities of continuity, timelessness and durability. Repetition fashions the particular qualities of judicial legitimacy. It works to carry the status, values, power and so on from one member of an elite group to another, from office holder to office holder.

Piper suggests that viewing these portraits is more like reading heraldic compositions. Each picture is an assemblage of signs and symbols that communicate information about social status, power and authority. As an aesthetic code dedicated to the portrayal of 'rulers' and their deputies it is perhaps not surprising to find that it is used in the portraits of New South Wales senior members of the judiciary from the nineteenth to twenty-first century. It is a code that enables the senior judiciary to be made not only in the image of the power and legitimacy of the law but also in the image of political and social elites.

I want at this point to return to the face in the judicial portraits. What function does the face play in this context? While the face is a relatively unimportant part of the overall image, its function is not insignificant. The face in portraiture has a long and complex history. In part it is a history of techniques of image making dedicated to reproducing the likeness of the sitter. This has long been problematic as few had the skill to realize it.[53] The judicial face is also affected by political and philosophical factors.[54] The face connects portraiture to the Greco-Roman and medieval traditions of funeral effigies. Effigies as likenesses record the identity of the recently deceased. They also record that subject for eternity. Likeness performs a memorial function in portraiture.[55] However, likeness was not the only objective of this memorial function. The effigy/face is also intended to celebrate the individual as an ideal; as an enduring exemplar. 'Likeness' is mediated by the demands of perfection. While the faces of the judges in the portraits from the nineteenth to the twenty-first century are depicted (by way of light and shade) to produce a face that has depth, detail and complexity, the face is still produced according to the requirements that tend to eliminate signs of imperfection, play down idiosyncrasies, and remove blemishes, in order to portray the judicial sitter's exemplary qualities.

What does the repeated appearance of this aesthetic tradition in the judicial portraits of the Chief Justices of New South Wales tell us about these images in particular and about judicial portraiture more generally? First, it suggests that these portraits draw upon a long-established aesthetic tradition developed to represent social, political and institutional elites in a society. In line with that tradition of self-fashioning the surface of the portrait of each judge shows a preoccupation with the symbols of power, status and authority. The repeated use of the picture formats, poses, backgrounds, props etc. that make up this aesthetic code fashions the body of the office holder according to values and virtues of the institution, of majesty, higher authority, of dedication to the word, of endurance, continuity, consistency, repetition. Individual difference is marginal as each sitter's identity expresses the same qualities and virtues. The sitter's image (including the face) is shaped by the demands of making public the legitimacy of the institution's power. While this might suggest that likeness and individuality have little significance I would suggest a rather different approach is necessary. Likeness and individuality are produced according to the need to form the individual office holder as an exemplar, as an ideal of the enduring values and virtues of the institution he embodies.

Judicial portraits highlight the continuing importance of the long-established association between portraiture and effigies. In New South Wales the painted image of the judge only appears in public after the institutional (metaphorical) death of the sitter: after resignation or retirement. In some instances the memorial qualities of the image have been more literally expressed. The portraits of three Chief Justices, Sir Frederick Jordan, Herbet Evatt and Sir Leslie Herron, were made after the death of the sitters, being created from photographs of the deceased.[56] In part, the function of the judicial image is to inspire and orientate the viewer after the living subject of the image has departed.

But it would be wrong to conclude that the slavish reproduction of this long and elaborate aesthetic tradition totally erases differences between the various office holders. Let me give two examples. The first is the portrait of Chief Justice Kerr who was Chief Justice from 1972 to 1974. His portrait, which has many features in common with the portraits that precede and follow it is distinctive because he is shown holding (rather than wearing) his full bottom wig. How are we to make sense of this difference? One reading of the repositioned wig offered by retired judge Roddy Meagher is that the hand-held wig captures something of Chief Justice Kerr's personality: in this case his vanity. Kerr, Meagher explained,[57] was known to be particularly proud of his full head of hair. Another reading might be suggested by reference to a biographical note that accompanies a reproduction of Kerr's painted portrait in the book *Portraits of the Chief Justices of New South Wales.* During the short period of time that Kerr occupied the post of Chief Justice he played a key role in developing new administrative structures to reduce the developing bureaucratic burden that was affecting the judges. Quoting a fellow judge, Mr Justice Moffitt, Bennett explains, 'The Chief Justice by force of his personality has achieved these results...'[58] The wig in the hand, flouting centuries of tradition, may be a reference to not just the personality of the office holder but the fashioning of that personality as a sign of particular (and maybe changing) qualities and characteristics of the institution: the judicial virtue of strong personality, determination, and superior management skills.

A second example I want to briefly consider is the portrait of Chief Justice Spigelman (below). Again, in many respects this image follows the aesthetic tradition described above. But a more careful examination of the image suggests that such a conclusion is problematic.

The backdrop and the use of props is something of a departure. While this portrait follows the convention of using the book to fashion the character of the Chief Justice, it also makes use of a wider range of props than is to be found in any of the other portraits in this case study. The body of the judge is flanked on his left by a small set of scales

Figure 1: The Honourable Chief Justice Spigelman, Chief Justice from 1998–2011

and (on the right) by a carved figure, a bird that sits on top of the low bookcase. Above, and dominating the background, is a large painting. The painting is of an interior with two Chinese porcelain pieces. At the centre of the painting is a shaped opening (a window?) that looks out onto an oriental garden. The Chief Justice is positioned between the two painted porcelain pieces; a vase with a Chinese design to his right and the figure of a horse to his left. The opening/window and garden scene that frame his head and shoulders is made up of a cascading willow, water, bridge and an oriental building. In part the backdrop and props may tell us something of his keen interest and involvement in the arts. They may also refer to a longstanding interest in things Chinese.[59] Do these aspects of the portrait shift the focus of the image away from the institutional function of the image and towards the portrait of an individual? It certainly seems to be the case that the background detail adds layers of meaning relating to the sitter's character and personality. But I want to suggest that the image still works as an institutional image. The sitter's interest in things Chinese is here portrayed as a virtue of judicial office, maybe symbolizing the judicial importance of cultural awareness and the judicial virtue of sensitivity to diverse social and cultural experiences. While the traditional symbols of the office, and the virtues associated with them, still crowd the image, the change in the minor detail, such as the background and introduction of additional props, may also indicate an attempt to fashion the qualities of virtues of office differently.

Exceptions

If the preoccupation of my analysis so far has been the identification and analysis of the visual language that is common to the portraits that make up the case study, I now want to examine a number of visual 'exceptions'. The first examined under the title 'novelty as tradition' focuses upon a picture of the Honourable Sir Laurence Whistler Street (Chief Justice from 1974 to 1988). In contrast to the other pictures this is not a painted picture but a photograph. It is found in Bennett's book *Portraits of the Chief Justices of New South Wales*,[60] and used on the website of the Supreme Court of New South Wales. It provides an opportunity to reflect upon the impact of the technology of the camera upon the judicial image. A picture of Chief Justice Murray Gleeson (1988–1998) attached to his biographical file on the Court website is the basis for the second 'reflection', this time under the heading 'neo-tradition'.

The pose is radically different from that of the other portraits, being a cropped image that concentrates on the sitter's head and shoulders. Legal robes and props that might indicate his associations with the law are notable by their absence; they are totally missing. How are we to make sense of this very different aesthetic?

Novelty as tradition

The photographic portrait of Chief Justice Laurence Street is not a copy of the painted portrait of him that hangs on the wall above the vestibule leading into the Banco Court. The photographic portrait offers evidence of a different practice of judicial picture making: the photographic portrait. What interests me here is the impact the technology of the camera has upon the judicial image.[61]

There are some assumptions and expectations that painted and photographic portraits share. The first is the empirical quality of the image. Both the photographic and painted portraits of Chief Justice Lawrence

Street are images of that particular individual and both are a record of his existence. But this is also the point at which the two formats begin to separate.

The surface of the painted image tends to display signs of the fabrication of the image, particularly the painter's marks: the brush strokes. This may raise doubts about the empirical aspects of portraiture. Was it painted from life?[62] It may also draw attention to the truth claims of portraiture; how accurate or how manipulated is the painted image of the sitter? Some of the important assumptions about the nature of a photographic picture are captured in the following comment by John Tagg in his study *The Burden of Representation*:

> … there is an existential connection between 'the *necessarily* real thing which has been placed before the lens' and the photographic image: 'every photograph is somehow co-natural with its referent'. What the photograph asserts is the overwhelming truth that 'the thing has been there': this is a reality which once existed…[63]

This, Tagg explains, is the 'realist position' on the photographic image. It draws attention to an approach to photography that emphasizes the strong indexical qualities associated with the picture; that the photographic image is an unmediated record of the thing that is placed in front of the camera. The technology reinforces 'the realist position' by way of its apparent capacity to record objects in minute detail. Thus the photographic portrait appears to be an antidote to the apparent mediations of painted portraits, such as the tendency to idealize the face of the sitter or the manipulation that gives priority to the symbols of office over the idiosyncrasies of the sitter. The realist position suggests that a photographic portrait merely records everything as it is. If this is the case, then the impact of the image maker, the sitter and the commissioning parties on the image may also be affected; they are made redundant or are at best of reduced significance. How do these factors impact on photographic portraits of judges?

To answer that question I want to turn to a collection of photographic portraits of Chief Justice Laurence Street deposited in the State Library of New South Wales. It is made up of thirty-five photographic images of the Chief Justice, all dating from 1974, the time of Street's appointment.[64] While the Library catalogue makes no reference to the name of the photographer the institutional origin of the pictures is identified: the New South Wales Government Printing Office.

The thirty-five images show Chief Justice Street in thirty-five different poses. In some he stands, in others he sits. Sometimes he sits immediately before the camera, sometimes behind a desk. He stands to the side of the desk, by a marble fireplace or by a chair. Sometimes he is located close to the plane of the picture. In others he is more distant. There is less variation in the backdrop (a wall of books). Props are limited (the book dominates). The pose varies: sometimes the book is held close and high on the chest with both hands, sometimes it is lower, just above the waist. Sometimes the pose is more relaxed, with the book to the side of the chest held by just one arm and hand. Sometimes the hands come together without the need for a book. The face also takes on a number of poses. The gaze is to the left or right. Sometimes he gazes directly at the camera/viewer. At other times he looks down. His face tends to adopt enduring rather than quixotic expressions: of calm, tranquillity, reflection, and inner depth. In some pictures he manages a gentle smile, in others a frown. And then there is the question of the use of judicial robes. Scarlet, ermine and full bottom wig make an appearance in maybe half of the images. In others the sitter wears a smart, plain and sober business suit.

This archive of thirty-five photographs problematizes the 'realist' assumptions of photographic portraits of the judiciary. They offer evidence of the process and the compositional work that goes into fashioning the photographic image of the judge. While the photographic portrait of Chief Justice Street does indeed record a single moment in which the sitter appears before the camera, captured in previously unimaginable detail, that single moment depends upon (and needs to be re-connected to) a longer process of picture production and image management involving many social interactions, evaluations and decisions that impact upon the image.

Of particular interest here is the way in which many of the photographic images in this small archive show a clear connection between the different (and relatively new) technology of image production, the camera, and an aesthetic tradition that predates the advent of that technology. Many of the poses, backgrounds, props, facial expressions, hand positions etc. found in these photographic images come from the pre-photographic visual language of judicial portraits. The introduction of a new technology and techniques of representation does not lead to the wholesale abandonment of this earlier aesthetic tradition produced and associated with another type and technology of image production.

Applying these insights to the photographic portrait of Chief Justice Laurence Street, what conclusions can be drawn about the impact of photography upon the image of Chief Justices? One possible conclusion is that the 'new' image is unremarkable; its difference is barely recognizable. It is still an image that forms the subject of the picture according to a visual language that represents the subject as a member of a political and institutional elite. Dominated by the robes of office, the wig, in a well-established pose, playing down the individual and the idiosyncratic to fashion the individual's image conforms to the well-established conventions associated with depictions of the judge as a state official. Certainly in this instance the technology of the camera is made to connect to (and might be said to disappear behind) this older aesthetic tradition. It is put to work to reproduce an aesthetic code that has long been used to produce the image of institutional, political and social elites in a new medium. Tagg suggests that their appearance in photographic portraits may work to attach the 'aura' of the older pictorial tradition (in this instance the painted image) to the photographic image.[65] Rather than abolishing what Walter Benjamin called the 'cult' value of the painted picture,[66] this photographic portrait seems to reproduce it and re-deploy it.[67]

At the same time, this image of Chief Justice Street is also something of a dramatic departure from all of the images in my case study that preceded it.[68] In comparison with all of the earlier images it is unrivalled in its empirical qualities: in its ability to capture the detail of the individual office holder (the shape of his face and hands, in the likeness of his eyes and so on) and the accuracy of the reproduction. But at the same time, the resort to the long-established aesthetic tradition of 'scarlet and ermine' tends to blunt that novelty by way of an aesthetics that makes the individual little more than a mannequin for the display of the symbols of office.

Neo-tradition

The second 'exception' I want to explore centres on the photographic portrait of Chief Justice Gleeson attached to his biographical sketch on the web page dedicated to the Chief Justices of New South Wales. Unlike the painted portrait of Chief Justice Gleeson that hangs in the Banco court or his photographic portrait that graces the *Chief Justices* leaflet, this is a photographic image that does not make reference to the 'scarlet and ermine' tradition. This picture of a Chief Justice uses a very different visual language and composition. The face, not the body, dominates; it takes up over 50 per cent of the surface of the picture. The little clothing that is visible takes the form of a sombre business suit, a white shirt and a conservative tie. There appears to be no references here to the symbols or props of office of Chief Justice in particular or the institution of law in general. The composition and the pose of the face are also different. This is a 'head on' or a 'frontal' pose, not a three-quarter face. The gaze is direct, positioning the viewer at the same level as the sitter: not positioning the viewer below.

The composition, the focus upon the sitter's head and shoulders, is one that art historians associate with 'informal' portraits.[69] Its scale is associated with domestic and intimate spaces and not with public or state matters. The pose emphasizes intimacy, familiarity and closeness between the sitter and the viewer rather than remoteness, distance and hierarchy. The head and shoulders portrait is a pose more associated with the sitter's individual character and personality rather than an office or institution. In good part this is expressed in the importance given to the face. The emphasis upon the face brings together likeness and truth: identification with character and personality.

The use of this picture on the Supreme Court website suggests that the visual language and composition used to make this very different image have official support and currency. Its appearance suggests that some dramatic changes have occurred in expectations and assumptions that relate to the way the office holders are being imagined and presented. Gone are the iconographic conventions that have long been used to represent social and political elites in general and state officials in particular. Gone are the signs that have been used to signify its key qualities and virtues, of durability, legitimacy and permanence, behind which the individuality of the office holder appears to be obscured. The 'new' aesthetics seems to be one that suggests that the individual has a new visibility. It seems to visualize the judge according to new requirements of intimacy, according to new expectations of openness between those who govern and those who are governed. The 'realist' assumptions brought into play by the use of the camera exacerbate the truth of these intimate and individualizing aesthetic characteristics.

But we ought not to forget that this is still an 'official' portrait and as such it is located within a picture making tradition dedicated to the representation of the qualities and virtues of the institution. Now it fashions the judicial subject by way of an aesthetics apparently devoted to making the sitter an individual without reference to the institutional or social position that he might represent. Allard, commenting upon the emergence in the nineteenth century of this intimate and informal style of portraiture in the context of images of important political figures, suggests that the emphasis upon the individuality of the sitter rather than the symbols of office expresses 'democratic and bourgeois principles'.[70] The qualities and characteristics of the institution and the social status attached to the post and the post holders are not, he suggests, missing but are now coded in a different way. Status now has to be represented using a certain discretion. Status is now, '… not so much [what] is shown as the manner in which it is shown that betokens dignity and exemplarity of the illustrious man…'[71] The character expressed in the face of the sitter now carries much of the burden of representing the institution.

Does this emphasis upon the face of the individual reveal more about the office holder as an individual? Historians of photography have noted the importance of the 'head and shoulders' composition, the development and use of the full-face pose, the horizontal gaze, the blank background. All appear in photographic portraiture used to develop the 'sciences' of physiognomy and phrenology, in anthropological projects seeking to establish taxonomies of civilizations, cultures, racial and ethnic categories, in medical and criminological projects dedicated to the identification of the signs of pathology and deviance. It is an aesthetics associated with and designed to fashion not the image of the powerful and the elite in a society, but to produce the image of the weak, the dispossessed and the marginal in society. It is an aesthetics associated with new strategies of governance, with enhanced surveillance and increased subordination.[72]

A feature common to these projects was a desire to capture the individuality of the sitter in order to position the subject of the picture within a grid of meaning that enabled the viewer to differentiate between the normal and the pathological. While the camera appeared to be capable of capturing an abundance of detail, in order to be useful, this detail had to be managed: to be reduced. The head and shoulder composition produces 'more' information by simplifying: by reducing the information. It is a composition that works like a caricature.

The aesthetic that informs the head and shoulder portraits of Chief Justice Gleeson produces something of a paradox. On the one hand, it seems to resort to an aesthetics that was developed to create an experience of intimacy that appears to offer greater insight into the truth of the sitter by way of emphasizing the head and face, suggesting greater openness. At the same time, it resorts to a visual language that generates the identity of the subject by stripping away detail, by reducing the information.

When these insights are applied to the image of a Chief Justice, this leaves us with a conundrum. What does an image informed by the head and shoulder aesthetics communicate about the office of Chief Justice and about this particular office holder? When we look at the cropped photo portrait of Chief Justice Gleeson, what we see, in relation to the other images in this case study, is something of a radical (modernizing) departure. It potentially suggests a new intimacy and a new openness between the judiciary as a powerful political elite and the viewer, the people. It may suggest something of a new emphasis upon the individuality of the office holder as a key judicial virtue and a new way of fashioning the legitimacy of judicial office. Its veracity may also suggest that a new willingness to be public is also a judicial virtue: the idiosyncrasies of the individual's character and personality are not to be smoothed out or rendered obscure by way of the symbols of judicial office. In short, as an aesthetics that is associated with rulers in democratic contexts, its use in making images of judges suggests a change in the way the judicial role and the status of the judiciary is being understood and expressed.

At the same time, it is an image that resorts to a visual language that reduces information. This is a face that has had individual variation taken out by way of standardization. It is made using an aesthetics that 'makes public' by reducing the information it makes public. When used to fashion (to make public) the institution of the judge rather than being a subject that is obscured by the clutter of the 'scarlet and ermine', the individual subject is now obscured in an unexpected manner. The face itself becomes not only the symbol of office (the expression of its qualities and virtues), but it is also the symbol that obscures the individuality of the office holder. The face has become the visual assemblage that does the same symbolic work that in the 'scarlet and ermine' tradition was done by the robes and the books.

Conclusions: Judging the imagination

This is a study of a small sample of judicial portraits. It is an attempt to engage with an aspect of legal culture that has been neglected and more specifically it seeks to open up a new area of legal scholarship about the judiciary. The study of judicial portraiture provides a unique opportunity to examine the aesthetic forms of self-fashioning through which the qualities and attributes of judicial office have been made public at any one point in time and over a period of time. While the sample of pictures discussed in this case study is small and many are remarkably similar, they offer a rich resource. This chapter offers a fragment of an analysis of these judicial images.

This study of judicial portraits suggests that visual culture plays a role in generating the identities of not only those who are the subjects of these pictures but of those who were involved in the commissioning process and those who appear before them. The aesthetics chosen to fashion the image of the various office holders visualize and make public a range of key ideas, values and virtues about law in general and the judge in particular and make them accessible to the various audiences who view these images. Almost all of the images considered in this chapter visualize the Chief Justice according to an aesthetics long associated with representations of the sovereign. They depict the two bodies of the judge, the physical natural body and the symbolic body with priority being given to the latter.

While a key feature of judicial portraits may be their indifference to change, one portrait being almost indistinguishable from all of the others, the aesthetics of judicial images and the technology of image making is changing. Judicial portraits made and displayed before the advent of the camera were exceptional cultural objects produced by and for an elite. While the printing press in general and etchings, prints and so on made these images available more widely, the camera has not only changed the quality of the image but also extended access, making the picture of the judge one that is more readily available for mass circulation. But the potential for mass dissemination of these images does not necessarily mean that their impact will be more widespread. The greater availability of these images is occurring at a time when portraits are not only precious objects that are to be preserved, valued and venerated but are ubiquitous, disposable objects, viewed once, if at all, with indifference and then thrown away. An ironic effect of an epoch defined by way of the rise and rise of visible culture may be the production of an indifference to the visual and the creation of new invisibilities.

This fragment of an analysis suggests that much more research is needed to examine the production, use and circulation of these images. More detailed studies of the history of the use of portraiture by legal institutions, the various legal communities and the individual barristers, solicitors, judges depicted is needed. The preoccupation of this chapter has been 'official' images. This leaves many judicial pictures out of the frame. A detailed study of the different visual cultural formats, etchings, cartoons and caricatures, photojournalism, film, TV,[73] websites etc. is needed to examine the complexity of the visual cultural landscape at any one point in time and over a period of time. Detailed studies of the interaction between the painter and the sitter are another avenue of study that has the capacity to provide valuable insights into the factors that inform the process of (self) fashioning the image of the institution and the institutional character of the sitter.[74] Further work needs to explore the impact of the location of the pictures upon their meaning[75] and the viewer's reaction to the picture meanings. This chapter is merely the beginning of a project to examine the role of visual culture in the production of the idea of the judge that inhabits the professional and public imaginations.

Notes

1 This is not to suggest that the role of judges has not changed. In a criminal justice context, see David Garland, 'The Limits of the Sovereign State: Strategies of Crime Control in Contemporary Society', *British Journal of Criminology* 36, no. 4 (1996), pp. 445–471. And in civil disputes, see for example Mark Galanter '… A Settlement Judge, Not a Trial Judge: Judicial Mediation in the United States', *Journal of Law and Society* 12 (1985), pp. 1–18.

2 Australian research suggests that face-to-face interaction may be short in duration. See Kathy Mack and Sharon Roach Anleu, 'Performing Impartiality: Judicial Demeanour and Legitimacy', *Law and Social Inquiry* 35, no. 1 (2010) pp. 137–173.

3 See in general Peter Goodrich, *Languages of Law* (London: Weidenfeld and Nicholson, 1900).

4 For example, on architecture and the use of space, see David Brownlee, *The Law Courts: The Architecture of George Edmund Street* (New York: The Architectural Foundation, 1984); Paul Rock, *The Social World of an English Crown Court: Witness and Professionals in the Crown Court Centre at Wood Green* (Oxford: Clarendon Press, 1993); Linda Mulcahy, 'Architecture of

Justice: The Politics of Courtroom Design', *Social and Legal Studies* 16, no. 3 (2007), pp. 383–403. On theatre, see Paul Raffield, *Images and Cultures of Law in Early Modern England Justice and Political Power, 1558–1660* (Cambridge: Cambridge University Press, 2004). On dress, see John H. Baker, 'A History of Gowns Worn at the English Bar', *Costume: The Journal of the Costume Society* 9 (1975), pp. 15–27; John H. Baker 'A History of English Judges' Robes', *Costume: The Journal of the Costume Society* 11 (1978), pp. 27–39. On sculpture, see Denis E. Curtis and Judith Resnik, 'Images of Justice', *Yale Law Journal* 96 (1987), pp. 1727–1772.

5 For work on popular culture in generating the legal imagination, see for example Anthony Chase, 'Towards a Legal Theory of Popular Culture', *Wisconsin Law Review* (1986), pp. 527–569; William McNeil *Lex Populi: The Jurisprudence of Popular Culture* (Stanford: Stanford University Press, 2007); Steve Redhead, *Unpopular Culture: The Birth of Law and Popular Culture* (Manchester: Manchester University Press, 1995); Richard Sherwin, *When Law Goes Pop: The Vanishing Line between Law and Popular Culture* (Chicago: University of Chicago Press, 2000). Work on the judiciary focuses upon courts and the print media. See Florian Sauvageau, David Schneiderman and David Taras, *The Last Word: Media Coverage of the Supreme Court of Canada* (Vancouver: University of British Columbia Press, 2006); William Haltom, *Reporting on the Courts: How the Mass Media Cover Judicial Actions* (Chicago: Nelson Hall, 1998).

6 For example see Costas Douzinas and Lynda Nead (eds.), *Law and the Image: The Authority of Art and the Aesthetics of Law* (Chicago: University of Chicago Press, 1999).

7 John Denvir, 'Introduction to Special Issue on "Legal Reelism"', *Legal Studies Forum* 15, no. 3 (1991); R. Sherwin, *When Law Goes Pop*; Richard Sherwin, Neil Feignenson and Christina Spiesel, 'Law in the Digital Age: How Visual Communication Technologies are Transforming the Practice, Theory and Teaching of Law', *Boston University Journal of Science and Technology Law'* 12, no. 2 (2006), pp. 227–270.

8 For example there is a growing body of work on the use of photography, powerpoint, video, and digital images in trials. See Katherine Biber, *Captive Images: Race, Crime, Photography* (Abingdon: Routledge, 2007); Jessica M. Silbey, 'Judges as Film Critics: New Approaches to Filmic Evidence',

University of Michigan Journal of Law Reform 37, no. 2 (Winter 2004), pp. 492–571; Jessica M. Silbey, 'Filmmaking in the Precinct House and the Genre of Documentary Film', http://lsr.nellco.org/suffolk/fp/papers/20 (2005).

9 Philip N. Meyer, 'Visual Literacy and the Legal Culture: Reading Film as Text in the Law School Setting', *Legal Studies Forum* 17, no. 1 (1993), pp. 73–94; Richard Sherwin, Neil Feignenson and Christina Spiesel, 'Law in the Age of Images: The Challenge of Visual Literacy', in Anne Wagner, Tracey Summerfield, Farid Samir and Benavides Vanegas (eds.), *Contemporary Issues of the Semiotics of Law: Cultural and Symbolic Analysis of Law in a Global Context* (Oxford: Hart Publishing, 2005), pp. 231–255.

10 Peter Goodrich, *Languages of Law.*

11 Bruno Latour, 'What Is Iconoclash? Or Is There a World beyond the Image Wars?', in Peter Weibel and Bruno Latour (eds.), *Iconoclash – Beyond the Image-Wars in Science, Religion and Art* (Karlsruhe and Cambridge, MA: ZKM and The MIT Press), pp. 14–37.

12 On the resistance to images in historical scholarship, see Peter Burke, *Eyewitnessing: The Uses of Images as Historical Evidence* (London: Reaktion, 2001).

13 It has perhaps had a particular impact upon legal research. For an overview of work on images in criminological and sociological scholarship on criminal justice, see Robert Reiner, 'Media-Made Crime', in Mike Maguire, Rod Morgan and Robert Reiner (eds.), *Oxford Handbook of Criminology* (Oxford: Oxford University Press, 2007), pp. 302–337.

14 While there is artwork in the other public areas the only other public location of judicial portraits is the President's Court on the 12th floor with three portraits of past Presidents: Sir Frederick Jordan, Sir Bernard Sugarman and Justice Michael Kirby.

15 http://www.lawlink.nsw.gov.au/lawlink/supreme_court/ll_sc.nsf/pages/SCO_chiefjudges (last accessed 03/10/10).

16 http://www.lawlink.nsw.gov.au/lawlink/supreme_court/ll_sc.nsf/vwFiles/ChiefJusticesReduced.pdf/$file/ChiefJusticesReduced.pdf (last accessed 03/10/10).

17 Peter Burke, *Eyewitnessing*, p. 28.

18 Key texts in this field of scholarship include: Anthony Chase, *Movies on Trial: The Legal System on the Silver Screen* (New York: New Press, 2002); John Denvir, *Legal Reelism: Movies as Legal Texts* (Urbana: University of Illinois Press, 1996); Steve Greenfield, Guy Osborn and Peter Robson, *Film and the law* (London: Cavendish, 2001); Robert M. Jarvis and Paul R. Joseph (eds.), *Prime Time Law: Fictional Television as Legal Narrative* (Durham: Carolina Academic Press, 1998); Leslie Moran, Emma Sandon, Elena Loizidou and Ian Christie (eds.), *Law's Moving Image* (London: Cavendish, 2004); Barbara Villez, *Series tele: visions de la justice* (Paris: Presses Universitaires de France, 2005).

19 Ross Levi, *The Celluloid Courtroom: A History of Legal Cinema* (Westport: Prager, 2005).

20 Ibid. Other scholars have also noted the dominance of lawyers in 'legal cinema' plot lines. See *Picturing Justice* http://www.picturingjustice.com/

21 Ross Levi, *The Celluloid Courtroom*, and J. Howard Sundermann Jr., 'Judges in Film', *Picturing Justice: The On-line Journal of Law and Popular Culture* (2002), <http://www/usfca.edu/pjjudges_sundermann.htm (last accessed 24/11/08). Papke suggests that this state of affairs is changing in the US, see David Papke 'From Flat to Round: Changing Portrayals of the Judge in American Popular Culture', *Journal of the Legal Profession* 31 (2007), pp. 127–151.

22 David A. Black, 'Narrative Determination and the Figure of the Judge', in Michael Freeman (ed.), *Law and Popular Culture,* Current Legal Issues 7 (Oxford: Oxford University Press, 2005), pp. 677–687 at 678.

23 For an example where this does not occur, see Leslie J. Moran 'Projecting the Judge: A Case Study in the Cultural Lives of the Judiciary', in Austin Sarat (ed.), *Law and Film: Essays on the State of the Field,* a special edition of *Studies in Law, Politics and Society* 46 (2008), pp. 1–24.

24 For example see Robert M. Jarvis and Paul R. Joseph (eds.), *Prime Time Law* and Michael Asimow (ed.), *Lawyers in Your Living Room!* (Chicago: American Bar Association). Asimow's collection includes a section on television judges reflecting the changing profile of the judge on television.

25 Chuck Kleinhans and Rick Morris 'Court TV: The Evolution of a Reality Format', in Susan Murray and Laurie Oullette (eds.), *Reality TV: Remaking*

Television Culture' (New York: New York University Press, 2004), pp. 157–175.

26 Taunya Lovell Banks, 'Will the Real Judge Stand-up: Virtual Integration on TV Reality Court Shows', *Picturing Justice: The On-Line Journal of Law and Popular Culture* (2003), http://www.usfca/pj/realjudge_banks.htm (last accessed 25/11/2008).

27 Steven A. Kohm, 'The People's Law Versus Judge Judy Justice: Two Models of Law in American Reality-Based Courtroom TV', *Law and Society Review* 40, no. 3 (2006), pp. 693–728.

28 Suzanne Christie, 'Judge Judy: The Courtroom as Classroom', *Australian Feminist Law Journal* 13 (1999), pp. 86–97 at 87.

29 Ibid., p. 92.

30 The Civil law tradition, some scholars suggest, may provide opportunities for the judge to be a more important character. See Orit Kamir, 'Feminist Law and Film: Imagining Judges and Justice', *Chicago Kent Law Review* 75 (1999–2000), pp. 889–931.

31 See Leslie Moran, 'Judicial Portraits', *Portrait* 24 (Winter 2007), National Portrait Gallery, Canberra. On other legal portraits, see Peter Goodrich, 'Looking at the Overlooked: Portraits of Law School Deans', *Buffalo Law Review* 54 (2006), pp. 833–861.

32 Re-hanging tends to be associated with new court buildings.

33 For example, see 'The Right Honourable Sir Harold Barrowclough CJ', *The New Zealand Law Journal* (18 July 1967), pp. 300–303; 'Judicial Portraits', *New Zealand Law Journal* (April 1991), pp. 122–124; and William W. Scott, 'Roster of Judges of the Supreme Court of Appeals of Virginia 1779–1919', *Virginia Law Register* 5 (1919), pp. 185–188; Michael Kirby, 'On the Presentation of a Portrait by Josonia Palaitis' (2007), http://www.hcourt.gov.au/speeches/kirbyj/kirbyj_19nov07.pdfhttp://www.artafterhours.com.au/v1/content/29_mar_06/kirby_talk (last accessed 12/12/07). Mr Justice Michael Kirby has written about his experiences as a sitter: Michael Kirby, 'Judges and Art', *New South Wales Bar Association, Bar News* (2006): 51–54, and 'Hanging Judges and the Archibald Prize', *Media and Arts Law Review* 11, no. 3 (2006). The portrait in question can be viewed on the artist's website: http://www.jpstudio.com.au/galleryAll.php#85 (last accessed 03/10/10).

34 On visual images as evidence in historical scholarship, see Burke, *Eyewitnessing*. For examples of legal scholarship, see Baker, 'A History of Gowns Worn at the English Bar' and 'A History of English Judges' Robes'; John H. Baker, *The Order of Serjeants at Law* (London: Selden Society, 1984); William N. Hargreaves-Mawdsley *A History of Legal Dress in Europe until the End of the 18th Century* (Oxford: Clarendon Press, 1963), especially chapter 3.

35 Baker, 'A History of Gowns Worn at the English Bar' and 'A History of English Judges' Robes'.

36 Seals are another early form of judicial image. See Paul Brand, 'Stanton [Staunton] Hervey', *Oxford Dictionary of National Biography* (Oxford: Oxford University Press, 2006), http://www.oxforddnb.com/view/article/26326 (last accessed 24/11/08).

37 For an introduction to key themes of work on portraiture, see Richard Brilliant, *Portraiture* (London: Reaktion, 1991); David Piper, *The English Face* (London: Thames Hudson, 1957); Shearer West, *Portraiture* (Oxford: Oxford University Press, 2004); Joan Woodall (ed.), *Portraiture: Facing the Subject* (Manchester: Manchester University Press, 1997).

38 John Pope-Hennessy, *The Portrait in the Renaissance* (New York: Phaidon, 1966).

39 Ludmilla Jordanova, *Defining Features: Scientific and Medical Portraits 1660–2000* (Reaktion: London, 2000). Other work that engages with portraits of professionals includes Brilliant, *Portraiture*, and J. Ingamells, *The English Episcopal Portrait 1559–1835* (London: Paul Mellon, 1982).

40 Jordanova, *Defining Features*, pp. 14–15.

41 Ibid., p. 73.

42 Marianna Jenkins, *The State Portrait: Its Origins and Evolution* (USA: College Art Association, 1947). For a more general introduction to the image of the King, see Ernest. H. Kantorowicz, *The King's Two Bodies* (Princeton: Princeton University Press, 1957).

43 Jenkins, *The State Portrait*, p. 1.

44 Charlotte Townsend-Gault, 'Symbolic Facades: Official Portraits in British Institutions since 1920', *Art History* 11, no. 4 (December 1988), pp. 511–526 at 511–512.

45 Simon Schama, 'The Domestication of Majesty: Royal Family Portraiture, 1500–1850', *Journal of Interdisciplinary History* 17 (1986), pp. 155–183.

46 See Burke, *Eyewitnessing*, pp. 69–71.

47 Robert Rosenblum, 'Portraiture: Facts versus fiction' in *Citizens and Kings: Portraits in the Age of Revolution 1760–1830* (London: Royal Academy Publications), pp. 14–24 at 22.

48 The leaflet should be used with some caution. The images are edited: cropped. This affects their overall composition.

49 In the main the robes are the ceremonial robes associated with the office. There is one exception to this. The portrait of Chief Justice Herron shows him in the scarlet silk robes worn in everyday criminal proceedings.

50 On the book see Peter Goodrich, 'The Iconography of Nothing: Blank Spaces and the Representation of Law in *Edward VI and the Pope*', in Douzinas and Nead, *Law and the Image*, pp. 89–116.

51 Kantorowicz, *The King's Two Bodies.*

52 Piper, *The English Face.*

53 David Hockney, *Secret Knowledge: Rediscovering the Lost Techniques of the Old Masters* (London: Thames and Hudson, 2006).

54 Pope-Hennessy, *The Portrait in the Renaissance.*

55 The death mask was one technique used to make the effigy a 'likeness'.

56 John M. Bennett, *Portraits of the Chief Justices of New South Wales 1824–1977* (Sydney: J. Ferguson, 1977), p. 5.

57 Interview transcript Roddy Meagher 17/04/07 on file with the author.

58 Bennett, *Portraits of the Chief Justices*, p. 61.

59 During the course of his swearing in ceremony reference was made of his involvement (while still at school) in establishing an Asian Society to promote dialogue between Chinese and non-Chinese students. See The Honourable J W Shaw QC MLC Attorney General Of New South Wales, 'Swearing in ceremony of the Honourable J J Spigelman QC as Chief Justice of The Supreme Court of New South Wales', 25 May 1998, http://www.agd.nsw.gov.au/lawlink/supreme_court/ll_sc.nsf/pages/SCO_speech_spigelman_250598

60 Bennett, *Portraits of the Chief Justices.*

61 Other key questions relate to the history and contemporary use of photographic images of the judiciary.

62 The painted portraits of Sir Frederick Jordan, Herbert Evatt and Sir Leslie Herron were made after their death from photographs. See Bennett, *Portraits of the Chief Justices*, p. 5.

63 John Tagg, *The Burden of Representation: Essays on Photographies and Histories* (Basingstoke: Macmillan, 1998), p. 1.

64 The images can be accessed from the State Library of New South Wales at http://www.sl.nsw.gov.au/

65 Tagg, *The burden of representation*, p. 57.

66 Walter Benjamin, 'The Work of Art in the Age of Mechanical Reproduction', in *Illuminations* (London: Fontana Press, 1973), pp. 211–245.

67 Bruno Latour and Andrew Lowe, 'The Migration of the Aura, or How to Explore the Original through Its Facsimiles', in Thomas Bartscherer and Roderick Coover (eds.), *Switching Codes: Thinking through Digital Technology in the Humanities and the Arts* (Chicago: University of Chicago Press, 2011), pp. 1–13

68 I am not suggesting that this is the first photographic image of a Chief Justice of New South Wales. See the picture collection of the State Library of New South Wales for earlier photographs.

69 Piper, *The English Face*, p. 161.

70 Sébastian Allard, 'The Status Portrait', in *Citizens and Kings: Portraits in the Age of Revolution 1760–1830* (London: Royal Academy Publications, 2006), pp. 80–109 at 82.

71 Ibid., p. 83.

72 Tagg, *The Burden of Representation*, p. 5.

73 Moran, 'Projecting the Judge'.

74 Leslie J. Moran, 'Judicial Bodies as Sexual Bodies: A Tale of Two Portraits', *Australian Feminist Law Journal* 29 (2008).

75 See Marcia Pointon, *Hanging the Head: Portraiture and Social Formation in Eighteenth-Century England* (New Haven: Yale University Press, 1993). See Leslie J. Moran, 'Facing the Judge', *International Journal of Law in Context* (forthcoming 2011), pp. 61–80, for an analysis of the impact of context on the meaning of the portraits studied here.

12

This Is Not a Courthouse

Eva Löfgren

> [...] architecture, like all other cultural objects, is not made just once, but is made and remade over and over again each time it is represented through another medium, each time its surroundings change, each time different people experience it.[1]

Introduction

Since 1971, when the organization of the Swedish district courts was restructured, law court buildings and courtrooms have thoroughly changed appearances. Both the court institution and its accommodation have become more anonymous, some would say less intimidating, others less imposing. Today, most of us will never enter a court, and probably do not even know where it is located. The building of new courthouses is mainly a matter involving the developer and the architect. The National Courts Administration is responsible for providing the premises, but the buildings are let on the market and courthouses are neither publicly built nor publicly owned. There are standards which determine the design, primarily relating to security and working conditions, and as reliable tenants with particular needs the courts are considered self-evident participants in the planning of their new premises. The average citizen, though, is in no way involved in the process.

Historically, however, the situation was quite different. Between 1734 and 1970, according to the law code of 1734, the inhabitants of the judicial circuits of the Swedish rural areas were responsible for the building and maintenance of the local courthouse and jail.[2] The rural circuit courthouse, from now on referred to as 'courthouse', was to contain 'a hall [courtroom] as large as required and two [small] rooms' and there also had to be a jail where 'malefactors could be held'.[3] There are several reasons to believe that, unlike today,[4] there was a shared and consistent conception of what a courthouse should look like during the main part of this period. First of all, the local communities acted as both builders and property-owners, initially even as the actual workmen. Secondly, if we compare the drawings from the period, the architecture of all courthouses seems very similar.

In this article my aim is to examine what constituted a courthouse in the late eighteenth century. The subjects of the case-studies are Mönsterås courthouse in the south-east, and Kållängen in the south-west of Sweden, but other buildings will be used for reference and comparison. As for my choice of period, 1770–1820, seventy-five new courthouses were built during this time, generating a great wealth of unique drawings which make up eminent source material.[5] The majority of these early purpose-built courthouses were built in the counties south of Stockholm while the sessions of most of the northern judicial circuits were still seasonal. Since my focus in this article is on the purpose-built court accommodations, I will only discuss the courthouses of the southern counties. I am interested in finding out whether at this time there existed a shared conception of a courthouse, and if so, what kind of building was considered suitable for the function. What did the transformations from conception to reality look like and what knowledge can be garnered regarding the everyday life in and around the buildings? I will approach the questions from three perspectives: the stage of conception, the building stage and the buildings while in use.[6] By looking at the courthouses from these different directions, I wish to stay close to the notion that architecture should be regarded as a process and not as a static object or as a given result of a certain society or legal system.

The law of 1734: Conception of a spatial structure?

When examining the Building Code, ch. 26 sect. 4, of 1734, and considering the meaning of the formulation: 'a hall [courtroom] as large as required, and two [small] rooms', the question is whether the law refers to an actual building tradition. The fact that the exact same wording can be found in the corresponding section specifying the design of the vicarage seems to suggest that it had a specific purport related to a concrete, existing situation at the time. Even though the preparatory works of the law, from the late seventeenth and early eighteenth century, do touch on the courthouse section, there is no reference to the formulation specifying the number of rooms or the spatial structure.[7]

Today, many legal historians claim that the law of 1734, in its entirety, should be construed as a codification of practice, with particular reference to the appeal courts.[8] The aim of the law was systematization, not invention, and if we look for its models we must turn to the medieval laws.[9] Whether this means that the courthouse section laid down an already established tradition is difficult to assess and the sources point in different directions.[10] First of all there seems to have been both single hall buildings and courthouses with *more* than two rooms in addition to the courtroom. Secondly, it appears that the oldest courthouses were of the single hall type, known as 'court barns'[11] built without an antechamber, and that the customary division of the building into several separate rooms is a more recent development. In other words, there seems to have been courthouses with the spatial structure established in the law paragraph, but they appear to be the exception rather than the rule.

As I interpret the formulation of the law, it was intended to codify a spatial structure which had recently begun to appear.[12] The hall, or courtroom, referred to a room which was big enough to accommodate the rural circuit court, a group of fourteen men (the judge, the twelve lay assessors and the clerk), as well as the parties concerned, witnesses and the audience. The vagueness of the wording 'as large as required' may be read as a possibility for the controlling representatives of the Crown to demand larger premises to dovetail with the needs of the court. As for the two (small) rooms, professor of legal history Kjell Å Modéer suggests that the formulation should be interpreted as a reference to the dualistic relation of the judge and the panel of lay assessors.[13] From the point of view of the spatial structure, it can be argued that the wording reveals a courthouse conception which embraces other functions than as a courtroom. With the court came certain activities or needs requiring separate rooms, and thus the conception slowly came to imply more than a court-*session*-house. What I suggest is that the law of 1734 constituted a step towards a conception of the courthouse as a building containing not only different functions, but also different functional zones.

The drawings of the Superintendent's Office

As it turned out, courthouses built during the eighteenth century did not contain only a hall and two rooms, they were both built and perceived as much larger buildings. During the latter part of the eighteenth century, the Superintendent's Office in Stockholm was given the task of providing the judicial circuits with proper courthouse designs.[14] In 1776, a central decree established that all public buildings were to be built of stone or brick and the designs be approved by the government (the Crown), which referred the matter to the Superintendent's Office for consideration.[15] Courthouses were included under the decree since they were publicly financed.[16] Following the common procedure, a local public officer wrote to the Superintendent's Office on behalf of the inhabitants of the judicial circuit, requesting a drawing based on their expressed wishes. Information regarding measurements, construction material, number of rooms and their functions was included in the letters but the exact architectural design and the details were rarely defined. After a remarkably short period of time, the judicial circuit received a set of drawings, usually drawn on a scale of 1:140–1:170 and containing a plan, facade and section. The drawings were schematic and allowed local interpretation and solutions.

The law stipulated that the courthouse should be located 'where it was usually located' ('å vanlig tingsstad') but it did not specify on what kind of ground. As for the building site, the judicial circuits gave no information and the Superintendent's Office made no commentaries on the character of the locality intended for the courthouse. The letters of the circuits lack site plans and there are no documented discussions on the matter in the records of the Superintendent. Obviously, their courthouse conception did not encompass a certain kind of locality, such as a hill, secluded grounds or a church green. The Superintendent's Office appears to have been concerned with the actual shape of the building solely, but whether it was built next to the stables or in the middle of the fields was not an issue.

It seems reasonable to suggest that the drawings present the notion of the Superintendent's Office as to what a courthouse was, or should be. Certainly, the architects had the requests of the inhabitants to consider, but even when setting out from their wishes, they could still have created other spatial structures, designs and building types. There are some fifty Superintendent's Office drawings still in existence, and on closer examination they all turn out to have courthouses designed as small mansions.[17] These are classicist, symmetrical, one-storey buildings, the structure of which were originally inspired by French palace architecture and contain one large central hall for court sessions, a small antechamber and two or three rooms on each side of the courtroom.[18]

However, at the same time as the drawings seem to represent the conception of the Superintendent's architects, there is other source material implying that the conception was more widespread. Although the designs of the Superintendent's Office influenced the architecture of many parts of the country and thus the notions of what was suitable for different functions, I would suggest that the initiative to build courthouses with the structure and appearance of a mansion was also coming from the judicial circuits. Whether it emanated from the actual farmers is difficult to assess, but judging from the documents which describe the courthouse discussions, I am inclined to think that it did.

Mönsterås 1795–1800: Conception stage and courthouse building

In 1795, the Superintendent's Office received a letter and a project design from the small market town of Mönsterås.[19] The cover letter contained no mentioning of a stone construction and as most judicial circuits at the time, the inhabitants of Mönsterås appear simply to have ignored the decree of 1776 when first announcing their building project to the Office.[20] The procedure seems to be confirmed by the fact that very few of the petitions and letters regarding courthouses that are filed in the archive of the Superintendent's Office contain comments on the decree.

The Mönsterås drawing was clearly made by an amateur and intended to convey an idea rather than a precise form. From the cover letter we know that the inhabitants requested a revised design to be carried out according to the proposed dimensions, proportions, materials and number of rooms.[21] The drawing shows a symmetrical plan with a centred main entrance and two windows on each side, a low hipped mansard roof, and a spatial structure containing four rooms assembled around a large centre hall and a small antechamber. The rooms are named courtroom, antechamber, clerk's room, judge's room, kitchen, and the last and rather uncommon term 'larder', or housekeeper's room. This drawing indicates that the inhabitants of Mönsterås were concerned about the design of their courthouse, and not only about the materials and number of rooms, they also had a precise spatial structure in mind as well as a specific roof truss.[22] Their conception of what a courthouse should look like did in principle coincide with that of the Superintendent's Office.

In 1797, the final designs and written plan for the courthouse at Mönsterås were approved by the Crown and the contract to build the courthouse was put out to tender ('entreprenadauktion').[23] About three years later, in August 1800, the courthouse was finished and inspected.[24] This was a well-proportioned, symmetrical timbered one-storey building with a furnished attic, located in a mild incline above the main road on the south side of the small town. Unlike most courthouses built during the period, this one had a fairly large cellar. The walls had no panelling, but the timber was painted red according to the custom, and

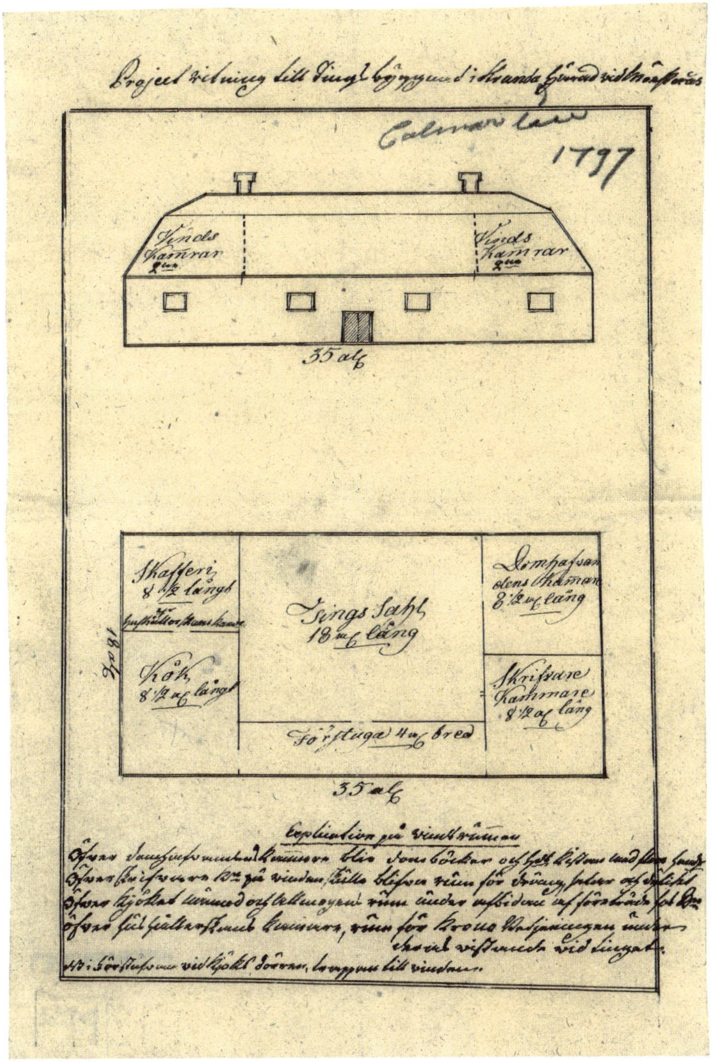

Figure 1: Drawing proposal of Mönsterås courthouse, 1797, made by an unknown talent. The lines below the drawing can be translated as follows: 'Above the judge's room are court records and the chest of the judicial circuit. Above the clerk's room in the attic is a room for farm-hand, fodder [or things, or sacks] and such. Above the kitchen, lay assessors and peasantry while waiting for the court [under afbidan af företräde hos Rn (Rätten)]. Above the house-keeper's room, room for the representative of the Crown when staying at the sessions. In the antechamber, by the kitchen door, the stairs to the attic.' Överintendentsämbetets arkiv (archives of the Superintendent's Office), Riksarkivet (the National Archive).

in his report, the surveyor remarks favourably on the mouldings.[25] The curb roof was covered with a double layer of birch-bark, then boarded and given a coating of tar. Centred on the south-west facade was the main entrance, with two large windows on each side of the decorative double leaf door. The north-east facade had six windows of which the four in the middle were adjacent to one another, thus indicating the position of the courtroom. As to the dimensions, the exterior measured 21 by 10.5 metres and the courtroom 10.5 by 6.9 metres, corresponding to many other courthouses constructed at the time.[26]

The spatial structure proposed in the sketchy proposal of 1797 was also the one that had been realized, but when it comes to the exterior design of the building, there were a few discrepancies.[27] The size and number of windows proposed in the sketch had been doubled in the actual building. Hence, every room had at least two windows and the

Figure 2: Mönsterås in 2007. Notice the extension of the courthouse, which forms the right part in the photograph and alters the proportions and symmetry of the late eighteenth-century building. Since the early 1970s the building has functioned as the public library. Photo: Claus Kempe, Mönsterås kommun.

courtroom had four, which of course made a great difference for the conditions during the hours of daylight. The drawing also showed a mansard roof with hipped top slope, while the realized roof was only curbed. There is reason to believe that the hipping of roofs had become a somewhat old-fashioned aesthetic ideal, but the deviation may also have been a result of difficulties related to the practical geometry of a both curbed and hipped construction.[28] During the first half of the eighteenth century, courthouses were often built with gable or hipped roofs. The mansard roof of the latter half of the century was not only an aesthetic ideal but also meant that the courthouses could have rooms on different storeys as it permitted gable rooms with windows and full ceiling height in the attic. The convenience of being able to put some of the rooms, and functions, on a second floor was thoroughly emphasized by the Superintendent's Office's architects.

To sum up the judicial circuit's courthouse conception compared to the realized building at Mönsterås, first of all, the decree requiring a stonehouse was not even discussed by the circuit, nor was it mentioned in the letters to the Superintendent's Office. A timbered construction seems to have been the only alternative ever considered. The conception conveyed by the sketchy drawing is that of a mansion. Yet, the building appears as what might be called traditional; the raw timber construction was painted red (as opposed to white or yellow which imply a more expensive oil-paint) and the boarded roof had a tar-coating.[29] In other words, the realization of the conceived courthouse set out from an established building tradition belonging to common people.

Kålländen 1783–87: Conception stage and courthouse building

My second case is situated in the south-west of Sweden. In the early 1780s, the old courthouse in the hamlet of Kålländen was in a state of dilapidation and the county sheriff raised the question of reconstruction at the ordinary court session.[30] As a result, the inhabitants of the judicial circuit[31] appointed a builder to examine the courthouse and suggest improvements. The (unique!) measurement drawing completed by the builder and the minutes from the court's discussion of the issue show that the old house was a large stone building with a huge hipped roof. What is indeed interesting is that the structure consisted of an antechamber, a central court hall, another five rooms and finally a kitchen – that is, the same spatial structure as the larger ones made by the Superintendent's Office. The measurement drawing seems to explain why the inhabitants proposed such a structure for their new house: it was established as a part of their courthouse conception.

The builder's first suggestion was to reduce the old courthouse by tearing down the north-facing front wall, thus removing the kitchen and the dining room and create an 'ordinary courtroom, four rooms and an antechamber'.[32] What was *ordinary* about the suggested courtroom is not specified in the court records, but judging from the new designs, it was smaller than the older room, square instead of rectangular, and

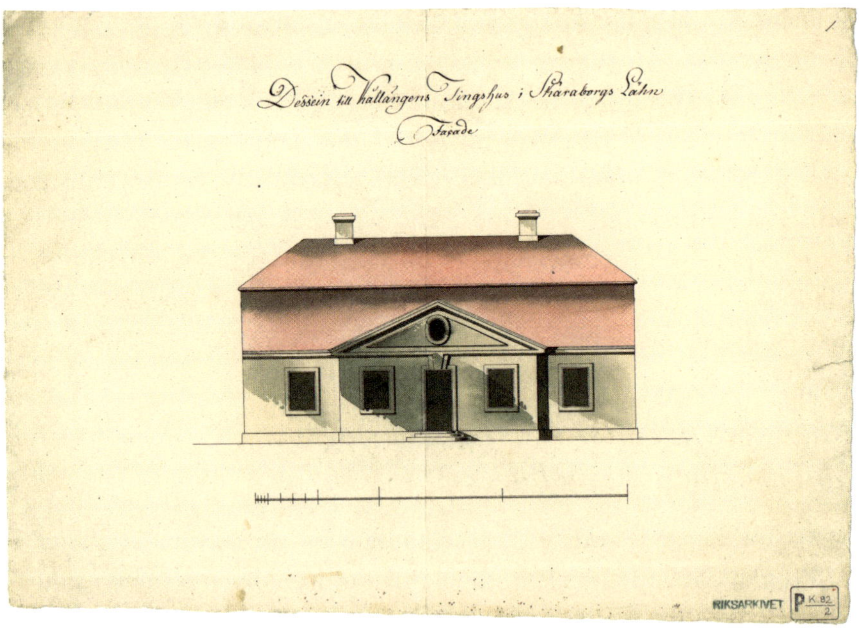

Figure 3: Kållängen courthouse. This final drawing of the Superintendent's Office was probably submitted to the judicial circuit around 1785. Överintendentsämbetets arkiv (archives of the Superintendent's Office) Riksarkivet (the National Archive).

with three and not five door openings leading to it. Curiously, despite this first proposition to remove the kitchen and keep the four rooms, the final drawing still includes a kitchen with a baking oven. There is no discussion on the matter documented in the minutes, but clearly the builder or/and the inhabitants of the judicial circuit could not imagine a courthouse without a kitchen. The great majority of all courthouse drawings from this period show a kitchen and seemingly this function was part of the courthouse conception. A courthouse most naturally included a kitchen.

In 1783, the Superintendent's Office received the Kållängen proposal, which consisted of a drawing and a cover letter. This was no simplified sketch but the coloured design of a person who knew much about proportion and construction, and who had scrutinized the old building well and truly. In the minutes from the court session preceding the drafting of this final drawing proposal submitted to the Superintendent's Office, the inhabitants expressed their deep worries about the costs of a new courthouse.[33] But even though the economic consequences of a reconstruction and the extra expenses due to the obligation to use stone were referred to, the inhabitants did not apply for an exemption or, as did other judicial circuits, simply ignore the decree of 1776. The old courthouse was made of stone which may have been re-used in the new building, yet a timbered or half-timbered construction would most likely have been less costly.[34]

The stone construction seems even more confusing when taking into account that the law stipulated a much simpler building. My studies of other late eighteenth-century courthouses show that those judicial circuits that bothered and/or had the means to build a purpose-built courthouse did not choose to build as cheap as possible. Either they built a large building, or they did not build at all but continued to hold the sessions in private homes or local inns.[35] However, the overwhelming majority of the purpose-built courthouses were wooden buildings. Despite the bad harvests of the late eighteenth century and other onerous building duties for the peasantry, the inhabitants of the particular judicial circuit surrounding Kållängen did not or could not conceive of a courthouse built of wood. First of all, this seems to indicate that the architects executed their tasks without attempting to adjust the original proposals in accordance with the decree of 1776, and secondly, that the stone construction at Kållängen was the result of a local debate.

We know that in order to build the courthouse at Kållängen, about seventy men were appointed by the circuit to carry out the different tasks of the process, some of them coming from other parishes and even judicial circuits.[36] The courthouse took three years to finish, and the result was a solid stone building, consistent in its symmetry and classicist features. It was built in one storey with a low slate-covered mansard roof with hipped top slope and light plastered walls. The single entrance, with narrow double doors and a limestone portal was placed in a projecting centrepiece crowned with a high-pitched pediment with a bull's-eye window. The four window frames of the front facade were of limestone, while the windows on the gables and in the back lacked stone

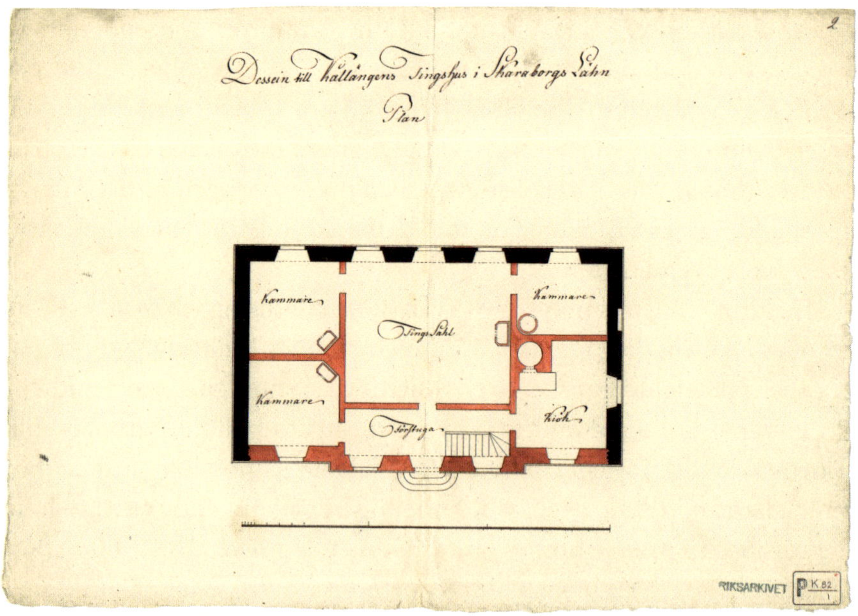

Figure 4: Kållängen courthouse, spatial structure. Except for the courtroom, the kitchen is the largest room in the building. The drawing also shows that there were no passages between the side-rooms. Överintendentsämbetets arkiv (archives of the Superintendent's Office) Riksarkivet (the National Archive).

frames. All details such as the mouldings and the limestone chimneys were plain and neatly finished.

To recapitulate the judicial circuit's conception compared to the realized building at Kållängen, the building that finally saw the light of day was almost identical with the one in the Superintendent's Office's drawing, at least if we speak of spatial structure and principal facade features. The greatest discrepancies concern the proportions. Since both the outer walls and the top slope of the roof were lower than intended, the building was overall lower and had a visually larger roof area compared to walling. It may have looked slightly heavier than the building the architect perhaps had in mind. Moreover, the pediment of the realized building was a higher construction with a more acute angle than the one in the drawing, the chimneys were thinner and the keystone above the entrance was of a simpler character.

Figure 5: Kållängen courthouse in 1968. Photo: Nils Fredrik Beerståhl, Picture archive of the Museum of Västergötland, bildnr A12866.

However, the simple lines on the drawings had been turned into slender mouldings, the dark holes representing the windows had been given frames and windows, and the fireplaces marked as triangles on the drawing had become either colourful tiled stoves or plain lime-washed stoves. As mentioned earlier, those elements were never defined in eighteenth-century drawings, and for some reason such concrete problems of detail were left to the builder.[37] Most skilled builders would have been familiar with the details and constructions which, so to speak, belonged to specific building types – it was part of their training and apprenticeship to learn the repertoire and probably to interpret the designs of the Superintendent's Office. At Kållängen, the result of the builder's interpretation of the drawings was a remarkable example of good workmanship.

Event and everyday life

In order to gain an insight into what kind of socio-spatial conditions the courthouses at Mönsterås and Kållängen produced, it seems important to delve into the everyday life that took place in and around the buildings. The question is what knowledge can actually be acquired regarding the everyday life? When it comes to the usage, the range of sources is limited and it is necessary to reflect along new lines. As a first step, I will look at the routines of the courts in general and scrutinize the commentaries on spatial structure made by the inhabitants of Mönsterås and Kållängen in particular. I will also study the surveyors' reports and check receipts from the building processes in search of items which indicate certain uses. Furthermore, I will consider the localization of the courthouses in order to understand the geographical context and detect possible overlapping activities.

We may assume that life in and near the courthouses centred around the recurrent sessions, but at the same time the sessions were not part of the actual everyday life in the sense of ordinary day life – on the contrary; they constituted an event. There were three ordinary sessions a year but in case of a serious crime the court could be summoned in between these gatherings.[38] At Mönsterås and Kållängen during the first two decades of the nineteenth century, there were normally about five or six sessions a year and they generally lasted between two days and a fortnight. During the remaining, greater part of the year, the buildings did not function as courts.

For the members of the court, and in particular the judge and the clerks who, it should be noted, served several judicial circuits, the sessions meant fulltime occupation and for a few days the courthouse became a residence which offered both board and lodging. As the circuit behind Mönsterås courthouse was geographically stretched out, those among the lay assessors with the longest way to travel had about 35 kilometres to the courthouse. At Kållängen, which was located in the middle of a very small circuit, nobody had more than 10 kilometres to travel. Sessions would begin at 9 a.m. and the first day always began with the local priest conducting a service which, at both Mönsterås and Kållängen, took place in the very courtroom. Since no case-agenda was put up in advance, there is reason to believe that on the first day of the proceedings, people crowded to hear what had happened in the circuit.[39] Unless there was a remarkable case coming up, fewer people probably attended the sessions during the following days. The law stated no limit as to when the day should end and there are sources which indicate that many proceedings continued late into the evening. This is also a reason why all members of the court stayed for several days, until the sessions were finished.[40]

In the courthouses of both Mönsterås and Kållängen, as in nearly all eighteenth-century courthouses, there was a kitchen and a baking oven. It seems remarkable that despite of the inn next door, public means were spent on the building of a kitchen. The function most probably brought about one or several women who were to bake and cook during sessions, and according to the drawing of the courthouse at Mönsterås, the house-keeper even had a room, right next to the courtroom. Both courthouses also had cellars, at Mönsterås they were vaulted and had iron hooks suspended from the ceiling, at Kållängen they comprised two pretty large rooms which were covered with slabs of sandstone and limestone. Since we know that there were separate jail-houses located close to these courthouses, the cellars were most certainly used to store food and not as jails. Cooking required cooling possibilities, even though it was carried out in a courthouse.

The surveyors' reports and lists of items show that the buildings at Mönsterås and Kållängen were equipped not only with a kitchen and a baking oven, but also with beds, stoups, buckets, tables, chairs and kitchen shelves.[41] However, there was not furniture enough to take all the members of the court to dinner. Either the court was seated in the courtroom itself, or the kitchen was built to serve the judge and the scribes only, in which case they would have their meals in the rooms intended for them.[42] When it comes to the courthouse as lodging for the night, the situation appears to have varied and it seems there were no established habits or taboos. Sometimes the judge and the scribes stayed at the inn, sometimes in the courthouse.[43] Some sources speak of a certain courthouse location as the most advantageous since 'lodging for the peasants could easily be found in the village', while others claim that many people, not only members of the court, slept in the courthouse itself.[44]

The scribbled lines, written on the first drawing of the courthouse at Mönsterås, give us further information on the kind of activity that characterized the building during the court sessions.[45] The author describes the functions of the four attic-rooms of which the one above the judge's room appears to have housed a farmhand, fodder (or things, or sacks – the handwriting is somewhat difficult to decipher) and such. We do not know on whose farm the farmhand normally worked and we can only guess what his tasks were during the sessions, but it should be noted that he was actually staying in the courthouse and that it was also used for storage purposes. Another man who also had a room in the attic at his disposal was the county sheriff. He probably had access to the room in between the sessions as well, since he was a representative of the Crown and in charge of controlling the courthouse. The third room was intended for the legal documents and the chest in which the judicial circuit kept its common means, in other words, a form of archive. Finally, the fourth room was built for the lay assessors and/or the peasantry – which may have referred to those amongst the audience who financed the building of the courthouse ('tingshusbyggnadsskyldige'). A picture appears of a court building crowded with people and bursting with activity on both first floor and in the attic.

During sessions, the court was seated at the far back of the room. The judge had the position in the middle and his desk slightly protruded in relation to the lay assessors' who were sitting on chairs or benches fixed to the wall. We do not know whether the court generally arrived before or after the audience, or if they entered from the side-rooms or the antechamber. But, in turn, security does not seem to have been an issue at the time, or it was interpreted quite differently.[46] Doors that lead from the court's space to the side-rooms certainly made it possible to withdraw without meeting the spectators, witnesses and parties. But normally the side-rooms did not have any passage to the antechamber since there was no door between the side-rooms, except for those buildings where the judge and the scribes had rooms next to each other.

Some courtrooms also had a bar, which closed the court's space and kept it separated. This bar is often interpreted as a symbolically important element which not only prevented the court from being compromised but also reminded of its objective position, apart from entangling relationships and dependencies. However, as unreliable as this source material may be, in a short-story written by judge and later on minister of justice, Louis de Geer, in the 1840s, both defendants and witnesses in fact stepped inside the bar when greeting the court. Some of the drawings of the Superintendent's Office point in the same direction, as does the existing interior of Fillinge courthouse in Östergötland, built in the 1790s. If we presume that all actors of the court sessions actually stepped inside the bar at one point or another, the bar seems to change meaning. Perhaps, at this time, it should not be understood as an absolute border, but more as a practical tool which guaranteed the court members a comfortable space during crowded sessions.

Certainly we do not know exactly how people moved around the courtroom in the eighteenth or early nineteenth centuries, but it seems that although there were bars and platforms, the socio-spatial situation of the courtroom was marked by motion and physical contact. Except for the court's seat, the courtroom was not divided into apparent functional zones. Receipts and protocols from Mönsterås and

Kålängen show that there were benches in the courtroom, but not enough seats for a large audience, with many people actually standing up. Parties and witnesses were placed side by side with the spectators who came and went during the sessions.[47] There was no specific area in the courtroom intended for the parties, which may be explained by the inquisitorial process of the time.[48] The trial or proceedings was not a matter handled by the two parties, but by the judge who questioned the person standing in front of him. As for those in custody, since both courthouses at Kålängen and Mönsterås lacked doors which led from the antechamber through a side-room and into the courtroom, these persons were presumably brought to the court through the crowd.

If the recurrent sessions represented an event, everyday life was presumably more affected by the practicalities related to the location of the building. Even though the courthouse drawings were approved by the Superintendent's Office and the buildings were given an exclusive classicist design, they were still part of the farmland. With few exceptions, Swedish courthouses in the eighteenth and nineteenth centuries were located in a village or a hamlet, close to the main road and the local inn. As inn-keepers at the time were farmers, the fields touched the facades of the courthouses, pigs were grubbing next door and people and horses passed by whether the court was in session or not. At Kålängen, the inn was located a few metres from the corner of the courthouse which constituted one of three buildings grouped around a paved yard.[49] In between sessions the local inn-keeper was normally allowed to use the building, and it was quite common until the end of the nineteenth century that courthouses were built as a combination of courthouse and inn. In these buildings, the inn was located on the first floor and the courtroom on the second.

Is this a courthouse?

When dealing with the late eighteenth-century courthouse conception, I have suggested that the law of 1734 did not represent a general conception, at the time, of what a courthouse was. Some sixty years after the law coming into force, the idea of a courthouse did not include a hall as large as required and two rooms, it embraced a much larger building with several different rooms for different functions. Thus, the courthouse conception implied more than a court-*session*-house as the activities of the court also entailed other functions. By the end of the eighteenth century, we can even distinguish the emergence of functional zones: The rooms of the judge and the scribes appear as a zone or unit which was normally put on one side of the courtroom, sometimes including a small archive room. On the other side, the kitchen and sometimes the larder or house-keeper's room constituted another zone, which in some cases could be reached through a separate side entrance in the gable of the courthouse. The last of the rooms surrounding the courtroom appear as less stable or defined units and were aimed either for the representative of the Crown, and/or for the lay assessors, or, as at Mönsterås, the house-keeper. What is important to emphasize is that since most courthouses at the time only had one single entrance, people

Figure 6: Kållängen courthouse in 1928, view from the south-west. The photograph shows the courthouse in its rural context in the middle of the farming landscape. The two-storey, panelled building on the left served at times as the local inn. Photo: Sanfrid Welin 1928, Picture archive of the Museum of Västergötland, bildnr A3046: A.

were still forced to meet in the antechamber. The idea of separate circulation routes did not appear until much later.

In the decree of 1776 it was clearly pointed out that the Superintendent's Office was to examine and approve all designs and financial accounts regarding public buildings. The character of the actual building site, though, was neither discussed by the inhabitants of the judicial circuit, nor was it considered by the Office. The Superintendent's architects were concerned with the architecture only and made new drawings of all of the proposed sketches or designs submitted to them, that is, no design appears to have been returned unmodified. However, the original wishes of the inhabitants of the judicial circuits always seem to have been accepted and I have even noticed formulations such as 'as the inhabitants wish' or 'according to the requirements of the inhabitants' in the memorials passing from the Superintendent's Office to the Crown for approval. What I have suggested in this article is that the inhabitants of the judicial circuits had exact opinions on both spatial structure and construction and a precise notion of what a courthouse should look like. The mansion-like character of the courthouse conception was both a result of the Superintendent's Office's ideals, and of the shared notion of the judicial circuits.

When it comes to character, proportions and measures of the realized buildings, both courthouses of Mönsterås and Kållängen were built in accordance with the drawings made by the Superintendent's Office. The difference between the conception and their materialization consisted in the realized courthouses being much more detailed and refined than the drawings implied. What seems striking when comparing the two buildings is that the spatial structure is very similar, while the materialization in several respects is quite different. The courthouse at Mönsterås was built by a fairly large judicial circuit and was located in a market town by the sea. Still, it was built according to a well-established building tradition as an unpanelled timber construction and a boarded roof with a tar-coating. The courthouse at Kållängen was built by a very small judicial circuit and located in the middle of an agricultural plain, indeed only twenty kilometres from a relatively large town. Unlike Mönsterås, this courthouse had an exclusive construction and design. For example the slates on the roof constituted a considerable cost as did the masonry of the frames. When it comes to similar buildings, we have to look for them among the mansions of the gentry.

The socio-spatial situation in and around the two courthouses presented in the article has in some respects appeared as paradoxical. Located in the middle of the hamlet or small market town, next to the everyday life of agriculture, the courthouses were still given the shape of a small mansion. When it comes to understanding the context, the current position of the eighteenth-century courthouses also confuses us. Originally, these buildings were not solitary monuments, but as great partitions and enclosures of land were carried out in the nineteenth century, the villages were split up as the farmers had to move their houses in order to live close to their fields. Even though the courthouses were rarely affected by these partitions, the restructuring made them appear as secluded buildings. Furthermore, when the courts moved to more modern premises, the courthouses were rebuilt into private homes which rendered them in picturesque gardens and in a quite different air.

The courthouse designs were made by the Superintendent's Office, but they were based on the requests of the local inhabitants who acted as professional builders in order to accomplish the objectives. The courthouses were indeed used as arenas where sentences were imposed and people's lives constrained, but at the same time the buildings contained a kitchen, a larder and even seem to have functioned as a festivity room and storage space. Considering the expressed ideas of what functions a courthouse was supposed to contain, the kitchen with the baking oven appears to be nearly as fixed as the courtroom. In the courtroom there was the platform and the bar which encased the court, yet the situation during sessions seems to have been marked by people coming and going, and the witnesses, parties and spectators sharing the same space.

Yet, are these really contradictory facts or only circumstances rarely considered in their simultaneity? Even though the judge and the housekeeper experienced the actual building differently, they almost certainly shared the idea that a courthouse included a courtroom and a kitchen. What seems important when trying to understand the spatial and social conditions of these past courthouses is that there was nothing contradictory about such a conception. Then again, it must be pointed out that when it comes to everyday activities and the question of accessibility, the courthouse was surely a different building to the house-keeper than to the judge. The late eighteenth-century courthouse indeed appears as a multi-functional building and should we want to explore its meanings, we would probably find a similar multitude.

Notes

1 Adrian Forty, Foreword in Ian Borden, Joe Kerr, Alicia Pivaro and Jane Rendell (eds.), *Strangely Familiar: Narratives of Architecture in the City* (London: Routledge, 1996), p. 5.

2 1734 års lag, Byggningabalken 26 kap. 4 § (Law code of 1734, Building Code ch. 26 sect. 4). The 'inhabitants' of the judicial circuits refer to those who had taxable land at their disposal. The range of the duty was related to the size of the land.

3 Law of 1734, section 26:4.

4 In *Celebrating the Courthouse: A Guide for Architects, Their Clients, and the Public*, ed. Steven Flanders (New York: W.W. Norton & Company, 2006), p. 13, justice Stephen G. Breyer argues that during the twentieth century, it became hard to define what a courthouse was supposed to look like. His description applies to the situation in the US, but many Swedish jurists would certainly agree with him. Kjell Å Modéer, professor of legal history, seems to express the same opinion when claiming that twentieth-century courthouses were deprived of such symbolic values which create identity ('avlövade på identitetsskapande symbolvärden'), Kjell Å Modéer, *Det heliga rummet. Domstolsbyggnadernas roll i det civila samhället* (Helsinki: Lakimies, 2000), p. 1067.

5 There are about 350 courthouses from the period 1700–1971 which are still standing. This number refers to buildings specifically built in order to hold court sessions. Since I have not examined the archive material of all 316 circuit courts of the time, the number should presumably be somewhat, though not considerably, higher.

6 In my doctoral dissertation I examine Swedish rural circuit courthouses from the period 1734–1970. Eva Löfgren, *Rümmet och rätten. Tinghus som föreställning, byggnad och rum i användning 1734–1970*, Institutet för rättshistorisk forskning, diss. (Gothenburg, University of Gothenburg, Stockholm, 2011).

7 Wilhelm Sjögren, *Förarbetena till Sverige rikes lag 1680–1736* (Uppsala, 1900–1909).

8 Claes Petersson, '1734 års lag – en medeltida lagbok eller en upplysningskodifikation? Till frågan om synen på lagändring i det förliberala samhället', in Robert Sandberg (ed.), *Studier i äldre historia* (Stockholm: Stockholms universitet, Historiska inst., 1985); Stig Jägerskiöld, 'Kring tillkomsten av 1734 års lag', in *Svensk Juristtidning* (1984).

9 King Magnus Erikssons landslag, the first Swedish code with kingdomwide application, was established during the fourteenth century and printed in 1608.

10 My work does not cover the eighteenth century but there are several interesting studies concerning specific circuit courts at the time, in which the issue of the most ancient accommodations is treated: Pehr Johnsson, *Östra Göinge domsaga, Broby som tingsplats* (Kristianstad, 1949); Lars Montelius, 'Tingshus i Östergötland', unpublished manuscript (1998), filed in the archive of Dokumentationsprojektet, Nordiska Museet, Stockholm; Folke Petersson, *Refteleboken* (kulturnämnden i Gislaveds kommun, 1976); Einar Persson, 'Tingsplatser och tingsbyar i Västra härad', in *Byarums hembygdsförenings Årskrift* (1974); Erik Wegraeus, *Ting och tingsställen i Nordals och Sundals härader* (Tingshusbyggnadsskyldige för Nordals och Sundals härader, Mellerud, 1970).

11 In Swedish, 'tingslada'.

12 1734, 26:2. The section on vicarages is far more detailed than the one regulating courthouses, but as regards the actual living premises the law only stipulates a hall, two rooms and a kitchen.

13 Kjell Å Modéer, personal communication, 16/05/2007.

14 The earliest document found in the Superintendent's archives, which concerns a courthouse, dates from 1756 and consists of a list of financial accounts and a letter, but no drawing. The first drawing dates from 1769 and the majority of the drawings were produced between 1770 and 1800.

Riksarkivet (National Archive), Överintendentsämbetets arkiv (Archive of the Superintendent's Office), Profana byggnader, DII ba:2 and letters Profana byggnader i landsorten, äldre serien FI baa 6.

15 'Kongl. Maj:ts Nådiga Förordning, Angående Hwad hädanefter wid Publique Byggnader kommer at i akttagas. Gifwen Ekolsund then 31 Julii 1776'. There had also been an earlier decree on the same subject: 'Kongl. Maj:ts allernådigaste Förklaring angående Stenhus byggnader i Städerna och på Landet, af den 19 januari 1757'. The aim of these decrees was mainly to reduce the risk of fire and limit the use of timber.

16 According to the source material filed in the local circuit archives and in the archive of the Superintendent's Office (National Archive, Stockholm), many judicial circuits built a new courthouse without any correspondence or the design being approved of beforehand. Of those circuits that did correspond with the Crown, most of them included a written description but no drawing.

17 At Riksarkivet (National Archive) in Stockholm, there are about fifty drawings, plans and sections, but some drawings have also been filed with local judicial circuit archives.

18 The hall is sometimes located to one side of the main entrance, but the most common structure is with the courtroom in the centre.

19 The name of the judicial circuit was Stranda.

20 Riksarkivet (National Archive), Överintendentsämbetets arkiv, Protokoll och handlingar rörande profana byggnader på landsbygden. Stranda härad, Mönsterås tingshus. There are all in all five letters or/and petitions filed under the Mönsterås courthouse, written between June 1795 and July 1797.

21 Official letter from the representatives of the county of Kalmar, dated 22 June 1795, Riksarkivet (National Archive), Stockholm. Överintendentsämbetets arkiv, Protokoll och handlingar rörande profana byggnader på landsbygden.

22 The designs and cover letters were sent to 'Kungl. Maj:t', H. M. Government the Crown, which submitted them to the Superintendent's Office for consideration. The proposal of the circuit of Stranda (Mönsterås) arrived at the Superintendent's Office on 1 July 1795: Riksarkivet (National Archive) Stockholm Överintendentsämbetets arkiv.

23 Unfortunately these documents have since then been misplaced, but we still know quite a lot about them as both the agreement set between the entrepreneur and the inhabitants of the judicial circuit in 1798 and the surveyors' report from 1800 refer to them in detail.
24 Surveyors' report: Landsarkivet Vadstena, Stranda härads arkiv, AIa:53, utdrag ur domboken 13 augusti 1800.
25 Surveyors' report: Landsarkivet Vadstena, Stranda härads arkiv, AIa:53, utdrag ur domboken 13 augusti 1800.
26 Measurement drawing from 1971, Uppmätningsritning av f.d. tingshuset i Mönsterås, Arkitekt & fritidsnämndsbyrån Sjöholm – Lindgren AB, Mönsterås. Most courthouses at the time were given dimensions between 110 and 250 square metres in one storey.
27 Surveyors' report: Landsarkivet Vadstena, Stranda härads arkiv, AIa:53, utdrag ur domboken 13 augusti 1800. Measurement drawing from 1971, Uppmätningsritning av f.d tingshuset i Mönsterås, Arkitekt & fritidsnämndsbyrån Sjöholm – Lindgren AB, Mönsterås 29.7.1971. Stranda hembygdsförenings arkiv.
28 Several courthouses from the period were given mansard or gable roofs instead of the mansard roofs with hipped top slope that were indicated in the original drawings proposed by the Superintendent's Office. Around 1800, flat gable roofs were becoming more current, a construction that did not leave room for any activity in the attic unless there was a frontispiece.
29 Surveyors' report: Landsarkivet Vadstena, Stranda härads arkiv, AIa:53, utdrag ur domboken 13 augusti 1800.
30 In the 1780s Kållängen included four farms. Enskifteskarta Kållängen 1823, Lantmäteriets historiska kartor (National Archive of Land surveys).
31 The name of the judicial circuit was Kinnefjärding.
32 Sven-Axel Hallbäck, *Kring Kållängens tingshus: en minnesskrift/utg. av tingshusstyrelsen i Kinnefjärdings, Kinne och Kållands domsaga* (Lidköping, 1970).
33 Ibid., pp. 22 ff. He refers to the judgement book of 1781, the protocol of 19 October.
34 Ethnologist Gösta Arvastson has pointed at the fact that in north-eastern Skåne, in the south of Sweden, the costs for building a stonehouse in the mid-eighteenth century were twice as high as a half-timbered building,

Skånska prästgårdar. En etnologisk studie av byggnadsskickets förändring 1680–1824, Skrifter från Folklivsarkivet i Lund no. 19 (1977), p. 101.

35 As was mentioned earlier, many eighteenth-century courthouses have been demolished and replaced during the nineteenth and twentieth centuries, but source material such as fire-insurance documents and financial accounts have made it possible to reconstruct what should be considered quite a proper picture of these buildings.

36 Hallbäck, *Kring Kållängens tingshus*, appendices 1–4.

37 No thorough research has been conducted on this subject. Göran Alm, Ph.D., Head of Bernadotte Library in Stockholm, has touched upon the subject in 'Arkitekturen och inredningskonsten', in *Signums svenska konsthistoria* (Lund: Bokförlaget Signum, 1997). In this article, he discusses the differences between the designs of Royal Palace architect Carl Hårleman and the resulting architecture, pp. 42–43.

38 Law of 1734, section 2:3.

39 The fact that there were no case-agenda put up was pointed out to me by Kjell Å Modéer, personal communication 2007–05–16.

40 The tradition among judges to write their autobiography has been treated by Kjell Å Modéer, in 'Rättens aktörer: den juridiska biografin som litteraturform', in *Kungl. Humanistiska vetenskapssamfundet i Lund, Årsberättelse* (2003/2004). In this article, I have used two biographical texts, Louis de Geer's *Minnen* part 1 and 2 (Stockholm: Norstedts, 1892), and Hugo Hamilton's *Min farfars journal 1809–1811: anmärkningar och anteckningar* (Stockholm: Geber, 1923).

41 Surveyors' report: Landsarkivet Vadstena, Stranda härads arkiv, AIa:53, utdrag ur domboken 13 augusti 1800. Receipts from the building process at Kållängen, 9 May 1787, Hallbäck, *Kring Kållängens tingshus*, 1970, appendixes 1–4, and Landsarkivet Göteborg, Kinnefjärdings härads arkiv.

42 During the period, there were courthouses which contained a dining room, for example the previous courthouse at Kållängen or the courthouse at Fillinge, Östergötland. We do not know, however, who dined there.

43 Hugo Hamilton, *Min farfars journal 1809–1811*.

44 Courthouse of Fillinge, 1737–1754, Bankekinds häradsrätts arkiv, Landsarkivet Vadstena. Ethnological recordings at Folklivsarkivet, 'Archive of Ethnological Collections', Lund, Manuskripserien M 3803, published in

Anders Salomonsson, 'Ting och rättvisa i Folklivsarkivet', in *Tingshus i tid och rum* (Jönköping, 1992).

45 Överintendentsämbetets arkiv (archive of the Superintendent's Office), Riksarkivet (National Archive) Stockholm, Protokoll och handlingar rörande profana byggnader på landsbygden. Stranda härad, Mönsterås tingshus.

46 Both the design of the courthouses and the lack of such discussions in the written sources point in this direction.

47 Louis de Geer, in 'Urtima ting', a short-story based on experiences from the courthouse in Fjälkinge and published for the first time in 1843, in *Valda skrifter del I* (Stockholm: Norstedts förlag, 1892), Reenstierna Märta Helena, *Årstadagboken Journaler från åren 1793–1839*, part 1–3, published by Sigurd Erixon et al. (Stockholm: Generalstaben, 1946–1949).

48 The history and realization of the Swedish Code of Judicial Procedure has been treated by Kjell Å Modéer in 'Den stora reformen. Rättegångsbalkens förebilder och förverkligande', in *Svensk Juristtidning* (1999).

49 According to a map of 1823 there were four buildings enclosing the yard (Lantmäteriets historiska kartor, Enskifte 1823).

13

Staged Justice

Lisbeth Fullu Skyberg

The present chapter examines the spatial and procedural staging of criminal cases, the intentions behind the interior decoration and how users in court feel that this design impacts on their social practices in Norway. In my analysis, I use metaphors from the theatre – not an unnatural choice in light of the following images.

Another important aspect of the function of the courts that has been much clearer in the public debate in Norway in recent years, particularly in connection with the proceedings in some major criminal cases, is that in addition to serving as the conflict-solver in specific cases, the court also functions as a kind of public stage where society determines where borders for what is right and wrong are to be drawn in our culture. My approach is in itself not new, as several renowned defence lawyers have previously used the terminology of the theatre to describe their activities in court. But I must admit that comparing the court and the theatre offends both institutions because a tempting deduction is not only that the court is entertainment, but also that the theatre is dull. The comparison nevertheless does focus attention on one important common trait: The court and the theatre both present understandings of reality, and in both the world of fiction and reality it is necessary to use rhetorical techniques when telling narratives.

Figure 1: Photos of the District Court Building in Oslo. In the first photo, characteristic theatrical masks decorating the Norwegian Theatre can be viewed through the court's glass pane. In the second photo, the inscription immediately below the sign-posting for Oslo Tinghus (the District Court Building) reads 'DET NORSKE TEATRET SCENEINNGANG' (Entrance to the Norwegian Theatre).

In this chapter, I shall restrict myself to dealing with two topics connected to the building of a new courthouse in Oslo and the restoration of Norway's Supreme Court. The arguments used in the selection of architectonic expression are thus relatively fresh, allowing us to compare the designers' intentions as to what the buildings should appear like in the eyes of the users. I will divide this chapter's topic into two parts:

1) What intentions lie behind the design of the courtrooms in question?
2) How do the various user groups perceive the effect of the staging on the proceedings?

The empirical basis for my analysis comes from interviews with interior architects, the then Director for Cultural Heritage in Norway, judges, lawyers and defendants. In this presentation I will be particularly interested in the perspectives of interior architects and judges.

Part 1: The symbols of power

The Danish scholar Jens Tonboe suggested in his book *Rummets sociologi* (Spatial Sociology) that the physical environments in which all phenomena and events take place are not irrelevant for the process and its outcome. Bearing this in mind, or based on sign theory or socio-material thinking in general, the material and physical environment of a courtroom will have communicative features.

Carsten Smith, the previous Chief Justice of the Supreme Court in Norway, thus wrote in the preface to *Norges høyesterett* (Norway's Supreme Court), which was published some years ago, that 'wandering in an old court building one may – if one has a finely tuned ear – hear the legal ideas resounding in the building'. In connection with the opening of the newly restored Supreme Court in 1996, Liv Gjølstad, a Supreme Court justice, stated in the Norwegian daily *Aftenposten* that she felt that the environment of the Supreme Court constitutes a whole where everything 'sings together'. The question then is what is the song about?

The interior architects stated that their principal challenge when designing fixtures and the interiors of courtrooms was to determine the intentions to be embedded in the material. They stated that four central areas were essential to their work, *floor plans, dimensions, symbol use* and *choice of materials*. They believed that these four factors were vital to how a room is perceived in general, but that it was particularly important to be aware of the choices as there was a clear risk of creating the expression of suppression by using architectonic techniques in a room designed for the exercise of power. At the same time, they also wanted the rooms to express seriousness and solemnity. One interior architect stated:

> When you've made it all the way to the court, then it's serious business, really. Then it has to be very solemn, and you should feel that you are in a special room. You must be given this sense of having to catch your breath, as in now, now's the time, this is it.

Thus the interior architects set about their task torn between the risk of expressing suppression and the wish to express solemnity.

Perhaps one of the most striking impressions you have when you walk into a courtroom is the clearly delineated staging. A courtroom is probably one of the rooms in our relatively egalitarian society where it is easiest to see that there are differences between people. The interior appears suitable for structuring the events because it draws a picture of the roles to be filled during the legal proceedings and of the status attached to the various roles. There are, according to the interior architects, no written guidelines determining the appearance of a courtroom. They also state that they feel it is impossible to start from scratch with respect to the notion of how a courtroom should appear since one has traditional ideas in one's mind. Also, perhaps needless to say, relations between man and objects are not deterministic in the sense that a given symbol does not necessarily cause a defined reaction but rather one that depends on the context and the interpretation. An example of this could be the Norwegian national coat of arms, which in Norwegian courtrooms hangs on the wall behind the judges as a graphic alibi for the exercise of power, just as churches have their altarpieces. I cannot say whether this should be interpreted as analogous with the advertisement claiming that Norway's most famous painting is Munch's *Scream*, while Denmark's most famous painting is Krøyer's *Hip Hip Hooray*. The Norwegian national coat of arms nevertheless shows a rampant lion holding an axe in the direction of his gaze, while the Danish one shows three resting lions, comfortably ensconced and surrounded by hearts.

Floor plans – establishing spheres

Traditional Norwegian courts have a straight judge's bench with the prosecutor's and defence counsel's desks placed at right angles to it.

The witness stand is placed in the middle of the room facing the judge's bench. The audience and press are placed at the back of the room. They represent the general public and thus a collective element. This group is also seated on benches, a traditional way of expressing that one is part of a larger whole and has no individual role, in contrast to those given a chair.

The positions of the parties are built around the courtroom's *centre axis* and *transverse axis*. The first is used to signify equality, the second to signify difference. The transverse axis divides the room in a manner that makes the parties on the floor equal, but separates judges by representing a qualitative difference, creating a distinctness and imperturbability.

This is emphasized by the fact that judges arrive and leave the room through their own door, while witnesses, lawyers and the spectators must use a common entrance. The bench is thus a dividing line, but also a meeting point. The dividing line is intended by the designers to symbolize the neutral, incorruptible and sovereign position in the legal process, and thus its dignity. The principal interior architect, Beate Ellingsen, stated: 'Never was it more natural to use the centre axis for all choices, and never have we met greater understanding of axes and symmetry than among the judges'. To continue the song metaphor used by Justice Gjølstad, we may thus state that through its division into spheres the room sings about the dignity of the court.

One of these two spheres is also expressed by some classical symbols of power that emphasize authority. This may be linked to the fact that by law, the judge is not merely an objective and neutral party, but also the one who undisputedly controls and decides the legal process. The interior architects saw the need to express this power relation spatially by allowing the room to impart the sense of this underlying hierarchy.

The judges do not only sit separated from the other actors, they also sit higher than them. This is a very familiar expression of authority. (Moses walked up the mountain to obtain God's Commandments; churches and castles are often placed on hills; teacher's desks were often placed on a podium.) Using height differences to symbolize rank has long ceremonial traditions – and such is also the case in courtrooms. Practical considerations are also interesting. How does one quantify a qualitative difference, in the sense of precisely how high judges should be elevated in our modern times? One of the interior architects stated that this indeed became an issue:

> Yes, like when the judges enter in their black robes, and they are always seated higher, they sit a minimum of 17 cm higher than the others down on the floor, because they must have eye contact with the person on the witness stand. In some cases we have used up to 34 cm. There are some judges who like to sit even higher, to look down on the person on the stand.

Another classical expression of power that can be found in the courtroom is the floor plan. French sociologist Pierre Bourdieu has stated that distance is an expression of power that is at least as important as crown and sceptre, because as he says, 'Architectonic rooms, with their quiet dictates direct on the body, achieve (…) that the body shows deference, shows the respect born by distance'. Being assigned that which is greater in many situations is a way of displaying recognition. Metaphorically, giving somebody larger space will be recognition of this person's interests and needs. The interior architects told me that, indeed, the floor plans become a central issue during the process of designing the courtroom. One of the interior architects put it this way:

> I should not have caved in when we were discussing how much space we should give to the judge's bench, this is a message about who one is to take into consideration which is embedded in the floor plan for the rooms. It is their [the judges'] demonstration of power, something that is not fair, the other areas have to be smaller. There are many interests in a room and areas are important, where is your zone?

We can thus say that the room also sings of the power of the court.

Hannah Arendt has stated that authority cannot survive without support from religion or tradition. The past may give authority and power a self-rationalizing element, contributing to allowing movement into the unknown guided by what is known. Tradition thus functions as a narrative by anchoring actions and phenomena in a narrative structure that imbues them with meaning by being organized in a particular way. Linking today's courtroom expression to tradition was also an important goal when designing the courtroom. In the Supreme Court the wish to place today's court in a special court tradition to create continuity and belongingness was given a concrete expression in the lobby. The Director for Cultural Heritage in Norway stated that there were some rooms the original architect had not had the funds to decorate so that they were now empty, without knowing what the plan for these rooms had been. The Director for Cultural Heritage in Norway therefore proposed:

> [T]he architect had drawn all these fields and they were naked and empty. And then I said, what if we put marble slabs there with statutes on them. And what was really amusing was that the judges thought this was a brilliant idea, and when choosing the statute texts, they really went all hammers and tongs into the task. And I was absolutely certain that they would include section 11 of the Constitution, [spoken solemnly] 'The Supreme Court pronounces judgment in the final instance', and then they laughed, you know, then they laughed.

Thus a range of quotations spanning a thousand years of legal thinking – from the twelfth century Gulating laws and up to the European Convention on Human Rights – has been put on the lobby wall. A legal tradition filled with discontinuity and changes of content is therefore displayed as continuity where the Gulating laws are on the same footing as the Constitution and the European Convention on Human Rights. Yesterday's law is made part of today's law, implicitly giving a rationale for tomorrow's law.

It may thus be stated that the room does not only sing of the court's durability, but also of its self-evidence.

Oslo Courthouse and Norway's Supreme Court have been built during different epochs, and also have their own distinctive expressions. Both buildings nevertheless express the same scenography, with the judge's

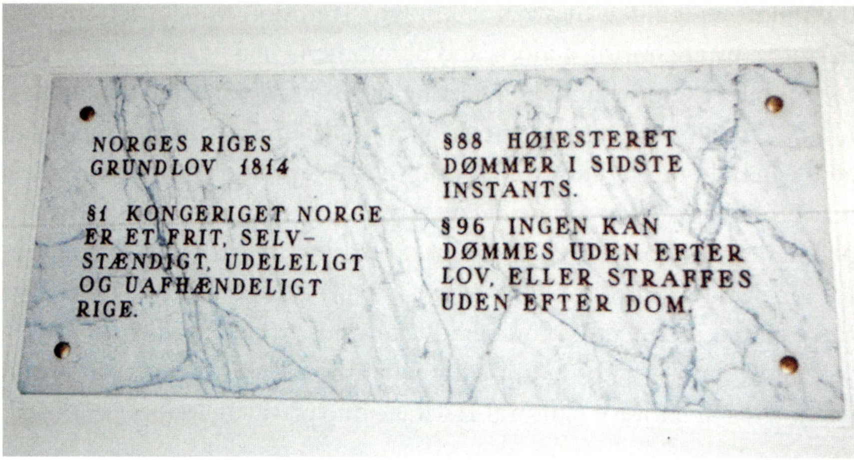

Figure 3: Detail from a plaque at the Norwegian Supreme Court Building bearing excerpts from Norway's Constitution.

dais, clear axes, favouring the area for judges and so on. An interesting difference is nevertheless that in both these buildings the law has been expressed in the lobbies. While the question in the Supreme Court was whether the quoted statutes should be set in stone or cast in bronze, the quotations in the Courthouse wind their way, at times laterally inversed, at times diffusely, and handwritten, across a column of ceramic tiles. While the Supreme Court thus displays a statute with the same finality as the inscription on a tombstone, Oslo Courthouse displays a law that is occasionally completely incomprehensible.

It is quite possible to say that both representations stand on equally firm ground, because even if a law is crystal clear in its consequences, it is nevertheless utterly incomprehensible to most people. The question is then what motivates these different expressions. Perhaps the law is clearer in the final instance, and perhaps it is easier to ladle on symbolism in a building from another style epoch? The issue is whether this may be interpreted as more than a time-based stylistic difference.

The courtroom is a place where much can be read about state authority, but not all symbols and material techniques have been placed there to express power. The interior architects were quite pleased to receive feedback that the courtrooms denoted a democratic expression, as this

Figure 4: Detail from the Oslo District Court Building.

was also a quality they had attempted to imbue the rooms with. In the words of an interior architect:

> There must be a certain sense of equality. Therefore we put the same decorations on the witness stand as on the chair of the president of the court, to balance things against the judge's bench. We had a fully deliberate attitude to the witness stand, we put up a small moulding to screen off the heart, this is so subtle that I dare almost not say it, but it is to provide security or a form of protection.

During the period when considerations of democracy and protection of the rights of defendants and witnesses gained in importance over the last century, it is reasonable to believe that this is also reflected more clearly in Oslo Courthouse, built in 1994, than in the Supreme Court, which was completed in 1903.

Another example is that one of the interior architects stated that even if many judges want even bigger benches, taller backs on their chairs and an even higher dais, there were also some judges who wanted to tone down the symbolic expression of power. By participating in user committees the judges are able to influence the design of the courtrooms, and, according to an interior architect, one district court judge felt that the architects should not use too fine birch in the furniture:

> He didn't want it to look so stylish, as it were, because as he says 'There are actually quite a few rustics in the court', so the factory had some problems finding adequately imperfect materials.

Finally, one can state that the room sings in a duet with its surroundings.

I have here said something about the symbols of power; the power symbols actually have does not only depend on the intentions one has tried to put into them, but on how users interpret the expressions. As honour can only exist through its reputation, courtroom symbolism can only support the court's authority and dignity if it is able to engender such trust in the interpreters.

Part 2: The power of the symbols

In this final part I shall briefly mention some of the judges' observations from their user perspective.

The designers aimed to embed four principal messages in the rooms and their materials: The room had to communicate the court's dignity, power, eternity and self-evidence. Basically many of the judges and legal officials were of the attitude that the room did not play any role in relation to the processes in the court. In the words of one appellate court judge: 'Little work has been done on how a court should appear, this theme has never been taken entirely seriously by the lawyers'. The judges were nevertheless in agreement on some things: first, that the staging was practical and, second, that the courtroom radiated authority, and this, as it turned out, was often two sides of the same coin.

The informants generally felt it was positive that the room signalled the court's authority. On closer questioning, most of the judges and lawyers also had many opinions as to what the room more specifically contributed to the court process. They had preferences when it came to what type of courtroom they liked, and as far as it was possible they would deliberately use particular courtrooms at particular points in time in the proceedings to establish different moods and ambience.

What the judges and lawyers saw as the clearest and most important signal from the courtrooms was that the room expressed authority and dignity. This primarily contributed to respect. The fact that the courtroom expresses solemnity and authority was seen as a way of helping in the court's primary function, to resolve conflicts. The authority must not only work inside the courtroom, it must also work outside it. According to a Supreme Court judge, 'Distance and signalling difference are important for authority. The idea is also that the court's decisions must be accepted without too much fuss, that somebody calls to a halt'.

The judges feel that the basic idea behind this signal is the emphasis on distance. One judge stated that it is important to remove the court's decision from the judge as a person, and this is easier if spatial distance, daises, robes and symbols are used. The judges describe this distance as good and useful. In the courtroom it should be felt that society is making the decisions, not the judge. As one of the judges emphasized about his robe, 'It is my function that is important, not my person'. It was the judges' hope that in the court no one would feel that the proceedings and decision were a private vendetta, rather they should feel that the public punishment was the result of a situation that society insisted on addressing, and that it was necessary to have signals communicating this.

The judges also feel that an architectonically formal room with large distances and a solemn mood makes it easier to keep a strict regime, with less small talk and informal conversation. One judge said that it is often maintained that the closer people get to one another, the better the communication flows, and the better quality it has. However, one condition for this, he felt, was that people had to be on an equal footing, which he thought was not the case in a courtroom. Another judge stated that as the system is applying societal power it would be counterproductive to have this take place while enjoying a nice cup of coffee together.

The judges also felt that the room presented underlying ideas of fairness and justice, neutrality and equal treatment. According to an appellate court judge:

> In smaller courtrooms everything is more intimate for better or worse, and then individual matters relating to the defendant, the prosecutor and the defence counsel may take on more importance. We had such a courtroom in the old courthouse, which was a bit too small, and I really must admit that I placed more importance on such things there, because you were much more on top of each other.

Another stated:

> In Sweden they have tried much more of this without robes and all, but I'm afraid that this actually will … – and this is only thinking out loud on my part, really – but I think this will give the stronger party in this setting greater influence, because if these things are not formalized, those who are most reticent will simply not have a chance. It is typical that proceedings are quite often dominated by those with authority.

Thus in court we can find the idea that communication based on distance contributes to justice – equal matters are dealt with in an equal manner. In this there is also possibly the inherent condition that different individuals will have equally good or poor opportunities to influence a more formal framework, but I shall not discuss here and now whether this position is tenable.

The emphasis on distance also contributes to protecting judges. One Supreme Court judge states:

> It is really quite a terrible thing to sit there and decide who is a murderer, for example. You are like God, in a way. And I have not had occasion to study what the rituals in the courtroom and the physical arrangement there mean as protection for people who are set to do so serious things. But if we look at God's hand by Michelangelo in the

> Sistine Chapel in Rome, then we understand that God is not a man chit-chatting with those He is weighing on judgement day.

The judges did, however, also see unfortunate effects from this traditional staging, seeing problems in the room design, such as making people more nervous and accentuating conflicts. If witness testimony is a central element of the total evidence, and the witness's nervousness undermines the testimony, this is needless to say unfortunate. In the words of an appellate court judge: 'Without a doubt in some cases the design of the room may be such that witnesses feel so out of place that they are unable to explain what they should have done'.

The judges also found it unfortunate that in some cases the formal mood also hardened the lines of conflict between the opposing parties in court. Even if this polarization made the case clearer for the judges and they therefore deemed it useful, the same polarization also hardened the conflict between the parties. The judges therefore felt that in a case where the aim is to negotiate a settlement, it would be preferable to use rooms that facilitated for a 'small-talk ambience'. This also applied to cases where the parties would need to continue to cooperate after the case had been settled in court, as, for example, when determining custody of and visitation rights for children, where the judges preferred rooms that were less conflict-intense.

One Supreme Court judge also pointed out that an unfortunate aspect of building respect for the court through distance and respect for authority might be that the court is not called to task enough and court practices are not adequately criticized:

> It goes completely without saying that the exaggerated trust we have had in sentences being correct is not rooted in reality. This is hardly right, nor is it unimportant that we should have this unlimited trust in the administration of justice. So you might say that in one way or other, the way it's been is that the dignity of the court has, in part through the legal rules and in part through the lack of criticism and lack of acceptance of criticism within the system, obviously led to quite a few miscarriages of justice over the years that have never been rectified. And this might be

connected to the fact that this has been considered as a kind of operating expense that has to be paid to give the court the authority it has.

Conclusion

In a sign-theory understanding, both the court's material design and its actors will have communicative aspects. Hence both actors and material design may exercise power by guiding the social interpretations and practices of others. As communicative actors, however, the material design and the social actors are furnished with different qualities; they have different qualities as sign carriers. The material design functions as a continuous transmitter of messages. The court, the judge's robe and the judge's dais do not, in contrast to the judges, live and breathe. On the other hand, the staging or material design will depend on the recipient's interpretation, while a judge's power of decision is not connected, to the same degree, to how he or she is interpreted.

Most of the architectonical and symbolic expressions in court have both a practical and symbolic rationale. One may nonetheless wonder which of utility value or symbol value proves to be most practical. German historian Theodor Mommsen delimits authority to being more than persuasion and less than an order. It has been said that authority that is threatened is pleading. If authority must to some degree display its authority, it is already undermined. If judges need to hammer their gavels to quiet their courtroom, their authority and sovereignty are already under question. If the objective basis of power that the court rests on proves to work also as a symbolic power, it will be interpreted as a legitimate content of meaning, an expression of some sort of natural order which opens the way for the exercise of the objective power. The staging can affirm interests without interested parties themselves needing to argue for them. Thus the material design is like tacit lobbying. The message in the symbols of power tells those of us who understand the codes that we are in the presence of power, without the powerful needing to tell us so.

14

From Stone Circle to Transit Hall

Law and Art in the District Court Buildings in Ängelholm and Helsingborg

Martin Sunnqvist

When one walks across the cobbled square Tingstorget[1] in Ängelholm, one's eye is caught by the district court building. It was built in 1860–61 in one storey, to which was added in 1924 another storey and an apse to the courtroom. The middle and side sections of the red plastered facade are marked by yellow pilasters and the roof is a hipped saddle roof crested with a lantern with a sceptre and balance on the top. Above the old entrance door in the middle of the facade, there is a balcony with the armorial bearings of the circuits[2] Södra Åsbo and Bjäre; a bear rampant for Södra Åsbo and St. Tora holding a book and a palm branch for Bjäre.

In 1954–56, a new building for the secretariat of the court was added to the west of the old courthouse and connected to it via a passage building. In this passage, the new main entrance was placed, surrounded by a mosaic by the artist Ralph Bergholtz.[3] Ralph Bergholtz has himself described the thoughts behind the mosaic:

> Beginning in the characteristic angle of the new gable, the play of the lines moves in waves through the mosaic and finally fades out in the pilasters of the old court building. The variations of the colour between greenish-yellow and brick-red emphasizes the motion. The intention

> has in other words been to have the mosaic work as some sort of heart which sets the lines of the facades in rhythmic motion.[4]

He has also stated that the idea of the work of art was 'an organic connection between old and new – the continuity in the development of the sense of justice'.[5]

In the left part of the wall

> one perceives three caryatidic[6] figures alluding to the extension of legal community over wider and wider areas: The justiciar who himself kept the law for the people of the settlement. [...]. Valdemar Sejr,[7] who wrote the first Scanian law[,[8]] bears the Danish colours on his shield. Gustaf Cronhielm, president of the law commission, which composed 'The Swedish Law Code'.[9] They are accompanied by symbols of faith and power – the hammer of Thor and the sword, the cross and the executioner's axe, the Swedish lion.[10]

In the upper part of the mosaic, there are architectural details which symbolize the phases of the development of civilization, and in the lower part the development of the sense of justice is shown

> from the 'law of the stronger' via duels, ordeals, communitarian revenge, imprisonment and penal servitude towards a more liberal understanding of penal law. The symbols of law, the sword and scales, lead – above the entrance – to the right part of the mosaic, where falling bombs form the background to the planting of a new tree, alluding to a common legal order organized in root, stem and branches. The epoch is suggested by the buildings of The League of Nations and The United Nations.[11]

In this manner, Ralph Bergholtz has placed the district court building of Ängelholm in the centre of the legal development from the medieval travelling justiciar to the international legal order of today. The purchaser of the work of art was Tingshusbyggnadsskyldige, a special territorial corporation which until 1971 was responsible for building and maintaining the courthouse of the circuit and where the circuit

Figure 1: Mosaic by Ralph Bergholtz, 1954–56. Photo: Martin Sunnqvist.

judge and the lay assessors made the decisions.[12] They were conscious of the symbolic meaning of the mosaic and of their possibility to exert an influence on it, but if they really used their possible influence on the artist is not known.[13] The message of the mosaic is still of immediate interest, and we are still in the last epoch of its time axis. The only circumstance which reveals that fifty years have passed since the mosaic was made is that the symbols of today's international legal order are placed somewhat in the periphery, as if they were waiting around the corner, while they now are of central importance.

If one now walks through the entrance door and then left, one comes to the courtroom, which is inside the old entrance door. The room is impressive, with dark wooden walls and with the court placed in a semicircle in the apse. The window behind the chair of the judge has stained glass, a work of art made by the same artist, Ralph Bergholtz, in 1946, twenty years before the mosaic.

In the centre of the picture, there is a circle of stones[14] with an oak in the middle. There is also a justiciar, an assembly and parties, of which one accuses and the other takes an oath. To the *dexter,* i.e. to the left from the viewer's point of view,[15] of the stone circle is a peasant with a balance in his right hand and an axe in his belt. The background is a log cabin and a newly ploughed field and a rider with a fiery cross with runes. To the *sinister* of the stone circle is *Magnus Rex,* King Magnus Eriksson of Sweden, Norway and Scania. Magnus is wearing his crown and holds a sword and a scroll with his name in Latin. He stands in front of a stone building and a writing monk. Far down to the *dexter,* there is a group of people who seems to want to take the law into their own hands, and opposite them, there is a group of people who listen to the law.

In the top centre is Jesus Christ in a mandorla.[16] His hands are raised, and the people to his right are expiating their crimes while they to his left are looking towards Heaven. To the right of Christ is the coat-of-arms of the circuit of Södra Åsbo, *Argent a bear rampant Sable,* and to his left is the coat-of-arms of the circuit of Bjäre, *Or a female (St. Tora) with clothing Gules and coronet Or, holding in her right hand an open book Gules and in her left hand a palm branch Gules.*[17]

The picture is divided with a clear vertical line. The right half – in the perspective of the justiciar in the stone circle and of the onlooker – contains the prosecutor or plaintiff, the law, the King with his name in Latin, the listening subjects, the faithful who look towards Heaven and the coat-of-arms with the saint, the book and the palm branch. The left half contains the defendant, the fiery cross with runes, the peasant, the rebellious, the penitents and the coat-of-arms with the bear, which actually – in defiance of the *courtoisie* rules[18] of heraldry – repudiates Christ in turning his back on him. Three parts unite the picture and annul the opposition: Christ, the stone circle, and the symbol of justice where the peasant holds the balance and the King the sword.

Altogether, the picture symbolizes the legitimacy of law and its historic and popular roots. The law was made in alliance between God, king and people; the law which is God's law,[19] the legislation of the king and the legal practice of the people at court. The Form of Government (Constitution) of 1809 was built on the idea that the

Figure 2: Stained glass window by Ralph Bergholtz, 1946. Photo: Martin Sunnqvist.

power was with the king and the estates, which established independent courts to administer justice. However, the courts were placed under the king. The question whether the constitution of 1809 built on Swedish tradition or influences from abroad has caused extensive discussion,[20] but during the 1940s, the historical view was influential:

> [The king] also sits as a judge himself and he does so as the final court of appeal. And this is the way it has been for more than half a millennium. Already in the Svealand codes from the thirteenth century, the idea that the King was the fountain of all justice was implied, and in the common

> law code of the realm [c. 1350], it was made explicit that the King within his realm has received from God the highest authority over all temporal judges.[21]

The fact that almost all stone circles were built as graves, and that they have got their judicial importance, if any at all, later[22] is no obstacle for the interpretation of the picture; neither is the fact that the general code of law of Magnus Eriksson did not include Scania and thus not the circuits of Södra Åsbo and Bjäre. The stone circle and the king as legislator are used as metaphors of judging and law-giving. The oak is central – the justiciars were said to sit under oaks.[23] As a source for his creativity, Ralph Bergholtz used the stained glass artisans of the thirteenth century,[24] which, in combination with the fact that the circuit judge and the lay assessors made the decisions about the decoration of the court building[25] and that Ralph Bergholtz also was a church artist, gives further aspects to the historic and sacred features in this stained glass window.

In this courtroom, in June 2005, a murder case was tried, when the District Court of Ängelholm, which by then had become the Ängelholm division of the District Court of Helsingborg, was closed down. The court moved to the new court building in Helsingborg, and the trial continued, as if nothing had happened, in one of the modern courtrooms there.[26]

Also in the new district court building in Helsingborg there is a large work of art, which is an integral part of the building.[27] Since the building explicitly has been built for the district court and the work of art has been made with this in mind, I suggest in the following that it offers an image of law. A relevant question could otherwise be whether the same work of art could have been made for a hospital, a fire station or a port office, for example.

The outward form of the work of art can be described as a horizontal rectangle, which half way up is cut by a floor. In this manner, the work of art is in two corridors above each other, and on the opposite walls of the corridors there is a glass wall which is next to the entrance to the court building. In the centre of the painting is a black rectangle, encircled by a green, then a blue, thereafter an orange and lastly a yellow rectangle. Within the painting, there are hardwood veneer doors to courtrooms and other rooms.

The artist behind the work is Ann Edholm,[28] who has been commissioned by the National Public Arts Council (Statens konstråd). The district court no longer makes its own decisions as regards the decoration of the court building. Such decisions are made by the court, the National Courts Administration, the National Public Arts Council and the house owner[29] in consultation with each other.[30] The work of art is entitled *Transire*, and the thoughts behind it have been analyzed by the art critic and author, dr. phil. Tom Sandqvist on the website of the Public Arts Council.[31] Sandqvist's point of departure is that the word *transire* etymologically means to 'cross' or 'transgress' and connects to 'transitio' and 'transit', 'going through'. This meaning is reflected in the work of art in that the doors to the courtrooms

Figure 3: *Transire* by Ann Edholm, 2005. Photo: Martin Sunnqvist.

> so to say [...] have been placed directly on the painting at the same time as they have been integrated in the immediate shape of the picture as functional openings to the rooms behind the painting. The title also refers to the fact that the ceiling and floor which divides the glass wall cuts through the painting at an angle of 90 degrees. Besides the fact that the courtrooms themselves can be seen as a sort of transit rooms, it is, in view of the court building being placed close to the harbour of Helsingborg, not insignificant that the word 'transire' is also used in international shipping regarding the customs documents stating the goods that the ships have to declare in the relevant foreign harbour.[32]

Sandqvist further writes that *Transire* is not

> just any abstract wall painting, if it even is abstract regarding both the most concrete doors in the painting itself and the immediate bodily effect of it. It cannot be stressed enough that Transire is one single large painting which keeps the storeys together in a thematic visual comprehensive picture where the glass wall mirrors the divided picture at the same time as it is revealed as a painting in its entirety once it is seen through the glass facade from outside. The upper and lower parts of the painting are in different rooms inside the facade at the same time as the painting is combined to the desirable totality only in the outer perspective.
>
> As a visual figure, Transire is based on a sort of ingenious perspective effect where, moreover, the escape lines in the painting itself focus towards the black central part, which in its turn plays with the black body of the building above the glass wall. On the floors, the 60 centimetres wide fields give the feeling of 'wading in colour' up to the knees, as Ann Edholm expressed it in her description of the project. At the same time, the impression from for example the parking space below the court building or from the harbour awakes and enhances the experience of the composition, which is based on the central perspective. A fundamentally decisive aspect is also the fact that the meeting between the painting and the wall, exactly where the glass wall 'ends' at the third pillar in the direction of the wooden panelled entrance part, is constituted by a several

> millimetres high relief, which allows the painting to be understood as a body, jabbed by doors and openings, in correspondence with the own body of the visitor in the room.[33]

Sandqvist continues with relating the work of art to other aspects of the artistry of Ann Edholm, while I am looking for ways to relate the work of art to the court building of which it is an integral part. Sandqvist finally mentions this aspect:

> Also the two rooms inside the glass facade suddenly look like a kind of transit room for the gaze which looks for the overall picture, the gaze that from the outside sweeps over and penetrates the facade and in the two rooms bounces on the doors and in thought penetrates the openings and transgresses the boundaries of the room and the concrete reality, if you do not happen to be a judge, a lay assessor or a prosecuted person, because then you walk into the painting just like Wu Tao Tzu walked into the picture in the Chinese legend. Here, the transgression waits.
>
> Thinking of the title, Transire is truly a transcendental painting in the most literal meaning of the word.[34]

The painting has thus been interpreted as a transit room, which is characterized by the fact that people pass through it with different backgrounds and different goals. The gaze looks for something that perhaps is not there, bounces and transgresses the boundaries. It is not far-fetched to understand this as an expression of the view of our time on the law, where we look for justice, legitimacy and coherence, and when we do not find any of these, we force the law into a capricious structure and walk by.

The three works of art can be seen in one context. The reflections I present in the following are those of a lawyer, especially of a judge and legal historian.

One way of analyzing the works of art is by help of an insider-outsider perspective.[35] The stained glass and the mosaic were both commissioned by the Court Building Corporation (Tingshusbyggnadsskyldige), where the circuit judge and the lay assessors were influential. They have in all probability chosen the artist themselves and they have been able to influence the work of art. Regarding the mosaic it is clear that they were aware of this possibility even if we do not know whether any influence was exerted. The task of building courthouses has been transferred to the state, which lets a private entrepreneur – in this case G[eneral] E[lectric] Real Estate – build a courthouse which the state then rents. *Transire* has been commissioned via the National Public Arts Council. Even if the district court staff – judicial as well as administrative – has had the possibility to say their opinion and take part in the direction of the interior decorations, there have been no channels for direct influence from the judges on the artist.

It is not a far-fetched assumption that the stained glass and the mosaic mirror the court members' view on their mission; that judging is legitimate because of its historical roots. The stained glass shows the medieval origins and the mosaic gives a picture of the movement from the Middle Ages until now. *Transire,* on the other hand, gives a completely different image of the law; one sees distinct structures but from an outsider's perspective where the onlooker does not really realize how and why. If, on the other hand, it is the judge's picture of him- or herself which is mirrored in the painting, we have received a manifestation of the fact that the locally rooted, well-known circuit judge has been replaced by an anonymous, square – but paradoxically enough colourful! – civil servant.[36]

In the science of literature, Erich Auerbach has written about the figural method or the figural interpretation regarding finding the connection of meanings between two events. Particularly the narratives in the Old Testament have been interpreted as presages and premonitions of the narratives in the New Testament. The earlier event heralds and promises the later one, which fulfils and completes the first, without any temporal or causal connection between them.[37]

If one sets *Transire* in relation to the stained glass in the court building in Ängelholm, one finds stain and glass in both cases, but the stain and glass have been separated. The colour in the small fields of the stained glass window has been arranged in larger units. The obvious vertical boundary in the stained glass window has been transformed to an almost over-explicit horizontal boundary. The actors of law have disappeared, and all that remains are the naked structures that they built, but the memories of their history and why they were built are lost. The picture suggests that the historical roots have been replaced by confusion and emptiness.

The light is essential: In the stained glass, the light from the world around comes into the courtroom via the mediation of the symbols in the stained glass. Through the picture of Christ and the Christian metaphor of the light, this interpretation is strengthened. In *Transire,* the light only comes to the corridors between the glass wall and the courtrooms, but never entering the courtrooms.

If one continues Sandqvist's metaphor of Wu Tao-Tzu, law is beyond hope. Wu Tao-Tzu made a mural in an imperial palace. In the picture, he had made a door in a mountain. He clapped his hands, entered the door – and was lost forever. If that is what the actors of law have done, we are back in the land of the lawless down to the *dexter* in the stained glass picture. Sandqvist's metaphor with the painting as jabbed with doors and openings in correspondence with the body of the onlooker stresses this further.

But the stained glass can also be seen as the thesis and *Transire* as the antithesis. If one enters one of the doors, one does not disappear forever, but rather one ends up in another door in another work of art, namely in the mosaic in Ängelholm. There is a synthesis between on the one hand the historic roots of law and on the other the latest legal development with the sometimes conflicting legal principles that the internationalization bears with it. There, the contradiction between the old oak and its transformation to hardwood veneer doors is annulled in that a new tree is planted. There are the waves of change and the heart of law, the connection between the ancient, the contemporary and the future, symbols of faith and power, legitimacy and broad-mindedness. Between the still pictures of petrified historicity and rigid structuralism is a living presentation of the development of law by the actors.

Seeing it this way, the chronology is different. The stained glass is rooted in a time marked by the Second World War,[38] *Transire* mirrors the 1970s and the 'murder of the holy room,[39] and the mosaic in Ängelholm still mirrors the continuous development of law[40] in a way that is relevant in the legal order of today, where Swedish law is part of a common international and European legal system.[41]

Notes

1 While 'torg' means 'square', 'ting' means 'circuit/district court session'; cf. 'tingsrätt' ('district court') and 'tingshus' ('district court building').

2 In Swedish 'härad'; cf. English 'hundred'. The older jurisdiction 'härad' is translated as 'circuit', 'häradsrätt' is translated as 'circuit court' and the newer 'tingsrätt' as district court.

3 Ralph Bergholtz (1908–1988). Cf. *Svenskt konstnärslexikon* I, p. 151.

4 My translation of 'Med utgångspunkt från den nya gavelns karaktäristiska takvinkel rör sig linjespelet i vågor genom mosaiken för att slutligen tona ut i det gamla tingshusets pilastrar. Färgens växlingar mellan gröngult och tegelrött understryker rörelsen. Avsikten har med andra ord varit, att mosaiken skulle fungera som någon sorts hjärta, som sätter hela fasadkomplexets linjer i en rytmisk rörelse.'

5 My translation of 'ett organiskt samband mellan gammalt och nytt – kontinuiteten i rättsmedvetandets utveckling.'

6 A *caryatid* was in classical architecture a pillar shaped as a sculptured female figure. Here, this refers to three mosaic males standing on the stone base and in a symbolic sense supporting the roof with their heads.

7 King of Denmark (1202–1241).

8 More accurate: during whose reign the Scanian law code was written down.

9 'Sveriges Rikes lag', 1734.

10 My translation of 'urskiljer man tre karyatidiska gestalter syftande på laggemenskapens utvidgning över allt större områden: Lagmannen som själv "gömde lagen" för boplatsens folk [...]. Valdemar Sejr, som skrev den första Skånelagen[,] för de danska färgerna i sin sköld. Gustaf Cronhielm, ordförande i lagkommissionen, som utarbetade "Sveriges Rikes lag". De åtföljas av symboler för tro och makt – Torshammaren och svärdet, korset och bödelsyxan, det svenska lejonet.'

11 My translation of 'från "den starkares rätt" via envigen vid tinget, "järnbörden", samhällets vedergällning, frihetsstraffet och straffarbetet mot en allt vidsyntare straffuppfattning. Rättens symboler, svärdet och vågen, leder över entrén till högra väggfältet, där mot bakgrund av fallande bomber ett nytt träd planteras, syftande på en ny allomfattande rättsordning med dess organisering i rot, stam och grenar. Epoken antyds av NF:s och FN:s byggnader'. The quotations are from 'Tingshusmosaiken; beskrivning av konstnären Ralph Bergholtz', in *The Archives of Tingshusbyggnadsskyldige in the Circuits of Södra Åsbo and Bjäre*, The Regional State Archive (Landsarkivet) in Lund.

12 26 kap. 4 § byggningabalken (the book of buildings in the Swedish law code). See Kjell Å. Modéer, *Den svenska domarkulturen – europeiska och nationella förebilder* (Lund: Corpus Iuris Förlag, 1994), pp. 32–35, 67–69.

13 At an extra assembly of the courthouse building corporation 'before the circuit judge in the circuits of Södra Åsbo and Bjäre – in the circuit court building in Ängelholm March 17th 1954' the corporation approved an extension of the building and appointed a committee to make all decisions which were not reserved for the board of the corporation. The committee, which consisted of circuit judge (*häradshövding*) G. A. Eriksson, chairman, circuit police superintendent and public prosecutor (*landsfiskal*) Erik Söderholm, lay assessor, later premier lay assessor (*häradsdomare*), Stefan Svensson and master builder Jean Christiansson, 18 May 1955, received a message from the municipal architect (*stadsarkitekt*) Arne Lindström, who was the architect of the additional building, that the artist Ralph Bergholtz was working on a proposal of a mosaic for the passage building. At the next meeting of the committee – 23 May 1955 – a sketch was available. The committee thought it appropriate to let the board of the corporation 'decide whether the proposal – unaltered or after some revision – should be realized'. Having researched all the documents of the corporation except the verifications, I have not been able to find the protocols of the board from 1955 or earlier. This means that I have not been able to find out anything about the discussions leading to the appointment of Bergholtz or reactions, if any, to his sketches. A protocol of the board from 16 January 1956 is, as far as I have been able to find, the oldest surviving protocol; the archive, which is in the Regional State Archives in Lund, is still unregistered and in

total disorder. Members of the board were the circuit judge and a few lay assessors. On 7 July 1955 Bergholtz was present at the meeting of the building committee and presented a sketch of the mosaic above the entrance door. No decision was made, and Bergholtz informed the committee that he in due time would present a life-size sketch of the entire mosaic. The same day, however, a contract about the work was made. The work had to be finished by 1 November 1955.

14 Stone circles are in Swedish called 'domarring', literally 'judges' circle'. It is no longer assumed that the stone circles were used for law court purposes, but the word remains. In English, the most convenient word is 'stone circle'; an alternative is 'cromlech', which in Welsh means a construction with a flat stone resting upon upright stones but which in Brittany means a stone circle. See *The Oxford English Dictionary,* vol. IV, 1989, p. 38.

15 I use the heraldic terminology which sees the motive from the angle of the bearer.

16 According to Therese Andersson, there is at Skissernas museum (Museum of Sketches) in Lund a sketch by Ralph Bergholtz from 1948 with an almost identical image of Christ for the church at Kvistofta; the difference is in the position of Christ's hands. See 'Ralph Bergholtz. En glasmålning på Ängelholms tingsrätt', essay within the course Nordisk konst (Nordic Art), Spring semester 1994, Lund University (in the file for Ängelholm Court in the Court Building Documentation Project, see www.raa.se), p. 10. Cf. *Svenskt konstnärslexikon* I, p. 151, where it is stated that Bergholtz has made six large stained glass pictures with Biblical motives for the church at Väsby in Scania. Regarding the Court Building Documentation Project, see Ylva Blank and Eva Löfgren, 'Tingshusen – en väg till kulturhistorien', in *Byggnadskultur* no. 4 (1999), pp. 22–25. This is, as far as I know, the only courtroom in Sweden with a picture of Christ. In this perspective, the words of Beate Ellingsen, 'The churchroom has the altarpiece, the courtroom has the royal coat-of-arms', are especially interesting ('Rom og rett', in *Nordisk tidsskrift for kriminalvidenskap* (1995), p. 301). Beate Ellingsen discusses in detail the interior design of courthouses in relation to her work with the district court building of Oslo, Norway.

17 These are the older circuit arms, in Swedish blazoned *i fält av silver en upprest svart björn* and *i fält av guld en med gyllene krona krönt rödklädd*

kvinnofigur (S:ta Tora) hållande i höger hand en röd uppslagen bok och i vänster hand en röd palmkvist respectively. In 1955 H. M. Government (Kungl. Maj:t) granted *Or a pile concavely enarched Vert between two branches of beech Vert* (*i fält av guld en störtad grön inböjd spets, på vardera sidan åtföljd av en grön bokkvist*) to the circuit of Södra Åsbo and *Gules a female with clothing Or and coronet Azure, holding in her right hand an open book Azure and in her left hand a palm branch Azure* (*i rött fält en i fotsid dräkt klädd, stående kvinnogestalt av guld, krönt med en blå krona och hållande i högra handen en uppslagen blå bok, i den vänstra en blå palmkvist*) to Bjäre.

18 The figures in coats-of-arms are generally oriented to the *dexter*, since they then seem to move in the same direction as the person who holds his shield in his left hand; the sword is held in the right hand. The exception is the rule of *courtoisie*, where the shield is reversed to show respect to something to the *sinister*. *Dexter* and *sinister* (right and left) are used in the perspective of the bearer of the shield. Already Bartolo da Sassoferrato, or rather his son-in-law and editor Nicola Alessandri, discussed *courtoisie* in *Tractatus de insigniis et armis*; however, the present-day editors of the text have not understood the significance of the rule (see Osvaldo Cavallar, Susanne Degenring and Julius Kirshner, *A Grammar of Signs: Bartolo da Sassoferrato's Tract on Insignia and Coats of Arms* (Berkeley: University of California Press, 1994), p. 156 note 8).

19 The wording '... I will and shall with my best wisdom and conscience do the right in all judgements, no less to the poor than the rich, and I shall apply the laws and legal statutes of *God and Sweden*...' ('... jag vill och skall efter mitt bästa förstånd och samvete i alla domar rätt göra, ej mindre den fattige än den rike, och döma efter *Guds och Sveriges lag och laga stadgar*...') [italics added here] was part of the judicial oath until 1 July 1959, when the mention of God was removed; cf. Martin Sunnqvist, 'Domareden och dess religiösa inslag', *Rätt, religion och politik, Rättshistoriska skrifter 9* (Stockholm, 2008), pp. 85–113.

20 Emma Rönström, 'Forskardebatten kring 1809 års regeringsform – Till frågan om grundlagens härkomst', *Statsvetenskaplig tidskrift* (1997), pp. 448–467, with references.

21 My translation of: '[Konungen] dömer också själv och det i sista instans. Och så har det varit sedan mer än ett halvt årtusende. Redan i 1200-talets

Svealagar framträder tesen om konungen såsom källan för all domsrätt, och i landslagen säges klart ifrån, att konungen har i sitt rike av Gudi högsta dom över alla världsliga domare', in Fredrik Lagerroth, *1809 års regeringsform. Dess ursprung och tolkning* (Stockholm: Norstedts, 1942), p. 63. Cf. Henrik Munktell, *Det svenska rättsarvet* (Stockholm: Bonniers, 1944).

22 Birger Wedberg, 'Domarringar', *Svensk juristtidning* (1942), pp. 425–426; K. E. Sahlström, 'Domarringarnas härkomst', *Fornvännen* (1942), pp. 115–135.

23 Sven Tito Achen, *Symboler omkring oss* (Stockholm: Norstedts, 1975), p. 54; John Watts, 'Looking for the State', in Peter Coss and Maurice Keen (eds.), *Heraldry, Pageantry and Social Display in Medieval England* (Woodbridge: Boydell Press, 2002), pp. 243–267, esp. p. 249.

24 Therese Andersson, 'Ralph Bergholtz', p. 3.

25 The protocols of the board of the Court House Building Corporation are, as mentioned in note 13, probably lost. The protocols of the Corporation assembly have been preserved, but they only refer to more general issues.

26 From 1 September 2004 until 15 August 2005 I was deputy district judge (*tingsfiskal*) at the District Court of Helsingborg. I sat mainly at the Ängelholm division, but was not, of course, judge in the murder case. The courthouse in Ängelholm today functions as the private John Bauer school.

27 In Helsingborg, there are also former court buildings at Gasverksgatan 9 (in use 1971–2005 by the District Court of Helsingborg) and at Kaliforniegatan 3 (in use 1896–1970 by the Circuit Court of Luggude). These buildings do not have a similar work of art. The works of art in the city hall, where the Magistrates' Court (Rådhusrätten) sat until 1970, reflect the history of the town of Helsingborg.

28 Ann Edholm, b. 1953, was professor at the Royal University College of Fine Arts (Kungl. Konsthögskolan) in Stockholm and the Valand School of Fine Arts (Konsthögskolan Valand) in Gothenburg and is a fellow of the Royal Academy of Fine Arts (Kungl. Akademien för de Fria Konsterna); www.statenskonstrad.se (last accessed 1/11/2006).

29 Most court buildings are no longer owned by the state.

30 Here follows an illustration of the mechanism of decision-making: At a 'users' meeting' (*brukarmöte*), in which representatives of the District Court,

the National Courts Administration, the architects (Pyramiden Arkitekter, later Plain Arkitekter AB), WSP Jönköping, Ecoscape AB and GE Real Estate, on 11 February 2004 (the protocol by mistake dated 2003), the architect Carl-Åke Bergström presented ideas of artistic decorations, after which it was decided that the court or the National Courts Administration should send a letter to the National Public Arts Council. According to a protocol of 27 February the court had sent such a letter with the purpose of arranging a meeting with representatives of the court, the art council, the National Courts Administration, architects and the interior designer. According to a protocol of 26 March, such a meeting had taken place. According to protocols of 28 May and 24 June, such meetings were to be held again those days. According to the protocol from the 'users' meeting' on 18 August, the results of the contacts with the arts council had to be presented at the end of September, which, according to a protocol of 16 September, was postponed until 20 October. The architect Carl-Åke Bergström was appointed to 'look after the interests of the Court'. The arts council would present its proposal to the District Court on 4 November at 13.30. On 28 October, it was noted that the presentation on 20 October turned out very well. The meeting on 4 November of the 'group of interior design' (*inredningsgruppen*), where I was present (and assumed a somewhat sceptical attitude towards the symbolism of the work of art and its harmony with the building). The general opinion in the group was, according to the notes taken by the chairman, that the work of art was 'eminent and brilliant' (*utmärkt, briljant och strålande*). At the next meeting of the 'group of interior design', on 29 November, the representative of the National Courts Administration questioned whether the work of art, regarding the intensity and aggressiveness of the colours, could have an undesirable effect on people in the lobby. According to a note at the end of the protocol, contact was taken with the public arts council, which said that the fears were unfounded, since the intense colours only occur in 60-centimetre wide fields. The discussion ended with the National Courts Administration and the interior designer at a meeting on 10 December registering their dissent regarding the colours in the minutes. At a meeting on 25 February 2005 (the protocol by mistake dated 2004), the discussion was closed.

31 Tom Sandqvist, 'Transire – Ann Edholm i Helsingborg' and 'Ann Edholm', www.statenskonstrad.se (last accessed 1/11/2006).

32 My translation of 'så att säga [...] har placerats direkt på målningen på samma gång som de har integrerats i den omedelbara bildgestalten som funktionella öppningar in i rummen bakom målningen. Titeln hänvisar också till det faktum att det golv- respektive takparti som delar den glasade fasaden går tvärsigenom målningen i nittio graders vinkel. Förutom att själva tingssalarna kan betecknas som ett slags transiteringsrum är det med tanke på tingshusets lokalisering i direkt anslutning till hamnen i Helsingborg inte heller oväsentligt att ordet 'transire' dessutom används i den internationella skeppsfarten för de tulldokument med varor och gods som fartygen måste deklarera i den aktuella utländska hamnen.' This part of Tom Sandqvist's analysis is also presented in a brochure published by the National Public Arts Council and made available in the lobby of the court building.

33 My translation of 'är inte vilken abstrakt väggmålning som helst, om den ens är abstrakt med tanke på både de högst konkreta dörrarna i själva målningen och målningens omedelbara kroppsliga verkan. Det kan inte nog understrykas att Transire är en enda stor målning som håller ihop våningsplanen i en tematisk-visuell helhetsbild där glasfasaden samtidigt speglar den genomskurna bilden på samma gång som denna uppenbaras som en hel gestalt först då man utifrån blickar in genom fasaden. Målningens övre och undre parti befinner sig i skilda rum innanför fasaden samtidigt som målningen kombineras till den eftersträvade helheten först i det yttre perspektivet. // Som visuell gestalt bygger Transire med andra ord på ett slags sinnrik perspektivverkan där dessutom flyktlinjerna i själva målningen går in mot det svarta mittpartiet, som i sin tur leker med byggnadens svarta kroppsvolym ovanför glaspartiet. På respektive plan upplevs i första hand de 60 centimeter breda banden så att känslan uppstår av att 'vada i färg' upp till knäna, som Ann Edholm uttryckte sig i projektbeskrivningen. Samtidigt väcker och förstärker intrycket från t.ex. parkeringsplatsen nedanför tingshuset eller från hamnen ett stycke därifrån upplevelsen av den på just centralperspektivet byggda kompositionen. En fundamentalt avgörande aspekt är också det faktum att mötet mellan målningen och väggen i exakt den punkt där glasfasaden 'slutar' vid tredje pelaren i riktning mot det träbeklädda entrépartiet utgörs av en

några millimeter hög reliefverkan, som gör att målningen kan uppfattas som en av dörrar och öppningar genomstungen kropp i korrespondens med besökarens egen kropp i rummet.'

34 My translation of 'Även de två rummen innanför glasfasaden framstår plötsligt som ett slags transiteringsrum för blicken som söker helhetsbilden, blicken som utifrån sveper över och tränger igenom fasaden för att i de bägge rummen studsa mot dörrarna och i tanken sedan tränga igenom öppningarna och därigenom överskrida rummets och den konkreta verklighetens egna begränsningar, om du inte råkar vara domare, nämndeman eller åtalad, för då går du in i målningen som Wu Tao Tzu gick in i bilden i den kinesiska legenden. Här väntar överskridningen. // Med tanke på titeln är Transire en i sanning transcendental målning i ordet mest bokstavliga bemärkelse.' If you want to get another dimension to the analysis, see Lars Vilks's commentary at http://www.vilks.net/?p=264 (with the discussion further down on the page).

35 Kjell Å Modéer, 'Nordisk juristkultur en del av rättskulturen. Förändring och stabilitet', in Pia Letto-Vanamo (ed.), *Nordisk identitet. Nordisk rätt i europeisk gemenskap* (Helsinki, 1998), and idem, 'Vad är rättskultur? Om vår tids historiska skolstrid vid juridisk fakultet', in *Rätten. En festskrift till Bengt Ankarloo* (Lund: Nordic Academic Press, 2000).

36 Kjell Å. Modéer, *Det heliga rummet. Domstolsbyggnadernas roll i det civila samhället* (Helsinki: Lakimies, 2000), pp. 1060–1072. Cf. Modéer, *Den svenska domarkulturen*, pp. 55–63.

37 Erich Auerbach, *Mimesis. Verklighetsframställningen i den västerländska litteraturen* (Stockholm: Albert Bonniers förlag, 2002), pp. 58–59, 83–86.

38 Cf. note 21 above.

39 My translation of 'mordet på det heliga rummet', Modéer, *Det heliga rummet*, pp. 1071–1072. Cf. note 36 above. I thought of the 1970s already at the meeting on 24 November 2004, see note 30 above. I could not, however, *ex tempore* analyze the issue then.

40 Cf. e.g. Kaarlo Tuori, *Critical Legal Positivism* (Ashgate: Aldershot, 2002), pp. 147–196.

41 Modéer, *Det heliga rummet*, p. 1072; Per Henrik Lindblom, 'Rättegångssalens väggar – om domstolsprocessen i tid och rum', *Svensk juristtidning* (2002), pp. 1–11.

Contributors

LEIF DAHLBERG Born 1962. Ph.D., Associate Professor (Docent) in Comparative Literature, University of Stockholm, and Senior Lecturer in Communication, Royal Institute of Technology, Stockholm. Dahlberg teaches media and theoretical texts that range from the eighteenth to the twenty-first century. He has written articles and books on German Romanticism, European Modernism, narratology, media history, law and literature, advertising, and new media. His current research project investigates the construction and representation of legal spaces in law, literature and political philosophy in works from Greek antiquity to the present.

RAINER MARIA KIESOW Born 1963. Privatdozent, Dr. jur., Visiting Professor at the École des Hautes Études en Sciences Sociales (Paris), Professor (Privatdozent) at the Law Faculty of the University of Frankfurt and the Max-Planck-Institut für europäische Rechtsgeschichte. He is co-editor and director of the law journal *Myops. Berichte aus der Welt des Rechts* (C.H. Beck Verlag); He has previously published *Das Naturgesetz des Rechts* (1997), *Das Alphabet des Rechts* (2004), and *Kredite in der Risikogesellschaft* (2005).

PIA LETTO-VANAMO Born 1954. LL.D., Professor of Legal History specialized in European legal history, conceptual history and history of legal profession. She is currently Director of the Institute of International Economic Law at the University of Helsinki. She is a member of a Centre of Excellence for Foundations of European and Law and Polity research (http://www.helsinki.fi/katti/foundations/index.html) dealing with problems concerning legal cultural foundations of the European market. Her latest publications have concentrated on historical-comparative analysis of legal concepts and legal argumentation.

EVA LÖFGREN Born 1971. B.A. in Literature and B.A. in Conservation, D.Phil. in Conservation, University of Gothenburg. Recent publications include 'The Space of a Court, Conceived and Realised: Fillinge District Court-House 1789–1797' (2008), 'Architectural Inquiries' (web publication) (2008), 'Vardag i rättsskipningens periferi', in *Från Schlyters lustgård, Rättshistoriska uppsatser* 6 (2007) and her dissertation, *Rummet och rätten. Tingshus som föreställning, byggnad och rum i användning 1734–1970* (2011). Her main research topics include the history of ideas, and the realization and use of rural district courthouses.

DAG MICHALSEN Born 1957. LL.D., since 1997 Professor in Legal History at the Faculty of Law at the University of Oslo. He has published books and articles on the history of legal science, history of constitutional law and methodology of legal history. Among his most recent publications is the monograph *Romerrettsideologi* (Roman Law Ideology) (2008).

KJELL Å MODÉER Born 1939. Professor emeritus at the University of Lund. He was Professor of Legal History from 1977 to 2007. From 2005 to 2007 he held the Ragnar and Torsten Söderberg Professorate in memory of Samuel Pufendorf. He was published substantially within comparative legal history and law and religion and has been awarded three honorary doctoral degrees. He was the chairman of the steering group of the project 'Nordic legal maps in transition'.

LESLIE J. MORAN Born 1955. Professor of Law at Birkbeck College. He qualified as a solicitor in 1979 and in 1996 was awarded a Ph.D. He has been working on law and visual culture for many years. In 2004, with colleagues at Birkbeck, he edited *Law's Moving Image*. He is currently undertaking research on the judiciary and visual culture. Other publications include *Sexuality Identity and Law* (2006), *Sexuality and the Politics of Violence and Safety* written with Beverley Skeggs (2004), *Legal Queeries* (1998), and *The Homosexual(ity) of Law* (1996).

LYNDA NEAD Born 1957. Pevsner Professor of History of Art at Birkbeck College, University of London. Her main publications include *The Female Nude: Art, Obscenity and Sexuality* (1992), *Victorian Babylon: People, Streets and Images in Nineteenth-Century London* (2005) and *The Haunted Gallery: Painting, Photography, Film c. 1900* (2008). She is currently working on a book on the aesthetics of boxing entitled *The Art of Boxing: A Book in Twelve Rounds* and on a project on the artist's studio.

HANNE PETERSEN Born 1951. Professor of Law and part of the management team of the Centre for Studies of Legal Culture at the Faculty of Law, University of Copenhagen. In 1991 she received her doctoral degree (dr.jur.) on a dissertation about labour law, informal law, women's law and legal theory. She has worked as a consultant and facilitator since the 1990s on several courses concerned with human rights, women's law and methodology in African countries, Pakistan and the Middle East. She was Professor of Jurisprudence and Sociology of Law in Greenland from 1995 to 1999, Professor of Greenlandic Sociology in Copenhagen from 2001 to 2006, and since 2007 Adjunct Professor at Tromsø University in Norway. She has published *Home Knitted Law: Norms and Values in Gendered Rule-Making* (1995). She has also edited the volume *Love and Law in Europe* (1998) and co-edited *Legal Polycentricity: Consequences of Pluralism in Law* (1995), *Paradoxes of European Legal Integration* (2008) and *Law and Religion in Multicultural Societies* (2008).

KHALED RAMADAN Born 1965, Beirut. M.A. in Architecture, Royal Danish Academy. He is External Lecturer at the University of Copenhagen, and has done Ph.D. research in Media Aesthetics. He has published several articles and books, most recently *Peripheral Insiders* (2007).

CECILIE SCHJATVET Born 1966. Cand.jur. 2002. She has worked as an advocate at the Law Firm Hestenes and Dramer & Co in Oslo, Norway, since 2002. She represents clients in criminal cases, asylum cases and other human rights-related cases. She is the appointed member of the Human Rights Committee and the Asylum and Immigration Committee of the Norwegian Bar Association, and of the Norwegian National Committee for Research Ethics (NESH). She has an Associates of Arts from San Francisco City College (1998), and a B.A. in Creative Writing from San Francisco State University (1995). From 1989 to 1995 she worked on features, shorts, documentaries and commercials in San Francisco. She has several publications on the topics of international law and legal history.

LISBETH FULLU SKYBERG Born 1969. Research Fellow, Department of Criminology and Sociology of Law, University of Oslo. Her main research topics include sociology of law, legal epistemology, evidence of law, legal culture, rhetoric and communication.

MARTIN SUNNQVIST Born 1975. LL.M., University of Lund 2001, Law Clerk 2001–2003, Appeal Court Clerk 2003-, Deputy District Judge 2004–2005 and 2009–2010, Associate Judge of Appeal 2010–. Doctoral candidate in Legal History at the University of Lund 2005–, LL.Lic. 2009. His main research topics include the legal history of judicial review and judicial interpretation of statutes in constitutional conformity in the Nordic countries. He has also published articles on judicial oaths and researched legal symbolism.

PETER WAHLGREN Born 1955. LL.D., Professor of Law and Information Technology, Faculty of Law, Stockholm University. Professor Wahlgren has published many articles and several books on law and IT and legal science, including *Automation of Legal Reasoning* (1992), *The Quest for Law* (1999), *Juridisk riskanalys* (Legal Risk Analysis) (2003), and *Lagstiftning* (Legislation) (2008). Since 1999 he has been editor of the book series Scandinavian Studies in Law.